FDR's SHADOW

ALSO BY JULIE M. FENSTER

and available from

PALGRAVE MACMILLAN

The Case of Abraham Lincoln

FDR's SHADOW

Louis Howe,
The Force That Shaped
Franklin *and* Eleanor Roosevelt

JULIE M. FENSTER

palgrave
macmillan

FDR'S SHADOW
Copyright © Julie M. Fenster, 2009.
All rights reserved.

First published in 2009 by PALGRAVE MACMILLAN® in the United States—
a division of St. Martin's Press LLC, 175 Fifth Avenue, New York, NY 10010.

Where this book is distributed in the UK, Europe and the rest of the world, this is
by Palgrave Macmillan, a division of Macmillan Publishers Limited, registered in
England, company number 785998, of Houndmills, Basingstoke, Hampshire
RG21 6XS.

Palgrave Macmillan is the global academic imprint of the above companies and
has companies and representatives throughout the world.

Palgrave® and Macmillan® are registered trademarks in the United States, the
United Kingdom, Europe and other countries.

ISBN 978–0–230–60910–5

Library of Congress Cataloging-in-Publication Data is available from the Library
of Congress.

A catalogue record of the book is available from the British Library.

Design by Letra Libre, Inc.

First edition: October, 2009.
10 9 8 7 6 5 4 3 2 1
Printed in the United States of America.

CONTENTS

Eight pages of photographs appear between pages 132 *and* 133.

"Louis Howe was probably the greatest influence in both my father and my mother's lives."

—*Elliott Roosevelt*
June 20, 1979
Franklin D. Roosevelt Library,
Hyde Park, New York

PROLOGUE

April 18, 1936, didn't start out as a bad day at all to be the president of the United States, or to be Franklin D. Roosevelt. The news was mild, aside from unrest in Ethiopia. Congress was quiet and criticism of the president, while shrill, had yet to puncture the idolatry that made overconfidence the only real thing for Roosevelt to fear as he approached the end of his first term in office.

In the afternoon of that Saturday in April, Roosevelt made a surprise visit to the Corcoran Gallery of Art three blocks from the White House to see his own antiques on display: 192 naval prints and a dozen ship models on loan from his personal collection.[1] He may or may not have been disappointed to find that the object of greatest fascination in the exhibit was the painting of himself that accompanied it. A critic who eavesdropped on the people crowding around the portrait determined "quite clearly that they are not interested in the President's favorite subject at all but are keenly interested in the President."[2]

While Roosevelt was out that afternoon, he traveled to the Bethesda Naval Hospital, seven miles away, to spend time with Louis Howe, a long-time patient there.[3] Howe, the secretary to the president, was racked by health problems arising from poor breathing and circulation, though he was trying hard to rally in time to help Roosevelt in the coming reelection campaign.[4] On some days, Howe was not even coherent. But he was almost certainly lucid and conversant on the afternoon Roosevelt came to call—only a few hours later, his doctor reported having a "very cheerful" talk with him.[5] Anyway, Howe always brightened when he saw the Roosevelts, Franklin or Eleanor.[6]

April 18 was not a bad day to be the First Lady, either. That morning, Eleanor Roosevelt met a dozen girls from New York's elite Todhunter School—where she had once taught—and took them sightseeing in Washington. More than anything else, they wanted to go to the Federal Bureau of Investigation. Escorted past hundreds of other tourists, Mrs. Roosevelt and her party were taken on a tour by the director himself, J. Edgar Hoover.[7]

In the evening, President Roosevelt dressed in white tie and tails to attend the semiannual Gridiron Dinner. He and a couple of hundred other guests were regaled with songs and skits presented by members of the Washington press corps. One ditty spoofed the Civilian Conservation Corps.

> We joined the New Deal
> to see the world
> but what did we see—the C.C.C.[8]

Eleanor Roosevelt was also out for the evening, with somewhat less laughter, attending a conference of the Washington Committee on Housing, of which she was a member. She delivered a speech on living conditions among the city's African American population and then left for home at about nine o'clock.[9] The Gridiron Dinner lasted longer and was still noisy as the hour of eleven came and went, crowded by jokes poking fun at the Roosevelt administration.

> The government of checks and balances has become one of all checks—
> and no balances.[10]

Even if it was the stuff of college humor, the audience found the show side-splitting.[11] One of the skits featured "Alfreda Smith," a female version of Roosevelt's old political comrade, Alfred E. Smith, pioneer of the modern Democratic Party. Smith had recently baffled his friends—and even his old enemies—by joining the ranks of the Republicans and Roosevelt-haters. Alfreda, having just used her own pin money to get home from a date, whined:

I'm never going riding again with that Franklin Roosevelt.[12]

No one laughed harder than Roosevelt. After the stage show was finished, those in the room raised their glasses in a formal toast to the president and then called on him for a speech.[13] According to the rules of the Gridiron Club, his remarks were not to be reported by anyone who was present. But he was expected to be amusing and, no doubt, he was.

At the White House, a call came from the Naval Hospital at about 11:30 that night. By the time the president returned home, just before midnight, Eleanor was waiting for him with Stephen T. Early, the White House press secretary. Louis Howe had died at 11:10 PM.

The news was not a surprise to the Roosevelts, not on the face of it. Howe had lived with them for almost fifteen years. He had never been entirely well during that time, suffering most noticeably from asthma. During his final eight months, when he was staying at the hospital, he was still under their mantle. "I go to see Louis every day that he will see me," Eleanor wrote in January.[14] As for anyone on a vigil for the critically ill, that part of the Roosevelts' lives was a diary of enlarged details, epic only to those closest to the patient. Howe's secretary, Margaret "Rabbit" Durand, had sent a typically well-meaning, utterly helpless update to his family earlier that spring: "I hasten this note," she wrote, "to tell you that I think Mr. Howe is much better today than he has been since the 15th of March. Really and truely [sic] he seems more like himself in every way and I mean this in all seriousness . . . I think from the way he is going that it will not be long before he is back in his fighting cloths [sic]. Of course tomorrow might bring forth a different story, and I may regret writing the first paragraph of this note to you in which I sound so optimistic."[15] Within Howe's immediate circle, Rabbit and the two Roosevelts had carefully dampened their hopes during his upturns and steadied their expectations whenever he took a turn for the worse. Then suddenly, even that way of life was over for them all when, as Eleanor put it, "he simply slept away."[16]

As midnight approached that night, Eleanor attended to her obligation to telephone Howe's wife, Grace, who lived by herself in Fall River, Massachusetts. Steve Early left to prepare a news bulletin, which was released to the press at 12:10 AM.[17] As to Franklin Roosevelt, he was in some sense on his own for the first time in twenty-five years.

Roosevelt may well have been uncertain about just where he was without Howe, but *Time* magazine wasn't. "Admirers he had by the millions," the magazine would say of Roosevelt, "Acquaintances by the thousands, advisers by the hundreds, friends by the score, but of intimates such as Louis Howe he had only one."[18] The following morning, Roosevelt personally ordered that the White House flag fly at half-staff. Later in the day, he canceled all of his appointments and activities for at least two days, Monday and Tuesday. He remained in seclusion the rest of Sunday.

Eleanor wrote in her syndicated newspaper column that day, "We can, of course, think of little else today but the loss of our old and dear friend, Colonel Howe." (The military title was honorary; Howe had been named a Kentucky Colonel in 1932.) A paragraph of tribute followed, referring to his pity, warmth, and sincerity, and ending with a line that would normally be quite unremarkable, practically constituting boilerplate in any other eulogy: "His courage and loyalty and devotion to his family and friends will be an inspiration to them as long as they live."[19] One of the mysteries lingering after Louis Howe, though, was just which were the family and which the friends.

———◆◆◆———

Howe's wife, Grace, and their two adult children arrived in Washington on Sunday evening. After consulting with them, Franklin Roosevelt chose to hold the services at the White House, marking only the fifth time since 1920 that the White House was to be used for a funeral. The ceremony was scheduled for Tuesday, with calling hours beforehand.

Three of the Roosevelts' five grown children made plans to attend: James, Elliott, and Anna, the latter two flying from New York in rough weather. With plans coalescing on Monday, Eleanor appeared before the press. "He had an extraordinary sympathy for real need," she said of Howe, "He was kind and gentle and also a merciless critic of those for whom he felt responsibility."[20] She then described herself as a grateful recipient of that criticism, without recalling for the reporters that she had also once inspired Howe's sympathy.

Franklin Roosevelt was not seen at all on Monday, nor on most of Tuesday. While Howe was best-known as the "man who put Franklin D. Roosevelt in the White House,"[21] and had been working toward that goal for decades, some suggested that the president had outgrown his dependence on Howe's advice—that Louis Howe was a relic of the ascent with no place at the summit.[22] There were also those who thought the famed friendship was so one-sided that it barely fit the definition of the word, consisting in harsh terms of an indulgent boss who couldn't resist the adulation of his most ardent disciple. Roosevelt, for his part, made no effort publicly to cast light on his relationship with Louis Howe. On the eve of the funeral, he declined to see the press, as Eleanor had done. He didn't release a statement. He didn't volunteer to make any remarks at the funeral services, which would have been an appropriate tribute and one that might even have been expected of so effective an orator.

Roosevelt did answer the condolence notes that started to arrive, and which would continue to pour in for weeks. To many people, he acknowledged that Louis Howe had been "a grand soul." In Roosevelt's case, that wasn't necessarily high praise, however. He used the word "grand" with abandon, to describe trips, speeches, letters, or almost any other nouns in search of a boost. "Some [adjectives] did get overworked a bit," admitted Gabrielle Forbush, who had handled Roosevelt's correspondence during the 1932 campaign, "FDR always liked the 'grand' one."[23]

Roosevelt's more considered response went only a little further in reflecting his emotional state. On Tuesday, he dictated a letter in answer to a note about Howe sent by his friend, the maritime writer Ralph Cropley:

Thank you very much for that nice letter about Louis. We will all miss him but, of course, we feel that he has not enjoyed life for the past year and this makes his going much easier.[24]

Those who wrote to Roosevelt seemed more pained than the president himself. Frank Polk, a powerful New York lawyer who had worked closely with both Roosevelt and Howe over the years, expressed himself with a particular sense of the loss at hand:

The relations between you two was a great example of devotion and loyalty and also an example of what friendship should be. Your friends were not necessarily his friends, but beyond all question your enemies were his enemies. On your side, your devotion and understanding was just as real.[25]

To Polk, Roosevelt made his stock, pragmatic reply:

Just a note to thank you for your very nice letter about Louis. We all miss him but for him death must have been a blessed release. He had had such a long illness with no prospect of every [sic] being well again. My best to you and Lily.[26]

The insistence on finding a silver lining in the bleakest of situations was a seminal aspect of Franklin Roosevelt's character. But so was refraining from showing his deeper feelings, if any existed. Roosevelt didn't evince any need to make Polk's point about his devotion being just as real as Howe's. By the end of the day on Monday, though, he did make plans to attend Howe's burial in Massachusetts on Wednesday.

After the funeral services in the East Room late on Tuesday afternoon, the Roosevelts, with the Howe family, took a nine-hour overnight train to Fall River, Massachusetts, for the interment. The president would return to Washington immediately afterward, making for a trip of twenty hours, eighteen of them on the train.[27]

In Fall River, John and Franklin Roosevelt Jr., both students at Harvard University, met their parents at the railroad station and walked with them to a waiting limousine. After a short wait, their car joined a motorcade to the cemetery. During the ceremony, the president insisted on standing at the graveside, along with his family and the Howes. Eight Navy cadets served as pallbearers. An Episcopal priest conducted the rites. A Navy bugler sounded Taps.

On that day, Eleanor wrote, "There is a sense of emptiness that comes, when all that can be done for the person of a loved one is done. It is as though one were drained of all one's powers for a time."[28]

The feeling she described, President Roosevelt could not hide. As the casket was lowered into the ground, he gasped and struggled to keep from crying. Otherwise, he was at a remove, strangely distant and completely silent. "Mr. Roosevelt appeared oblivious to everything around him," observed a reporter.[29]

During the service, the president was supported by his two sons, each taller than he, and all of them bareheaded as a hard, cold wind blew.[30]

CHAPTER ONE

THE AIR IN SARATOGA

In October 1919, Louis Howe was in Washington, working by day and staying at the Hotel Harrington by night. His family was in Fall River while he worked as the assistant to the assistant secretary of the Navy, Franklin Roosevelt. One night, Howe "had plenty of time to lie still and think everything over," as he put it in a letter to his wife. His mind was at its best when he lay down on a bed or a couch, the floor, or occasionally even on a dresser, in order to think: just think. When he wrote to his wife, he felt a longing for his seven-year-old son, Hartley, known as "Bubble" or "Bubkins" or just plain "Bub." His other child, Mary, he complained, looked on him only "as a checkbook."

Mary Howe, nineteen, was a student at Vassar College and one of the few people in the world who would think to look to the perennially strapped Louis Howe as a checkbook. Much of the rest of the letter, in fact, was devoted to his latest attempt to keep the family solvent, juggling payments to take care of the rent and Mary's tuition. Financial troubles dogged Howe, but they were only distantly connected to the despair of the letter, an emotional frustration that revealed itself in many of his letters home, especially in the late 1910s and early 1920s.

As Howe neared the age of fifty, he was still unsettled, perhaps because his upbringing failed to prepare him for the life he faced as a man. Louis Howe was not meant to be poor. He was not meant to be working in a bureaucracy, with scant call for his creativity. He wasn't meant to be alone in his heart. He'd been promised much more, although in that regard he was hardly unique in middle age. The difference between Howe and a million others was that he was more stubborn than fate. Even when his hopes withered, as on the night at the Hotel Harrington, his inability to compromise remained.

If the points of Howe's early years had determined a straight line, it would have led straight to a position at the head of a newspaper, and his close-knit family would be at home a few blocks away. The line hadn't been a straight one, though, and so it was that Louis Howe was lying perfectly still in a hotel room in 1919, his only friend a boy of seven, four hundred miles away.

Howe had his share of friendly acquaintances. There were the people at St. Thomas' Episcopal church where he sang in the choir. And the amateurs in the theater troupe where he helped to put on plays. They were not the ones he had in mind, though, when he assessed his life in the letter from the Harrington and concluded that everyone who knew him—save Bub—viewed him with indifference, hatred, or opportunism. He meant the people about whom he cared, the Roosevelts and the Howes. The proper order was not certain as he scribbled away on letters in the night, yet it couldn't be ignored: the Roosevelts and the Howes. The Howes or the Roosevelts.

———— ·•·•· ————

Howe made a stark first impression, and those who knew him the least found it easiest to describe him. According to the universal opinion of casual acquaintances, he was slovenly, gruff, odd-looking, and completely oblivious to rank or social manners. One woman went so far as to state that he was low-class, and that people in the upper "caste," as she put it, naturally found it hard to accept him.[1] If Howe chose to be coarse, though, caste had nothing to do with it.

Louis McHenry Howe was born into a very rich home in Indianapolis, Indiana, on January 14, 1871. As a matter of fact, the house itself was among the more costly in the city, valued at a steep twenty thousand dollars.[2] Louis' mother, Eliza, known as "Lide," was part of the Indianapolis establishment. Her father, James M. Ray, had been an early pioneer in the area—so early that he was part of the federal commission that purchased land for the city and its surroundings from the local Native Americans. Ray later served as president of the Bank of the State of Indiana and made a fortune investing in mines. As soon as he could, he dedicated a great deal of his time and money to improving local education, especially through schools for females and for the blind.[3] Lide's first husband, James Sharpe, was another Indianapolis business leader, an executive with the Indiana and Illinois Railroad.[4] The couple had two daughters, Maria and Cora, before Sharpe's death in the early 1860s.

In 1867, Lide married Edward P. Howe, a native of Massachusetts whose family had settled in Cincinnati in the 1850s. Howe's parents had built a successful store there and then purchased a share of a wholesale business, which gave their children a comfortable start in life. Edward, the oldest of four, was a bright boy who graduated first in his class in high school. The year of his graduation, however, was 1860.[5] In the nervous climate of the times, he was anxious to see whether regional tensions would actually escalate into war. His focus on the national situation was a luxury that didn't last, though: soon after he graduated, his family lost the wholesale business.

Going broke was especially easy in the later part of the nineteenth century. Opportunity was easy to find and so was money on credit—and so were reversals, even on a local level. Those who borrowed heavily to make money were not uncommon, but they were the first to be ruined. For that reason, great families in that era were not judged on the initiative to make money, but on the discipline to keep it, which was rarer by far.

In the face of the downturn in Cincinnati, the Howe family moved to Indianapolis, where Edward's father took a job as a clerk and rented a home for his wife and children. When the Civil War began in April 1861, nineteen-year-old Edward was just starting a clerkship at a law office near Indianapolis. In September, he enlisted and late that autumn he was mustered into the 57th Indiana Regiment.[6] As the regiment marched through Tennessee, Howe served as a quartermaster, working his way up steadily. After two years, he held the rank of captain. Though his skills in supplying the regiment were crucial, he requested field duty toward the end of the war, when the 57th was fighting in Georgia. He apparently saw action at several sites between Chattanooga and Atlanta. After fighting in the war for three years, Howe then helped to write its history, which took even longer. Returning home late in 1864, he worked as an assistant to the adjutant general of Indiana, preparing the record of the state's involvement in the war, *The Report of the Adjutant General of the State of Indiana, 1861–1865*. When it was finished in 1868, the *Report* stretched to five thousand pages and filled eight volumes.

Captain Howe, as he was known for the rest of his life, was ambitious to secure his place in the upper class that his wife Lide occupied naturally. At the time of their marriage in 1867, Lide owned their house, and as of 1870 she controlled assets of $5,000. Edward had $3,000 of his own, but he had plans to increase it. He soon found an executive position with an insurance firm.[7] He also tried politics for the first and last time, running for the state senate on the Democratic ticket, as well as the Liberal Republican line. Apparently, there weren't enough voters of either type in Indianapolis, because he lost, although he had the consolation of running ahead of the other losing Democrats.[8] The Republicans, who had emerged from the Civil War with a more reformist reputation than the Democrats, dominated both national and Northern politics in the 1870s.[9] Captain Howe was more progressive than most others in his party, but his loyalty never wavered, as he persevered through many long years when "Liberal-Democrat" was a contradiction in terms.

When Louis McHenry Howe was born in 1871, his father was thirty, his mother thirty-nine, and his stepsisters, Maria and Cora, nineteen and fourteen.[10] In effect, the baby had four parents to fret over him. And they did hover over him, in part because they were affectionate people and in part because they soon discovered that the baby was sickly.

Julia G. Sharpe, who lived near the Howes, was a cousin of Eliza's first husband, James Sharpe. She described the Howes' son as "a rather pathetic little person—with large dark eyes and emaciated figure."[11] His family certainly didn't regard him as pathetic, though. His parents and stepsisters considered him a rare jewel, and handled him accordingly. "Louis, born late in the lives of his parents, was a very delicate child," Miss Sharpe wrote in a letter years later, "and it was said that his doting parents took him every morning to a doctor for a physical examination."[12]

By the time Louis was three, his condition was still troubling. Only one thing had really changed: the Howe family was practically penniless. Captain Howe had speculated in real estate and other ventures, probably using his wife's connections and certainly using her money. Unfortunately, Captain Howe's big chance to make a fortune came along just before the Panic of 1873, which instigated five hard years of economic depression. Anyone dependent on borrowed money was in trouble, as values dropped and loans were called in. Even Lide's father, James Ray, one of the city's founders and a symbol of its prosperity, was toppled at the age of seventy-three. No longer serving as a philanthropist, he was out looking for one. Before long, with the help of friends, he found what was later described as "an easy, but well paid position in the Treasury Department at Washington."[13]

For several years, Edward and Lide Howe managed to take care of their family. To save their fragile little boy from having to walk long distances, they bought him a miniature phaeton, a stylish type of carriage, with a pony to pull it. They tucked him inside and then escorted him to the doctor or elsewhere. The neighbor children couldn't help but gawk. "Such a program," Julia Sharpe noted dryly, "had been lacking in our lives."[14]

As an underweight child afflicted with asthma, Louis was a ripe candidate for early death, especially in the late nineteenth century, when air quality in cities was not very good and illnesses such as tuberculosis and typhoid swept through without warning, clearing out the weak—such as a skinny, wheezing little boy—along with many of the strong as well. The Howes took a conservative route, protecting their boy from both exertion and exposure, picking him up and carrying him when the pony phaeton wasn't available. The sense of need may well have been theirs as well as his. The special treatment gave them the benefit of having Louis with them constantly, to be hugged and held, enjoyed and indulged, included in conversations and closely nurtured. Some parents chose, on the contrary, to build up weak children through a rough-and-tumble regimen. Theodore Roosevelt, who was also small and asthmatic during his childhood in the 1860s, eventually adopted that path for himself.[15] So did others in Howe's era, such as the writer Ambrose Bierce and Woodrow Wilson.

The "strenuous life," as Theodore Roosevelt later labeled it, mandated vigorous exercise as a way for children "to overcome . . . difficulties."[16] That approach certainly had its success stories. It is somewhat harder to compile a list of potential celebrities who never made it to adulthood as a result of insistent relatives and their theories about hard living. The Howes chose not to take any chances with Louis. His breathing problems undoubtedly provided more than one stark episode to justify, for them at least, a constant sense of caution and a way of life that made the household revolve around the boy. "Some of the mothers of the neighborhood," recalled Miss Sharpe, "were inclined to criticize his bringing up as being pampered and thought he would have developed better had he been allowed to play with other children and not under the eyes of older and too solicitous people."[17] And yet by the time Louis was seven, he was no longer the main problem. Edward Howe's health had collapsed, probably from some combination of exhaustion and disappointment over that the fact that he could no longer care for his family. Lide's family stepped in to help.

L ide had a stepsister named Anna, who had married Sylvester E. Strong, son of the nationally known Sylvester S. Strong, an authority on the rehabilitation of invalids.[18] Both the father and son were physicians in Saratoga, New York, where they owned Strong's Sanitarium, a thriving institution that offered a full range of services along the medical spectrum. People could check into Dr. Strong's whether they were gravely ill, mildly run down, or just urgently self-indulgent. In Saratoga, the differentiation wasn't important. Everyone went there to feel better in one way or another.

In the nineteenth century, Americans, especially those from big cities, were more anxious to escape heat and humidity—and the diseases they cultivated—than snow and cold. Cool, clean Saratoga, located about twenty-five miles north of Albany in eastern New York State, answered the demand for respite and grew into an exclusive summer resort. It catered to rich people and gamblers, two groups that invariably excited one other, at least when the season was still young. Gambling casinos operated illegally and openly in the middle of town. Opulent hotels lined the main street. By day, their long front porticos formed the axis of life in town, as people sat outside, unabashedly perusing the people on the walk. By night, the ballrooms at the great hotels brought the same pastime indoors and set it to music.

Sylvester S. Strong, who had started his career as a Methodist minister, aimed to add a wholesome, productive element to Saratoga when he opened his "Remedial Institute," as it was originally called. Although his sanitarium was a private hospital with four or five physicians on staff, it also helped to pioneer restful palliatives such as massage therapy and formulated mineral baths, which have remained popular at spas ever since. "A casual observer would not observe its medical character," noted a travel book. "There is no appearance of invalidism, and its prominent features are those of a first-class family hotel."[19]

In 1878, when Louis was seven, the Howes lost the house in Indianapolis and moved permanently to Saratoga, where they checked into Strong's Sanitarium. Louis would benefit from the town's clear air and healthful waters, while Edward's health would benefit from the fact that his whole family could live at the sanitarium for free. Although he had given up on real estate investments for the time being, he hadn't lost hope of recouping his fortune (and Lide's) in some future business venture. First, though, he had debts to repay and a family without a home of its own. Looking back on his literary experience with the *Report of the Adjutant General of the State of Indiana,* he accepted a job as a reporter at the town's leading newspaper, *The Saratogian.* With that, he was able to support the family again, in a rented home in town.

The Saratogian was a first-rate paper, and, like Saratoga itself, more potent than its size would suggest. It had just one flaw, from Captain Howe's point of view: It was Republican. In 1882, the captain purchased a smaller paper, the overtly Democratic *Sun.*

For about five years, Louis continued to lead a cloistered life, receiving his education at home. Finally, at the age of twelve, he was allowed to go to school. The fact that the institution selected was otherwise a girls' school did not make it any less appropriate from the Howes' point of view. The main point was that it was located across the street from the home they had rented. Whatever the distance, Louis was finally out of the house. On his own with other children, he took pride in the French spelling of his first name and insisted that it be pronounced "Louie," unlike the English "Lewis," with which there was no option except the hard and formal.

Whether the town worked its wonders on Louis, or he just outgrew some of his earlier maladies, he turned from a weakling of a boy into a very lively teenager. He was still skinny and sometimes asthmatic, but no one had to carry him around or plop him into a pony phaeton. The challenge was just to keep up with Louis as he played tennis, acted in school plays, and helped his father at the *Sun*.

In later life, Louis Howe never spoke of himself as a Midwesterner. He came into his own as an upstate New Yorker in Saratoga and he knew it as well as anyone, taking pride in its history before and after the Europeans arrived. In an article written in 1905 for *The New England Magazine,* Howe described the occasion in 1767 when William Johnson, an Irishman and large landowner in upstate New York, was suffering from a wound to his leg received in battle twelve years before. The Mohawk Indians voted in tribal council to escort him to the springs at Saratoga for treatment. Johnson was the first person of European descent allowed the privilege. After a few days, he was cured and when he returned home, he spread the word about the healing powers of the mineral water. "In 1783," Howe wrote, "George Washington, accompanied by Alexander Hamilton and Governor George Clinton, visited the Spring. Washington was so favorably impressed with its virtues that he made inquiries with a view to acquiring the land and building thereon a summer home, although at that time the spring lay in the heart of the wilderness, and one log hut sheltered all the inhabitants of the place."[20]

Saratoga grew quickly starting in 1831, when it was the destination of the second railroad to be constructed in the United States. By the time of the Civil War, the town was the unofficial summer capital of the country and its government, drawing the leaders of business, the arts, sports, and politics, all into one small town. "As a political observatory no place can be more fitly selected," boasted an article in *Harper's New Monthly*. "Information from all quarters is received daily; and it is the best of all places for politicians to congregate."[21] Howe's own article on Saratoga carried the tone of a memoir as he described the summer schedule in a town preparing to grow into a perpetual house party of fifty thousand:

> All during May, the inhabitants of what is then a quiet, pretty little village, boasting not over fifteen thousand inhabitants, have been making ready. By the first of June, the whole village, spick and span with new paint, with well-swept and graded streets, sits expectantly to greet the coming guests. Silently, quietly, almost unnoticed they slip in—wise old-timers, who have learned that June is the most beautiful month of the year at Saratoga, except possibly September. The small hotels now throw open their doors . . . and each of the innumerable boarding houses boasts a guest or two. They are a quiet, health-seeking, rest-seeking folk, these early comers, drinking in the wonderful air that sweeps down pure and fresh from the Adirondack balsam forests and sets the nerves tingling with new-born life. . . .
>
> As July approaches, the great hotels strip off their winter garments, and before the last of the small army of house cleaners has wrung her mop, the first visitor greets the smiling clerk. . . . At the Grand Union Hotel, Victor Herbert, with no ordinary summer orchestra, but a special band of fifty trained musicians, begins his concerts, and the empty seats on the broad piazzas grow fewer each day. . . .
>
> Then, suddenly, the first of August comes. For two days previous, a curious quiet has settled upon the town. It is as if every one had stopped to draw a good long breath before plunging into the exciting days to follow. . . . To the stranger, the first of August brings with it a wonderful surprise. If he is lucky enough to have a friend who knows the proper thing to do upon this eventful day, he joins the crowds upon the piazza of the United States or the Worden hotels where he can command a view of the short, wide street leading from Broadway to the station.[22]

In August, the racing crowd swelled the population with the richest citizens of every other town in the country, jamming the sidewalks on that hectic first of August. By nightfall, all the newcomers had accommodations somewhere. "There is nothing stranger," Howe observed, "than this apparently unlimited capacity of Saratoga to absorb people."[23]

For a wide-eyed boy such as Louis Howe, Saratoga in the summer was itself a college of the world, and he knew every corner of it as his own. It shaped him, made him wise in the appearance and use of power, and it turned him into a terrible snob—not about money, which could be somewhat laughable in Saratoga—but in the remarkable quality of influence. He was a small-town boy with one foot, as it were, in the court at Versailles.

For a time, according to Howe's later accounts, he planned on attending Yale University.[24] His grandfather, James Ray, had attended Columbia University fifty years before, and so Lide probably had hopes of college for her son, but Howe never matriculated at Yale, if he even applied.

Later, Louis Howe explained that his parents worried that his health was not equal to the rigors of academic study. There is no reason to doubt that, but, in addition, college was expensive, and classical studies were of no particular use to a budding reporter. Louis took a few courses at a local prep school, but he was impatient to enter the real world, joining his father at the *Saratoga Sun*. As a consolation, Captain Howe found freelance work as a travel writer and took his son on trips through Europe, the Middle East, and the Caribbean. A noticeably bright young man, Louis finished his education where he was most comfortable: utterly unbound and at his father's side.

———————

A profile of Captain Howe that later appeared in a book on the New York State Democratic Party was almost certainly written by Louis; it carries both his style and a long tribute to his working relationship with his father. The description of Captain Howe's war experience is rich in the sort of detail recalled in the front parlor, boasting that, "Although barely of age, and one of the youngest captains in the army, Captain Howe made a record for fidelity and efficiency, and also for gallantry in battle not surpassed by any of his comrades."[25] That was the lore to which Louis aspired and to which he gave his ultimate loyalty.

Captain Howe's lonely fight for the Democrats in upstate New York became Louis', too. The Captain's allegiance was rewarded, at least temporarily in the 1890s when Buffalo's Grover Cleveland was elected president on the Democratic ticket. As a result, Captain Howe was appointed Saratoga's postmaster, giving the family an extra source of income and its most comfortable standard of living since the sunniest days of Indianapolis.

At the *Sun,* Louis took on all chores. His father borrowed money for a color printing press and so, in the off-season, Louis tried to find outside jobs to keep it occupied. He didn't mind the work in sales; his travels gave him an intimate knowledge of the countryside and its inhabitants. During the summer, though, he was a busy journalist, using his reporter's credentials to gain access to the celebrities and politicians who passed through the resort. Both Edward and Louis wrote articles for the *New York Herald,* its sister paper, the *Telegram,* and the Boston *Herald,* as well as the *Sun.* They covered the social and political news emerging from Saratoga and also filed stories from the state capital at Albany.

The neighbors back in Indianapolis might have been surprised to see that Louis Howe was not only alive at the age of twenty, but energetic and popular. He was a good talker and had developed a snappy personality. One friend later called him "a gay blade," which in the parlance of the 1890s meant that he was very smooth with the ladies.[26] Howe's appearance was unremarkable, but he presented himself well and, anyway, in his era, looks were not everything in the eyes of the average young lady. Dancing skill was. And Howe had a reputation as an excellent partner on the floor. He also knew his way around town, and that was an attractive quality in a place rife with newcomers. Others came to the resorts and left, but for Louis at twenty, the great hotels were his, all summer long.

"The Grand Union has made the piazzas and lobby of that hotel by common consent the rallying place of Saratoga's gaiety in the evening," Howe wrote. "The spectacle is brilliant beyond description; evening gowns and gems of fabulous price are the rule, and in the marble-lined central office, the light from a hundred electric fixtures, tossed back from one flashing jewel to another, to be finally lost in a sheen of iridescent silk or fold of priceless lace, affords a sight unknown save in Saratoga."[27] For an article in the *Sun,* Howe recruited experts on jewelry, couture, and finance to circulate in the ballroom of the Grand Union Hotel on one perfectly average evening. According to the calculations of Howe's circulating appraisers, the aggregate value of the gowns in the room was $1.25 million; that of the jewels was $2.4 million and the total wealth of only fifty of the notable men present totaled $550 million.[28] That was the atmosphere of Louis Howe's neighborhood dance around the time he was coming of age.

Howe loved the theater, and so it followed that Louis Howe productions were soon everywhere—at schools and hotels, at commercial theaters and, when all else failed, at Dr. Strong's Sanitarium. Howe designed and painted sets, he wrote several plays, and he was a good actor who could get his laughs or draw a tear, but he was at his best as a director, meticulously coaching the players.[29] In his spare time, he also embraced two of the paramount fads of the 1890s, tennis and bicycling, indicating that his health was far stronger than it had been when he was a child.

Howe and the other young men of Saratoga had an enviable perch when it came to the hunt for a girlfriend or even a wife. Single women were plentiful during the resort season, since families on holiday tended to keep their daughters close at hand, even while encouraging their sons to go on vacation by themselves. Of course, some young men did choose to go to Saratoga, but a more common sight at the hotels was one parent or two registering at the desk with a slightly stifled daughter in tow. So it was that in 1896, Louis Howe noticed Grace Hartley, then twenty, in the lobby of Dr. Strong's Sanitarium, checking in with her mother, Mary.

Mary Borden Hartley and her ex-husband, Dr. James Hartley, also had two sons, who were as much as twenty years older than Grace. The Hartleys were from Fall River, Massachusetts, a port city on the water near Rhode Island. When Grace was a child, her parents divorced, leaving Dr. Hartley bitter toward everyone even remotely involved, except for his daughter, whom he was allowed to see only once a month. He especially hated his ex-wife's family, the Bordens, citing "the great wrongs, losses and personal insults which I have sustained from certain of [my wife's] relatives."[30]

With the divorce settlement from Dr. Hartley, Mary Hartley continued her upper-middle-class lifestyle. She was a good-hearted woman, although in conversation she could be very quick to boast that Cook Borden, one of Fall River's great industrialists, was her father.[31] That made her one of *the* Bordens. What she was slower to mention was that her niece was the infamous Lizzie Borden, who had been acquitted of killing her own parents in Fall River four years earlier. That made Mary one of *those* Bordens. It is very likely that Louis Howe, a veteran reporter at the age of twenty-five and a facile lobby hound since childhood, knew all of it, good and bad, even before the desk clerk had slid Mrs. Hartley the room key. In any case, Howe was instantly smitten with Grace Hartley.

Grace had just finished her freshman year at Vassar College. She was a prim young woman, noticeably intelligent in her manner. She was also very close to her mother, who was stiffly protective, having rejected Grace's most recent suitor either because he was Irish or because she suspected that he might take her daughter to Ireland—much too far from Fall River. The city of Fall River had a deep hold on the Hartley women, mother and daughter. For the moment, though, in the summer of 1896, none of that mattered to Louis Howe as he arranged to receive an introduction to Grace. She later told his friend and biographer, Lela Stiles, that she "was not a bit impressed with Louis Howe at that first meeting."[32] Howe didn't give up. His courtship of Grace was something of an echo of his father's interest in Lide Sharpe. Both aimed high, pursuing attractive women with more money, better connections, and a finer education. No one could doubt that Louis' feelings for Grace Hartley were sincere, judging by the ardor of his letters to her over the following two decades, but in a variety of ways, he followed in his father's pattern. Watching for a woman of consequence was one of them.

"Dear Miss Hartley," Louis wrote sometime soon after they met, "It is such a nice day don't you want to take a walk" (the grammar, or lack of it, is his).[33] Grace soon discovered that he shared her love of flowers and they would walk in the fields, gathering blossoms. Eventually, they saved the most beautiful ones, pressing them into a Victorian keepsake known as a flower book.[34] Grace tended to be reserved and Louis brought out her sense of humor. They danced at the hotels on Saturday nights. The following summer, Mrs. Hartley and Grace returned to Dr. Strong's, though Grace's situation had changed in the interim. She had decided to leave Vassar. "I roomed with two other Fall River girls," she recalled years later, "and every time one of us would get a letter from home we'd all devour it and then cry with homesickness."[35] She had spent two years at the college.

Early in the same year, 1897, Dr. Hartley had died, leaving an estate of $35,000. After giving $5,000 to the couple who had cared for him during his final days, he left Grace $30,000—minus two dollars, one for each of his sons. The only contingency was that she could not live with any member of the Borden family except her mother, or loan them money. He implied that he made that stipulation to protect her. When Grace arrived in Saratoga for the summer of 1897, she was a young woman of considerable means, worth approximately $30,000 more than Louis was.

With Edward Howe in charge of the Saratoga post office, Louis was then tacitly running the *Sun*. James Clarke, later a vice president of the Banker's Trust Company in New York, started as an apprentice reporter at the *Sun*. "You took the trouble to show me how to write my first newspaper story and I have never forgotten it," he recalled in a letter to Howe much later. "Probably you have forgotten it but it was a big moment for me. We stood against the desk in that little office of the *Saratoga Sun* with the smell of molten lead coming through the pressroom door, Brother Hastie trotting through telling me to hurry, and smiling Ethel Riley behind the counter giggling as usual."[36] (James Hastie was the printer; Riley, then a teenager, was another employee of the small paper.)

Louis continued to pursue Grace. Frances Perkins came to know both of them in about 1910. Perkins, the secretary of labor in the Roosevelt administration, considered Louis Howe a rather strange match for Grace, since he was neither collegiate nor social, in the class-conscience sense. "She wasn't a woman, as I knew her," Perkins said of Grace, "who ever would have been limited in her choice of husbands. She would have been likely to have had a reasonable opportunity to marry several perfectly ordinary people. But she did love Louis."[37]

Howe had qualities that set him apart. If he was not yet rich, he had prospects that gave him an aura of excitement. If he was something less than imposing in appearance, he could nonetheless make a lasting impression on those with whom he chose to try. From the start, he was flexible in sharing the interests of someone he liked—Grace liked flowers. That was one of the first things Louis learned about her. And he found it easy to appreciate them, too. She loved antiques and he entered into the search for rare ones at auctions and shops in the countryside. Howe was not the first person in love to adopt a hobby or two in the name of conquest, but the degree of his zeal was both unique and sincere, and an early introduction for Grace to his empathetic nature. If her interests became his, so, in time, did her problems. Grace was drawn to him and, it follows, began to consider what a future with him might be like.

At the time, Howe was ardently striving to be "ordinary," that trait upon which Frances Perkins' remark placed such a positive value, enveloping as it did acceptance of a comforting median for one's home and career. Nonetheless, Howe was not conformist by nature and he encouraged, even expected, individuality in those he respected. Grace, who had been indulged, but sheltered all of her life, was comfortable with Howe and came to return his feelings. He was a young man who could be trusted with intimate emotions. And he could dance.

After a two-year courtship, the couple became engaged and a wedding was planned for 1899. Mrs. Hartley must have approved, because in the fall of 1898 she allowed Grace to visit Saratoga on her own and stay with friends there. Of course, the person Grace was there to see was Louis. He could hardly wait to marry her. In fact, he couldn't wait. At the end of the visit, he volunteered to ride on the train with her part of the way to Fall River. En route, his sense of drama rose to the fore.

Louis told Grace that he was probably going to ship out to cover the Spanish-American War at any time and solemnly predicted that he might well be killed or else die from the strain. He concluded by making the case that they ought to be married that very day. According to Grace, the two of them scrambled off the main line and made a detour to Vermont, where marriages could be performed without a waiting period. They found a justice of the peace, said their vows, and completed the occasion with a pheasant dinner. Then Grace continued on home. She was only a little late getting to Fall River. Perhaps Louis was protecting Grace's honor in relation to some previous indiscretion. One can see how he might suddenly panic, imagining himself run over by a train and fretting about leaving her—potentially—as a single woman with a baby on the way. There is no evidence to think that was the scenario, except that it would explain Howe's rush. His mind worked constantly to meet just such possibilities with his own ready contingencies. Perhaps, on the other hand, he was just impatient to be a married man and if so, it's hard to think he and Grace could have had much time for romance in between the vows and the pheasant, or that if they did, he would have then deposited her on a night train to Fall River. With or without a logical reason, Louis tweaked the plan and, perhaps, his fate, leaving Grace again, but on his own terms, as her husband.

Howe returned home, still hoping to receive an assignment to cover the Spanish-American War. He would not have gone as the war correspondent for the *Saratoga Sun,* which barely had the manpower to cover Albany, let alone Cuba. The prospect involved the *New York Herald.* It was one of the better papers in the state, and Howe had carefully maintained his connection to it as a part-time "stringer" in Saratoga, filing stories as they arose. Whether or not the *Herald* was actually planning to send its man in Saratoga to cover the fighting in Cuba, the war effectively ended before the assignment came through.

Mary Hartley found out about the Vermont wedding by happening upon one of Louis' letters to her daughter and reading it, but she nonetheless gave Grace and Louis a resplendent society wedding in May 1899, as originally planned. Some of the guests probably knew that the vows were redundant, but no one spoiled the day about that. As a Hartley—that is, a Borden—production, the wedding was an indication of the family's belief that Louis' persona and his future were worth showcasing in a formal wedding for all of Fall River to see. The couple followed it with a wedding trip to Virginia, where they indulged their interest in antiques and found a Hepplewhite side table that they bought and took home, a present for themselves.[38]

Mrs. Hartley followed up the grand ceremony with an extraordinary wedding gift: a spacious house in Saratoga. As the year 1899 ended, Howe was just weeks away from his twenty-ninth birthday. He had overcome the worst of the health problems he'd faced as a youngster, and avoided the in-hibitions that might have been left by his family's response to those mal-adies. He wasn't a semi-invalid, confined to their loving front parlor, as he easily might have been. He had pulled himself up to become a busy newspa-perman, with every expectation of taking over the *Sun* someday. He had a wife about whom he was passionate and a home that he couldn't have af-forded on his own for another twenty years. Louis Howe could look back on the first part of his life as a struggle, but one that he had won.

CHAPTER TWO

UPSTATERS

During the first few months after the wedding, Grace didn't feel well, suffering from a number of minor maladies. She returned to Fall River often, but Louis wasn't resentful. In her absence, he wrote of their marriage with a kind of reverence. He had a need to believe in it and even admitted that when he went to church, he daydreamed about his wife. "Oh the wonderful places we have been to, you and I dear," he wrote, "while the stupid unimaginative congregation fancied me absorbed in the sermon."[1]

For the first three years that Grace was acquainted with Louis, during the courtship and engagement, she had known the Howe family to be comfortable and prosperous. Not long after she and Louis married, the situation changed. Captain Howe found himself in grave danger of ceding control of the *Saratoga Sun*. In the wake of Democratic reversals, he lost his sinecure as postmaster in Saratoga, and the *Sun* was in no position to make up the lost income, due to the liability of the color printing press. Rather than buoying the newspaper financially, the press was dragging it down—a debt that Captain Howe and his wife were unable to repay. As a member of the household, Grace could plainly see that Captain Howe was not equal to the challenge of rescuing the business. "There seems to be no hurry in him," she wrote to Louis from one of her frequent vacations to Fall River. She lamented her father-in-law's "lack of common sense."[2] It was true that the Captain couldn't be described as a natural-born businessman, with a record of making one fortune in his lifetime and losing two. In former days, though, Captain Howe had compensated for his failings with sheer drive. Once, there was indeed a hurry in him, but by 1899, he was tired and growing sick. It was Louis' turn. He had been bred to take his father's place and at the call, he gave it all he had. He had certainly inherited his father's stubborn ambition to succeed. Unfortunately, he had also inherited his father's business acumen.

In late 1899, Grace was in Saratoga when she learned she was pregnant and decided to go home. Louis might have pointed out that at the time she *was* home—in her own house in Saratoga—but to her, "home" was still her mother's house in Fall River. She made plans to stay there at least until June, when the baby was due. While she was away, Louis made a monumental effort to save the *Sun*. The paper needed an infusion of cash and he had only one source for it. He mortgaged their house. Grace presumably agreed, but it was nonetheless a desperate move on his part, and a heartfelt show of loyalty to his father. It was also tantamount to an act of larceny where his mother-in-law was concerned. She had given the house to Louis and Grace only months before in order to provide a basis of stability in their married life. That, it seemed, was as futile as Howe's effort to save the *Sun*.

When the *Sun* went out of business in 1900, the creditors sold it. Louis was left with nothing to show for his risky move except a heavy mortgage on the house and a tenuous job with the new owner of the paper. He was no longer in authority, but did continue reporting in his two areas of expertise: Saratoga, where rich people brought their scandals, to his mounting boredom, and Albany, where elected officials brought theirs—to his unending disgust. Captain Edward and Lide Howe, along with Cora, were left nearly penniless by the collapse of the *Sun*. They moved in with Louis, to save on expenses and to keep him company. Apparently, their housekeeping was lacking, giving Grace one more reason to stay in Fall River.

In the spring of 1900, Louis apparently took Grace to see one of her old friends, the sort of man she might have married. His comfortable house, fine horses, and general aura of well-being sent her into a new level of anxiety about her own plight. Having bolted right back to Fall River, she wrote to Louis about it darkly. He replied from his own new level of remorse. After swearing that his family was learning to live within its budget of five dollars per week, and promising that they would try to keep up with the housework in the future, he surrendered in anguish. He expressed in some detail his wish that for her sake he had died before their wedding and then he offered her a divorce.[3] She didn't seem to pursue the suggestion. She was, after all, pregnant with their first child.

By the time the baby, Mary, was born in June 1900, Grace had spent more of her married life with her mother than with her husband. As summer began, she and Louis made up with each other, after the recriminations and regrets of spring. Louis, traveling for work, saved enough money on his expense account by eating rolls for lunch and staying in cheap hotels to buy a train ticket for Fall River.[4] They still faced problems. After thirteen months of marriage, the bride and groom were each living with their own parents, and they were in debt. Grace returned to Saratoga with little Mary and stayed there over the winter of 1900–1901, chafing under the Howe family's combination of treacly affection and minute management of one another's affairs. Grace came from a crisper atmosphere in the Hartley/Borden tradition: cooler, perhaps, but with more individual dignity. Louis was still attached to his father's dreams and the plots the two of them had laid together. No one could blame the Howe family for being close-knit; their bonds had helped them through wrenching times with good cheer and optimism intact. Grace couldn't join them in either, though, not with a canopy of disaster hanging over the whole scene.

Indeed, after the Howes lost everything, matters could have been worse. And so they were when Louis was fired from his job with the *Sun*. Soon afterward, things managed to sink again. To Grace's shock and disgust, Louis returned to the *Sun* office and begged the owner for his job back. He got it. In Grace's family, nobody begged for anything, even if it

meant starvation on the street—which might have been next for the
Howes, in any case, because Louis soon lost the job once again. By then,
Grace and Mary were back in Fall River. Louis forfeited the house entirely
and lived with his parents in a boardinghouse.

In 1901 Louis helped his father launch another Democratic newspaper
for Saratoga. No one knew better than they did that the town didn't have
enough Democratic readers to sustain even the *Sun,* let alone yet another
paper. But they tried anyway, with a weekly called the *Saratoga Herald,*
largely compiled from the columns of the *New York Herald.* The publishers
were listed as "E.P. Howe & Son." The paper lasted until 1902, when Louis
left Saratoga for a full-time job in New York City as a reporter for the
Evening Telegram, where the managing editor, John T. Burke, had noticed
that he "showed an insight into New York State politics above the average."[5]
Within a month, though, Howe was back home in Saratoga. He said afterward that his health had collapsed while he was in New York.

———— ◦ ◦ ————

The same year, 1902, Eleanor Roosevelt began to see more of her distant cousin, Franklin, at social gatherings in New York. They had
known each other since childhood and, in fact, Eleanor's late father, Elliott
Roosevelt (the younger brother of Theodore Roosevelt), had been Franklin's
godfather. Eleanor, who had been educated in Europe, was dividing her
time between her dour grandmother, who lived at the Tivoli estate in
Dutchess County, New York, and her fun-loving aunts in New York City.
Aspects of both types of women seemed to vie for prominence in her personality. Never one to boast about herself, Eleanor did note that she had "a
quick mind,"[6] a prime characteristic and, in her, an irrepressible one.
Franklin was then a student at Harvard University, favoring courses in history and political economy. When he entered college, he was reserved in nature, but as an upperclassman, he began to exhibit an outgoing personality
that seemed to draw on endless self-confidence. Many people enjoyed talking with the ebullient young Roosevelt, but in 1902–1903, he sought out
Eleanor.

As Eleanor met more of the Roosevelt-Delano relatives, she was fascinated by the financial stability of their lives. Her immediate relatives lived elegantly, whether they could afford it or not, to the point that some of them literally spent their last dollar. And even then, they put on a fine appearance. In Eleanor's experience, the specter of ruin was never far away, and in times of disaster, her impecunious relatives were forced to turn to the wealthy ones for an income consistent with an upper-class lifestyle. "The Delanos," she wrote, "were the first people I met who were able to do what they wanted to do without wondering where to obtain the money."[7] She discovered that they watched their expenditures carefully, a trait that she found rather alien, but attractive at first, when it seemed to produce something her life lacked: predictability.

After Franklin graduated from Harvard in 1903, he asked Eleanor to marry him. She consented, admitting later that she didn't know very much about love or marriage at the time. Franklin, at least, had the advantage of seeing his own parents in a strong relationship up to the time of his father's death in 1900. He tried to assure his mother, Sara Delano Roosevelt, that marrying Eleanor was exactly what he wanted and wrote that he was "the happiest man just now in the world."[8] Nonetheless, his mother was unconvinced that either of them knew what they were doing and she did what she could to stall the wedding for at least a couple of years.

———◆———

In 1903, Louis Howe elected to start over in life. He decided to follow his old dream of becoming a freelance writer. He set his sights on the national magazines that guided American thought in the early twentieth century. He tried to sell fiction, without success, and feature stories, with small success. Fortunately, he already had a longstanding relationship with the *New York Herald,* to which he contributed articles as Saratoga correspondent. That kept him busy in summer, but during the rest of the year he found freelance work a trying way to earn a steady income.

Under the circumstances, the sensible move might have been to join Grace in Fall River and find a steady job there or somewhere in eastern

New England. He wasn't, in truth, much of a general reporter, lacking curiosity about even the most lurid crime cases, let alone the lesser stories on a city beat. Howe shone, though, in covering political and legislative maneuvering. With two state capitals, Providence and Boston, within a forty-mile distance, he would have had a good chance to establish himself in a comfortable job closer to Grace's hometown. He never tried it. He had a reason to stay where he was.

In the early years of the century, New York was the incubator for national politics, with the state entirely dominating the 1904 presidential elections. The Republicans were led by the president, Theodore Roosevelt of New York City. Howe had watched him rise from obscurity to the governorship in 1898 and then the vice presidency in 1900. In fact, working for the *Herald*, Howe covered Roosevelt's harried trip from the Adirondacks in September 1901 when President William McKinley lay dying in Buffalo from an assassin's bullet. Roosevelt renewed his party's liberal reputation, applying his brand of progressive politics to economic reform and several social issues. Party leaders made no secret of the fact that they missed the late President McKinley, an eminently reassuring moderate who had soundly beaten the prominent Democrat William Jennings Bryan in both 1896 and 1900. With no organized opposition, however, the Republican Party was entirely in Roosevelt's hands.

On the Democratic side, all of the major contenders for the 1904 nomination were New Yorkers. The probable winner, in the early opinion of party leaders, was William Randolph Hearst. Still boyish at forty-one, he had inherited a mining fortune and then enlarged it as a newspaper publisher based in New York. Hearst's father, George, had been a senator from California, and William was determined to take a prominent role in government. At least, sometimes he was determined. Other times, he didn't seem to care whether he succeeded in politics or not.

Hearst represented himself as a defender of the common man. As a two-term U.S. congressman elected in 1903, he was often labeled a radical or a socialist or both for pledging himself to government control of essential industries such as railroads and telegraph companies. He was also in favor of allowing the electorate, rather than state legislatures, to choose senators, on the basis that legislators were altogether too vulnerable to the influence of the powerful: specifically, through bribery.[9] As a candidate, Hearst had good ideas, some of them ahead of their time, but he was also marked by contradictions. Violently opposed to big business, he had built the nation's largest newspaper chain using cutthroat tactics. He despised bribery, and yet he was an accomplished practitioner of the art.

Aside from questions of character, though, Hearst was too liberal for many Democrats—nineteenth-century Democrats in spirit—who were hanging on to the party's pre-Bryan reputation for, as one observer termed it, "a dread of innovation," and a basic belief in business, big or otherwise.[10] An attempt was made to draft former president Grover Cleveland of Buffalo, who had been regarded as a moderate in his heyday in the 1890s. As of 1904, Democrats commonly hailed the three great presidents of the United States as Washington, Jefferson, and Cleveland. At sixty-seven, however, Cleveland had no intention of running for a third term. As the Democratic convention approached, the contest narrowed into a fight between Hearst and Alton B. Parker, the chief judge of New York's highest court. Parker was an old-fashioned type of Democrat, a throwback to the days before Bryan, the liberal, and even before Cleveland, the moderate.

Louis Howe ought to have been in his element in the 1904 campaign. People he knew personally, either from lobby chats in Saratoga's hotels or backroom confreres in Albany's capitol building, were taking hold on the national scene. All of the most crowded trains headed for the national conventions originated in New York, but Howe wasn't on any of them. Instead, he was helping to manage a businessmen's club in Saratoga in 1904. The job paid well and might even have turned into a career for him, in middle management and administration, but his mind was on politics. He was still submitting occasional articles to newspapers in the state, trying anything he could to stay in the political conversation. Yet the conventions were called to order without him. With the parties in a historic state of flux, he followed the news by reading about it in the paper.

Hearst may have possessed the power of his newspapers, but Parker had a tireless campaign manager in William F. Sheehan, a sharp and likable lawyer originally from Buffalo. Born into poverty in Buffalo in 1859, Sheehan had been a boat hand as a boy. An extrovert with the ability to juggle myriad activities, he became a lawyer and then a politician, with the memorable nickname "Blue-eyed Billy." He was a prodigy in New York politics, in line with the large body of Democrats who resisted reform, maintaining that government should manage itself and keep out of the lives of its citizens. At thirty-two, he rose to the level of lieutenant governor, the youngest in the state's history, and then retired from politics three years later, claiming that he was practically penniless.[11] That would change.

Leaving a career full of carping ward bosses and tangled favors far behind in Buffalo, Sheehan moved to New York City, where he kept busy with a day job as a corporation lawyer and, on the side, a host of rich friends; financier Thomas Fortune Ryan, for example, and others anxious to include him in their deals. By 1904, comfortably well-off, Sheehan returned to politics, promising to win the presidential nomination for his law partner, Alton B. Parker.

Many of the delegates at the national convention in St. Louis were looking for an antidote to William Jennings Bryan. Twice before, the Democrats had nominated Bryan and lost. A lot of smart politicians figured it to be Hearst's convention.

The silky smooth Sheehan came through for Parker, though, working through a deadlock in the delegate voting and finally staving off the Hearst forces by courting progressives from the Bryan camp. Not many people could have drawn liberal support to an incontrovertible conservative such as Alton Parker, but Sheehan did, by encouraging them to assume that Parker, the son of a farmer, would be as populist as Bryan. Only after the nomination was sealed did Sheehan release an urgent message from Judge Parker clarifying that he was firmly against Bryan's favorite issue: using silver in addition to gold to back the dollar (in order to free up credit crucial for farmers and small-business owners).[12] The Bryan liberals felt betrayed and the Democratic Party was instantly divided. But Sheehan had bagged the nomination for his man.

"It was clear," summarized a writer of the day, "that Parker represented, on the whole, the weight of conservatism, while Roosevelt embodied the spirit of progress, and that neither was typical of his party."[13]

In the general election, Theodore Roosevelt trounced Judge Parker, the last of the conservative, nineteenth-century-style Democrats ever nominated for president. Four years into the new century, the Democratic Party first repelled its liberal wing and then abandoned its conservative wing. All that was left, in New York State, at least, was the localized core controlled by the urban machines such as Tammany Hall—along with a vocal groundswell of people outside of the cities who were disgusted by urban machines—such as Tammany.

Tammany Hall, formally known as the Tammany Society, was a Democratic political club that rose at times to the status of a shadow government in the city of New York. With roots in the late 1700s, it flexed new powers in the late 1860s, even as it moved into its namesake building on Fourteenth Street in Manhattan.[14] "During the latter half of the nineteenth century immigrants were pouring into America through the Port of New York," explained Edward J. Flynn, a well-respected Tammany boss, "The so-called 'better element' would have none of them. The young Republican Party reflected this attitude. The immigrants, on the other hand, being human, wanted friends, jobs, the chance to become citizens. Tammany was smart enough to offer them all three, in return for lifetime, and often second-, third-, and fourth-generation fealty to the party. It was as simple and as obvious as that."[15] All the while, potential candidates were identified and nurtured. Those who were elected were expected to allow Tammany Hall officials to suggest names for appointments. Most obeyed; only a few of those who didn't stayed in office.

With control of so many elected officials in New York, most Tammany bosses reaped vast amounts of money through graft, skimming a share of the municipal contracts that their cohorts handed out. At the turn-of-the-century, Boss Richard Croker exerted enough control over the police department to offer protection to brothels and gambling halls, as well.[16] Having a lock on City Hall in New York, as long as its handpicked Democrats were in power, Tammany also reached into the state government in Albany, though with varying degrees of success.

Louis Howe was among those Democrats who wanted nothing to do with Tammany Hall, especially as it tried to solidify its control of upstate regions. As a reporter, he had seen for himself the crooked deals that had stifled state government for a decade or more. Not all of these deals could be traced to Tammany Hall, but Howe knew that it perpetrated the most extensive system of influence-peddling in the state. He rarely missed an opportunity to point that out in print. Yet there was no end in sight. Reporting such as his may have revealed corruption, but couldn't stop it.

———— •+• ————

Like the Howes, the newlywed Roosevelts found a house awaiting them when they returned from their honeymoon. They had been married in March 1905—choosing St. Patrick's Day because Eleanor's Uncle Theodore would be in New York City for the parade and could give the bride away. Franklin was a student at Columbia Law School at the time. As soon as the semester was over, the couple went to Europe and returned to a fully furnished house. "A tiny house," Sara called it, "just twelve feet wide— in 36th Street."[17] Her late husband had once expressed the opinion that parents should not live with their adult children and she followed his rule to the letter, keeping her own house around the corner on Madison Avenue and paying the lease on the one on Thirty-Sixth Street for Franklin and Eleanor. Despite the fact that they were just starting out, though, the young couple didn't actually need her financial help; they had assets of their own and might easily have rented an apartment.

Eleanor received an income of $5,000 in a bad year, $8,000 in a good one.[18] Franklin had a smaller independent income from the trust fund of $120,000 that he had inherited from his father.[19] Together, they earned approximately $10,000 annually in independent income at a time when a U.S. congressman, by way of example, was paid $5,000. Eleanor apparently mentioned the possibility of renting a flat for themselves, but the house on Thirty-Sixth Street was furnished and ready, and neither she nor Franklin was in a position to set up a household; she was pregnant when they came home from Europe and he was returning to his studies at Columbia. Like the Howes, they had high expectations that led them to gladly accept help from a parent and live in a home that otherwise would have been out of reach.

The news for Louis Howe in late 1905 was that the *New York Herald* called him back to reporting with a part-time job covering Albany politics during the legislative season, which would start in January 1906. He was to work as a second-string man, behind another reporter, but at least he was back in the fray, contributing articles to the *Herald* and its affiliate, the New York *Telegram*. Renting an apartment in Albany, he lived with Grace and Mary, though they were used to the fact that just because they lived with him, they didn't necessarily see him. "He never had any sense of time," Grace later recalled, "He was a newspaper man and night or day meant nothing to him."[20] With no permanent home of their own, the couple had come to plan their domestic arrangements one season at a time: spring (the Legislative session in Albany), summer (Saratoga Springs' flowering), and fall (election time). When Louis could afford it and Grace was willing, they rented furnished apartments and stayed together. More often, though, Grace opted for the congenial life she and Mary enjoyed in Fall River, while Louis stayed in boardinghouses or hotels, to save money.

The excitement later that year was that William Randolph Hearst was bouncing back from his run for the White House by announcing his candidacy for governor of New York. With the hearty backing of Tammany Hall, Hearst swept through the summer toward the nomination. The Tammany political machine was not merely a source of support, however. It was also a major issue in the campaign.

"The New York State Democrats around Rochester and Buffalo didn't want to be Tammany Democrats," Frances Perkins later recalled. "There were a good many fine old families up there . . . who were Democrats and wanted to be Democrats. They were Democrats philosophically and on a basis of the party platform and on the basis of free trade which was the standard policy of the Democratic Party in national politics." The struggle of the immigrant class for political power through Tammany Hall was not new in 1906, but it was still the basis of a draining struggle within the state of New York, where a motivated group of upstate Democrats resisted every inroad by the political machine. "They made it quite clear," Perkins continued, referring to the upstaters, "that they were against this misrule of the city by these 'low grade thugs.' It was the ancient conflict in American life between the old families and the newcomers, really. These 'thugs' were the Irish politicians who had just come up and who were presuming to say how things should be done."[21]

In upstate New York, Tammany's organization was patchy, but it was better than any other statewide machine. A wealthy Democrat in the small city of Auburn, Thomas Mott Osborne, sought to change that. He regarded Hearst as a demagogue who wanted mainly to lay waste to the old order, and he saw the Hearst-Tammany combination as a threat that was both personal and political. Even if Tammany was saddled with an unsavory reputation in much of the state, William Hearst was a master manipulator of public opinion, with the potential to recast the Tammany image. The combination provoked many Upstaters, notably Thomas Osborne.

Osborne was a feisty, impatient man. The son of a manufacturer of farm implements, he had successfully negotiated the sale of the family's business to International Harvester. Osborne emerged with millions of dollars, and that, too, served his impatient nature. When he disagreed with the politics of the local newspaper in Auburn, he simply started a new one, and backed it heavily until it came to dominate the market. Disgusted with the local political parties, he ran for mayor as an independent, and won. On a later occasion, when he suspected railroads of inefficiency in manpower, he did not wait for a standard investigation, he dressed as a hobo and road the rails to see for himself how employees were used.[22] To fight Hearst, he started by hiring the Metropolitan Detective Agency of Chicago to catch the publisher's representatives buying the votes of convention delegates. His insistent nature betrayed the outlook of a man who was used to having his own way, and was perfectly content to use shortcuts, when he could find them.

For the time being, in late 1906, Louis Howe didn't care what Osborne's inner character was. Osborne had offered him a job. After the Metropolitan Detective Agency failed to find a way stop Hearst, who ultimately won the Democratic nomination for governor, Osborne started working through the State Democratic Committee. Normally, a state political party might be expected to back its official nominee. But Osborne couldn't be bothered with such banalities. While the State Democratic chairman, William J. "Fingy" Conners, directed the Hearst campaign from his headquarters in New York City, Osborne engaged members of the Albany staff in his own schemes. In one of his initiatives, the State Democratic Committee—the Osborne branch of it—hired a cadre of six political reporters, including Howe, to make trips around the state. Their job was to marshal opposition to the Hearst/Tammany initiative.[23] The work was exciting, but it made for long days on the road. In Salamanca, a town in the western part of the state, Howe didn't finish until the middle of the night. And that was nothing unusual. Before he went to bed, he took a moment to write to Grace. "My schedule is this," he explained:

> At seven o'clock—more often at six—I get up and take the earliest train to the next town. All day I bustle around seeing men and at night consult with the party leaders. At ten o'clock I get a stenographer and dictate my story for the papers. After that a long confidential report of the . . . actual situation to Mr. Osborne. By that time it is generally half past one or two o'clock.

All of the Howes loved cats, and Louis told Grace that he had borrowed the hotel cat to keep him company. "I am dreadfully homesick," he wrote, "and she is purring away on my lap as I write."[24]

As of fall 1906, the New York State Democratic Committee had one official headquarters in Albany, underwritten by Osborne—and it also had another official headquarters in New York, underwritten by Conners and Hearst. Trying to find the true leaders of the party, an old-timer from Long Island spoke to a number of people in midtown Manhattan and then gave up. "Well, if this ain't the queerest campaign I ever saw," he said, "and I've seen some queer ones. Everybody seems to be afraid to commit himself."[25] That was just how Osborne wanted it. Howe later boasted that Osborne had caused "a complete breakdown in the old machinery of the State Committee under the exceedingly lax management of Mr. Conners."[26]

Hearst's opponent in the general election was Charles Evans Hughes, a reform Republican. Hughes was unstained by corruption, a lawyer who had worked so hard at his profession in his younger days that he habitually suffered nervous breakdowns in between cases and was forced to go away for rest cures. Joseph Choate, a fellow lawyer who was also active in Republican politics, had felt compelled to take him aside. "Hughes," he said, "if you don't get your fun as you go along, you will never have it."[27] In response, Hughes took up hiking. Whether or not he had fun, exactly, his health improved. In the 1906 gubernatorial election, the Democrats and the Republicans offered largely the same platform, including increased government regulation to protect consumers and workers, especially women and children. The contest would come down to a vote on leadership.

While most people either loved Hearst or hated him, the opposite was true of Hughes. Nobody loved him, in the public sphere, but nobody hated him, either, and everyone acknowledged that he was honest. Franklin Roosevelt was one of the many upstate Democrats who supported Hughes.[28]

For Howe, the 1906 New York gubernatorial election was a personal turning point. Rather than merely reporting on events as a disinterested observer, he was helping to create the news—and not only the current stories, but future ones as well, through the various machinations that he planned and perpetrated. He gained a respect for the detail and the potential of local organization. Meeting with town and county leaders, planting stories in local newspapers, speaking before small groups of influential voters: his work was hardly complex, but it gave him a taste of power that he had never had before. Osborne's anti-Hearst campaign allowed Louis Howe to edge onto the stage of politics, with a tiny step, perhaps, but one that let him turn and look at the world he had known so long from the opposite perspective.

For Howe and the other newsmen on Osborne's Democratic State Committee payroll, the frantic anti-Hearst effort lasted only a few weeks during late October and early November. Howe couldn't let it go at that, however. He was fascinated by the type of work he'd been doing, but, more than that, Thomas Osborne was a very rich man and Howe was drawn to him, as though for shelter.

Years earlier, Captain Edward and Lide had been rescued by the Strong family when they were in distress. Howe was in a similar position with Osborne, whom he saw as someone who could provide stability—and a regular flow of money—in his life. In early November, his erstwhile employer, the *New York Herald*, offered him a chance to go to Jamaica on assignment. Howe dawdled before replying. Meanwhile, he pursued a permanent job with Osborne.

After the election in which the Democrat, Hearst, was soundly defeated by Hughes, Osborne received congratulations from Democrats all over the state. One official wrote to him on New York State Democratic Committee stationery: "We have accomplished a wonderful work in these weeks," the official gloated, "and we are both hated and feared by the radical element. But Mr. Hearst has been balked in his ambition to be Governor and we have demonstrated our ability to do things."[29]

The only thing that the State Democratic Committee—or Committees— had actually demonstrated was a brilliant ability to elect Republicans. The Democrats had no platform to call their own; they fought each other to the point of fratricide, their leading candidates smelled like crooks compared to the pristine Charles Evans Hughes, and for all of the many millionaires in their ranks, they were flat broke. That was the status of the party that appealed as nothing else could to Louis Howe, on the outskirts and trying desperately to obtain a job as a Democratic operative, as well as to Franklin Roosevelt, confiding to a few people that he was hoping to run for office someday as a Democrat in New York.

CHAPTER THREE

HE DANCES
ON HILLTOPS

At the end of November 1906, Louis Howe sent Thomas Osborne a telegram of thirteen words bursting with gladness: "Letter received thanks," it ran. "I have notified herald [*sic*] to get another man for Jamaica."[1] Osborne had offered Howe the job he wanted, as political assistant. Howe happily bypassed the travel articles for the *Herald* in favor of a job in politics with Osborne, who was determined to reorganize the state Democratic Party—despite the fact that Fingy Conners remained chairman.

According to the new arrangement, some of Howe's work was not much above that of the skulking agents of the Metropolitan Detective Agency. His main asset, in fact, was his part-time job with the *Herald*, which gave him access to the halls and the backrooms of power. He was expected to keep his new boss informed of unreported news and rumor around the capital. He was to be a source of advice, but likewise, to be at Osborne's beck and call for political errands. Howe rather proudly described his role as that of "a confidential agent at the capital . . . in daily communication with the democratic state officers and legislators."[2]

By working for Osborne, Howe compromised his role as a newspaper-man, but in the early twentieth century, the lines of journalistic ethics were blurry. As a reporter for the *Herald*, he had access to conversations and information that he passed along to Osborne. But then, his position with Osborne made him privy to secrets and plans that could strengthen his reporting. If Howe was risking his newspaper career, though, he didn't regret it. In a letter to Grace, he savored the fact that Osborne wanted him as a "private secretary." In fact, he boasted about it to her, saying "That is the kind of job you have been always putting me up to getting."[3]

At the age of thirty-seven, Howe had devoted nearly twenty years of his life to newspaper work. That span coincided with the beginning of a golden age for newspapers, when they were growing in page length and devoting more space to articles than ever before. Good reporters were in demand everywhere, yet Howe could look back on only three positions as a fulltime reporter—and the only one that had lasted was his stint for the *Sun*, working for his father. Perhaps that was telling. When Howe worked for someone he respected, such as his father, he was the hardest of workers. Otherwise, he was only as robust as his interest in the day's topic. He was also becoming tougher as the frustrations of his career left their scars.

Around his family, Howe was yielding and sentimental, with a sense of fun that made him a one-man circus for Mary, arranging theatricals just for her benefit. Humor was an irrepressible part of him: if he wanted to be, he was the merriest person in the room. But not the pressroom. He had friends with whom he liked to talk late into the night at the bar in the Ten Eyck Hotel or some other tap room, but they didn't see Howe's soft and silly side. With every year that went by, as he clung to his perch as Albany's perennial part-time reporter, his moods were less well-disguised by convention and manners. He had a quick temper and a growing reputation for impatience with the shortcomings of others.[4] Cynical newsmen were to be expected, but Howe was an injured poet, as well, protecting an idealistic core. "He was not an easy man to get along with," said the financier and Democratic politician Herbert H. Lehman, who knew Howe later, "because he was temperamental and very self-opinionated, very impatient of any criticism or restraint or argument."[5]

With Howe's newspaper career having narrowed to the only work he liked, political analysis, other reporters—younger than he, with better jobs and more bylines—inevitably looked at him as a sad failure. He often professed to see himself that way, too, in letters to Grace. And yet his newspaper years were indicative of his stubborn nature. He couldn't fail at newspaper work because, ultimately, he didn't regard it as worthy of success. A reporter only reported events, after all. Great men steer them. When he found something to care about, he would find someone to care about, and in 1906, he thought the two came together in the person of Thomas Osborne.

———◆———

By the time Franklin Roosevelt passed the state bar examination in the spring of 1907, he and Eleanor already had a one-year-old child, Anna; their second child, James, would be born in December. Franklin duly found a job with a law firm, boasting in a letter to his mother, "I shall be a full-fledged office boy."[6] The joke wasn't far off. First, though, he took his young family to his mother's summer home on Campobello Island in Canada, near the coast of Maine. At twenty-five, he tore around the place with a special verve, exploring and sailing, playing with his children and all the while thinking it would be the last of his long summers at Campobello. Once he joined the ranks of the salaried worker in New York, he would be allowed only a couple of weeks for vacation.

The position at the law firm of Carter, Ledyard and Milburn was to be unpaid for the first year. As prestigious as Carter, Ledyard was in the field of business law, it was a poor choice for Roosevelt. At a less exalted firm, he might have been given intriguing work, even right out of law school. At Carter, Ledyard, surrounded by celebrated lawyers, he didn't have a chance. The firm handled trust litigation on the level of their most famous clients, John D. Rockefeller and J. P. Morgan. Roosevelt didn't get near those heights, but instead went in to his office every day only to assist the established attorneys. He wasn't inspired. Roosevelt was a man fueled by enthusiasm; he could be enthusiastic about birds, books, arcane facts, old houses, and faraway places. But he didn't like casework.

His bosses tried hard to tap his potential, eventually assigning him to their department of maritime law, in view of his interest in the sea. Apparently, he liked boats as transportation, but not as the object of detailed legal disputes. Even with every chance to develop a lucrative career at the firm, he seemed instead to be biding his time, doing the work necessary to keep his desk. Roland Redmond, a lawyer who followed him at Carter, Ledyard (and married into the Delano family), recalled in a 1978 interview that Roosevelt didn't seem to have any particular interest in the law or the details of practice. "Somebody once said he liked to dance on the tops of the hills," Redmond said.[7]

Eleanor Roosevelt spent most of her time in their house on Thirty-Sixth Street, though Sara Roosevelt was already planning to build her son and daughter-in-law a new, bigger house uptown on East Sixty-Fifth Street. Eleanor, during the first four years of her marriage, was in confinement for months at a time, pregnant and awaiting babies, but when she could, she met friends, went to the theater, and took classes to brush up on her language skills. She saw a lot of her mother-in-law and, by turns, enjoyed her company and chafed under her impeccable management of all of her households, along with that of Franklin and Eleanor. As a young wife, Eleanor learned that her husband was pleasant to a fault—and after four or five years of married life, his immediate disinterest in anything dire, gloomy, or upsetting began to strike her as a fault. She learned early on that whenever she deviated from a chipper frame of mind, she could not expect a discussion of more than a word or two about it. In response, she sulked. When her feelings were hurt or she was annoyed, she had the habit, as she later wrote, "of simply shutting up like a clam, not telling anyone what is the matter and being much too obviously humble and meek, feeling like a martyr and acting like one."[8] Eventually, she was worn down and quite often depressed, either by her new life or her own response to it. "I never talked to anyone," she reflected later. "That was why it all ate into my soul."[9]

The unwritten rule against introspection or, worse, self-pity that prevailed in the family of the Hyde Park Roosevelts had been absorbed early on by Franklin, but it may have eaten into his soul, as well. Sara Roosevelt once observed that she had never known fear in her life. It was an indication of the standard to which her son was raised. Yet Eleanor was surprised to learn that her husband did indeed know fear, even if it only emerged when all of his training was at bay: when he was sleeping. His nightmares surprised her on their honeymoon in 1905, as when he woke up in an English inn, shouting and trying to warn her that the ceiling beams were about to fall on them. In June 1907, during the summer before he started work, she described another nightmare in a letter from Campobello to her mother-in-law:

> I have quite forgotten to tell you about Franklin's dream two nights ago and I know you will be amused for it was so characteristic that I had to laugh when I got over being scared! He sleeps or rather slept until this night episode occurred on the side near the windows and suddenly leaped up, turned over a chair and started to open the shutters! I grabbed his pyjama tails and asked what he wanted and received this surprising answer: "I must get it, it is very rare, the only one and a most precious book." After some persuasion, he returned to bed, very angry with me and the next morning he knew nothing about it! Now I sleep on the window side as the middle of the room seems a better place to hunt for rare and precious volumes![10]

Even if he had recalled the dream, Franklin probably wouldn't have admitted it. Anxiety was not displayed in a household where moodiness was equated to weakness—not during waking hours, anyway. Eleanor followed his lead and they both followed Sara's lead in that respect. The letters that the couple wrote to her from their vacations were written jointly: one would start the letter, the other would add a few paragraphs, and it would revert back and forth until it seemed full enough to send. The handwriting was different, of course, but the tone was typically identical, breezy and affectionate, but never analytical. And never troubled, even if, as they filled up letters between shore dinners and poker nights, concerts and golf games, they were.

———— • ◆ • ————

In 1907–1908, while the Roosevelts settled into a state of respectability, with a lot of help along the way, Howe clutched at the post he'd found with

Osborne. He did his job, trying to turn the Democratic Party away from the Hearst-Tammany alliance. Meanwhile, Osborne accepted an appointment from the Hughes administration, serving as chairman of the state's prestigious new Public Service Commission, overseeing utilities and railroads. Osborne and Governor Hughes agreed that most of the utilities should be taken over by the state—a position that Hearst had long held as well.

Hearst's team watched Osborne's growing popularity in the state, warily expecting him to make a run for the governor's chair once Hughes stepped down. At the age of forty-nine in 1908, Tom Osborne was tall and ruggedly handsome, said to be charismatic in person, a comfortable speaker, and quite rich, though he was spending large amounts on his various hobbies. He had executive ability and understood business. A widower with four grown sons, he was regarded as a stable personality, and a man with a genuine desire to improve conditions for the underclass. All of it made him an intimidating future candidate.

After the summer of 1908, though, even Osborne's worst enemies knew that they had little more to fear. One night in Auburn, two hobos were arrested at gunpoint in a boxcar in Auburn, suspected of robbing bananas from a small store near the railroad station. One of the pair was rangy and the other was husky. Both were dressed in tattered, dirty clothes, with shaggy hair and beards. The big one, though, was wearing kid leather gloves that wouldn't have been out of place at the Paris Opera House. As the patrolman started to take the two bums off to jail, the one with the kid gloves pulled off his mop of hair, tugged his beard free and introduced himself as Thomas Mott Osborne, former mayor of the city. The patrolman recognized him, but insisted on arresting him, anyway. The bananas were still missing, after all.

When the Auburn police chief heard about the incident, the charges were dropped. In fact, the chief had already sent letters to other police departments in the state, requesting immunity for Osborne from possible arrest on vagrancy and other charges befitting a man dressed as a hobo. The mystery of who stole the bananas was never solved, though Osborne denied that it had been he. "I never had a gun aimed at me before," he later marveled. "It wasn't pleasant."[11]

Osborne's companion that night was twenty-four-year-old Louis Schaedeline.[12] They had met some years before when Schaedeline, a former elevator boy originally from Massachusetts, was in reform school. Osborne was a trustee of a reform school in western New York and was probably touring the school in Massachusetts as a research trip. Osborne's biographer, Rudolph Wilson Chamberlain, described Schaedeline's appearance: "Solidly, yet gracefully built, with dark skin and strong aquiline features, he was a perfect physical specimen."[13] By 1908, Schaedeline was living in Auburn, sometimes under Osborne's roof and working as a handyman around the property. He taught Osborne to ride motorcycles and drive fast cars. When Schaedeline sketched a design for a new kind of airplane, Osborne underwrote the cost of building it. He helped the younger man develop his interest in painting. Schaedeline took delight in Osborne's favorite hobby, as well, as the two men often dressed up in costume and went out looking for adventure.

With or without Schaedeline, Osborne assumed a variety of characters, according to his diary: "the Reverend," "MacDonald," "Dude," "Dr. Hurd," "Old Gent," "Mexican," "Italian," and "Colored Gent," among them. On one occasion while still the public service commissioner, he dressed as a hobo and, incognito, attended a speech by Governor Hughes—his boss. Going out in disguise had once been common for European monarchs. Peter the Great of Russia often went out as a common laborer, but his normal life as czar was so constricted that he used disguise as a form of escape. Osborne's life in Auburn wasn't quite so rarified, but apparently, his need for escape was still acute. He sometimes used masquerading as sociological research of a highly personal type: the quickest way to see what life was like for someone else. It was also a fetish he could not resist.

Word about Osborne's compulsion to dress up, along with his close relationship with Schaedeline, quietly spread in 1908 and 1909. His political friends dismissed it all as an innocent diversion: a hard-working man, getting his fun a little at a time, as Joseph Choate had once said. Osborne's enemies placed another construct on Osborne's secret life, deeming it evidence of what they contended was his homosexuality. As far as his political aspirations were concerned, the difference barely mattered. In Osborne's day, voters wouldn't knowingly allow a homosexual to occupy the governor's mansion, but then, they wouldn't want to find Dr. Hurd there, either.

Louis Howe, who made his living as a source of capital gossip, surely knew about Osborne's masquerading. He may well have witnessed it; one of Osborne's masquerades occurred right after a Public Service Commission meeting that Howe attended. A typical entry in Osborne's diary read:

Albany. Louis back from New York. Ψ Nig to Jingles.[14]

Chamberlain, Osborne's biographer, deciphered the code by assuming that the Greek letter Ψ (Psi) was an abbreviation for "Pseudomorphos"—dressed up. He didn't even try to guess at the meaning of "Nig to Jingles."

—•+•—

Howe knew that Osborne was not all that he seemed, but rather, an eccentric whose behavior in public wasn't easily explained outside of a drawing room comedy or a textbook on psychology. He also must have recognized that Osborne didn't stand a serious chance of becoming governor. Nonetheless, Howe kept his eye on his own goal. He was vying for a place in the battle for control of the New York State Democratic Party—the outcome of which would have a heavy influence over the national party. The avenues by which to reach his goal were limited. Tammany Hall, of course, loomed as one option. Howe had no place there; he derided and distrusted it. Beyond Tammany (or sometimes near it), the field of power was small. There were no natural leaders. There were no commoners. There were only millionaires—a small pack led by Hearst in New York, Osborne in Auburn, and Fingy Conners in Buffalo. If Osborne was something less than perfect as a political figure, let alone as a boss, so were they all.

Hearst had the reputation of a man "who would cause a war in order to make news," as a Syracuse *Post-Standard* editorialist wrote in 1907.[15] It was a reference to the well-documented campaign by the Hearst newspapers to first portray an 1898 explosion on the U.S. battleship *Maine* in Havana harbor as an act of Spanish aggression and then roil nationalistic outrage into what became the Spanish-American War.[16] The sensational style of most Hearst newspapers reflected back on the publisher: "the propaganda of evil," a correspondent named Jackson Searle called it in a letter to the *New York Times*. Searle made Hearst and his papers sound like something out of the New Testament: "In all that he produces we behold firebrands, holocausts, shipwrecks, blood, fury, sin and corruption. At the bottom of Hearst's heart is revenge, envy, and hatred, with a strong seasoning of malice and unchari-tableness."[17] In fact, few people, if any, knew what was in the bottom of Hearst's heart, or the top of it, either; he was well disciplined and un-demonstrative, and hard to follow when he did speak at length. Though married, he was known in newspaper circles to be adulterous. Yet that was-n't the sin that made even those more circumspect than Jackson Searle fear William Hearst and reach for their bibles for a point of comparison. "A man of undoubted force, self-contained, purposeful, undismayed by repeated de-feats, there is a certain majesty in his power," observed the sober *Current Literature* magazine, "but there is something sinister, somber and Satanic in that majesty."[18] Hearst was a generous employer, in a lordly way, but Howe could not have worked for him, either. He didn't like him or his egoistic vi-sion of the Democratic Party.

That left Fingy Conners, who started out as a stevedore and saloon owner in Buffalo. As an established businessman, he was still known to set-tle arguments with his fists.[19] He was tough and reckless, but never more so than when he was just a boy and received his nickname, "Fingy." He dared another boy to either chop or shoot his finger off, according to different sto-ries. Whatever the other youngster did, Conners was next seen running up the street, screaming, "My fingy's gone!" and the neighborhood didn't forget it. Conners went through the rest of his life with nine fingers. As the owner of large shipping concerns on the Great Lakes, Conners took ruthless ad-vantage of his former workmates, the stevedores. He became a millionaire and tried to improve his deportment, but he still looked like a pug and spoke like one. He said things such as—speaking to a reporter, "Say anyt'in' about Conners but nuttun'. When you say Conners, it means somet'in' or you wouldn't say it!" He also expressed the opinion that, "Brains is as cheap as tenpenny nails. I can buy tenpenny nails."[20]

Louis Howe would have been willing to sell. In fact, Conners might have been interested in buying brains in the form of political advice, but he already had all the "confidential agents" he needed. All three of the most prominent, nominally independent Democrats in the state owned newspapers. Hearst owned two in New York (and six more across the nation), Osborne one in Auburn, and Conners two in Buffalo. Hearst and Conners drew on their editorial staffs for the kind of information that Howe regularly fed to Osborne.

Howe knew his boss was unelectable, but then, the other two were problematic in their own ways. They were all difficult to work with, unrealistic at crucial junctures, or noncommittal, or both. All were encumbered with personal foibles that had to be kept in the shadows: dressing up, keeping chorus girls, or beating up rivals. For Howe, Tom Osborne was the best among those vying to take charge on Howe's home turf, the New York Democratic Party, and the one with the most appealing opinions. And he was the one who was paying Howe twenty dollars a week.[21] The salary Osborne paid, combined with that of the *Herald,* allowed the Howes to reunite in furnished apartments in Albany, at least during the legislative seasons of 1907 and 1908.

Howe attached his fate to Osborne's very vulnerable one, but the two never developed a friendship. Even though Osborne may have liked to dress as a low-class bum, he maintained his upper-class hauteur in daily life, regarding the majority of people as inferiors. To him, Howe was an employee, nothing more. Their correspondence was devoid of humor or personal news. In fact, throughout their working relationship, Howe typically sent telegrams to Osborne, with the sense of urgency that they carried, and Osborne sent Howe memos through the mail, with the sense of the mundane that they imparted.

———— • • • ————

For a year, Howe barely hung on as an employee, mainly writing reports, making contacts and performing political chores for Osborne. When work was slow or Osborne was busy with other things, Howe was laid off.

He invariably came back with a scheme, a bit of vital news or a suggestion for a meeting, none of which was very well disguised as anything other than begging of the sort that Grace considered unworthy of her husband. Osborne felt saddled with Howe, and was anxious to cut the ties between them once and for all, but it wasn't easy. At the end of 1907, Howe was out. In 1908, he was back and then fired again. That same year, Captain Howe died. With that, the essential partnership of Louis' life was over. He needed to find another, but the first had already left its mark. The honor that Louis felt in being Captain Edward P. Howe's son fired his ambition and, more than that, his sense of destiny.

Feeling ill and very depressed over his father's death, Howe was examined by an Albany doctor, who listened to his heart and reported quite confidently that Howe had no more than two months to live.

The news was bad, and Howe believed it. He also made use of it, letting Osborne know of the grim prognosis. Out of sympathy, Osborne took him back, treating him quite well until 1909 dawned. At that juncture—and in blatant violation of their last agreement—Howe was still alive and breathing. Once more, Osborne cut him loose, having no need for a political assistant and no use for Howe.

Nonetheless, he picked an odd time to fire a political adviser, as he started to think seriously about a run for the governorship in 1910. One explanation for the firing was that Osborne was running short of discretionary cash, with Louis Schaedeline's half-built airplanes draining some of his extra money. Howe muddled through the year, dividing his time between Fall River, where he stayed with Grace and Mary at his mother-in-law's house, and the Albany region, working part-time for the *Herald*. In Saratoga, he cultivated the attention of one of the wealthiest of the year-round residents, Spencer Trask, a Wall Street banker, philanthropist, and venture capitalist who had financed the reorganization of the *New York Times* in 1896. He and his wife, Katrina, owned the expansive and opulent Yaddo estate.[22] Spencer Trask was the head of a newly formed state commission looking for ways to promote Saratoga as a wholesome, healthful place. Howe heard that Trask needed someone to tour similar resorts in Europe and write a report about their activities and promotion. The two discussed the matter and laid out plans, though, tragically, Spencer Trask died in a train wreck on New Year's Eve in 1909.

As campaign talk began in earnest in the spring of 1910, Louis Howe was in Europe, traveling under the aegis of the late Mr. Trask's commission to study the management of mineral springs in Europe. Visiting famous resorts with Grace, Howe had an enjoyable trip, but he kept to the work at hand in his own dogged way. The result was that he was probably one of the few people ever to make a tour of European resort spas and return home ill from the strain. He wrote an effective report for the commission and then spent the summer in Massachusetts, recovering. Grace was not feeling well, either, but the cause of her discomfort was a happier one—she was expecting a baby, her first since Mary was born ten years before.

While Howe was abroad, Osborne was actually acting upon one of his suggestions. He called a meeting in Albany and formed the Democratic League, which was composed of disenchanted upstate Democrats looking for a way to create an organization of their own. By mid-June, Osborne's name was frequently mentioned as a potential candidate for governor. William Randolph Hearst, in France at the time, issued a statement on the subject. "I do not know a great deal about Mr. Osborne," he said, ever so casually. "I have only heard of him in connection with his intermittent whiskers, a hirsute adornment and artificial embellishment which, I am told, Mr. Osborne occasionally affects."[23] It was only a jab, but it was also a warning to Osborne that his enemies knew his secrets.

In fact, the rest of Hearst's statement about Osborne is enlightening, not for its repetition of the same basic point, but as a sample of Hearst's speaking style and an indication of the reason that he delivered so few speeches when he was running for office. Hearst decided to make a reference to Governor Charles Evans Hughes, who wore a beard all of his adult life:

> Since Mr. Hughes' uneventful and unrestful four years of public life, I have not had much faith in the political efficacy of whiskers, and still I would imagine that real whiskers must necessarily be more efficacious, politically and otherwise, than false whiskers; therefore, I would consider Mr. Osborne, if I considered him at all, very much less of a political attraction and party asset than Mr. Hughes has been.[24]

Hearst was one of the few politicians in history whose lieutenants maneuvered to make sure that he *didn't* speak at any well-attended events.

While the hopefuls were sniping and jockeying for position in the autumn election, Louis Howe was out of the fray, lying on the beach. Grace had found a place for her husband to recover from his exhaustion, renting a wooden house overlooking the ocean at Rhode Island Sound, about ten miles south of Fall River. "When we went over in early May," Grace later recalled, "there was a great spray of beach plum blossoms on the table. I swept out the sand and my husband came there and regained his health."[25] The spot, known as Horseneck Beach, was dotted with small houses, casual beach-shacks for people from Fall River and other cities in the vicinity. It was surrounded by sand dunes and beach grasses, which changed every year, although the atmosphere of fresh sea air never did. Howe delighted in the isolation. "Don't try to get down to the beach in the car," he advised a visitor. "They get rich down there pulling out cars from the sand."[26]

The beach house was a half-mile from the spot where the car could be parked, but in Howe's opinion, the walk was worth it. "One can't help but get well quickly at the Beach," he wrote.[27] He felt much better as the summer ended, but he still wasn't ready to go back to work. He and Grace were expecting their new baby in November and he opted to remain with his wife in Fall River.

— ·◆· —

Despite infighting as the election approached, the Democratic League maintained a semblance of unity at its core, rooted in every member's antipathy toward political machines, particularly Tammany Hall. Two League members from Dutchess County, a personable district attorney named John Mack and the mayor of Poughkeepsie, John K. Sague, allowed themselves to be swept up in the optimism and started looking for potential candidates in line with the League's thinking. They made a short list that included Franklin Roosevelt.

One of those who had previously discussed a potential political future with Roosevelt was Thomas Osborne. The two had met on a cruise to the

West Indies in 1904. As fellow Harvard alumni, they fell into conversation and Osborne emerged with a good impression, marking Roosevelt as a man to watch. Franklin Roosevelt was a Democrat and he was rich, or his family was. He would not be beholden to the machines, which were beholden to the financiers, who in turn needed certain legislation blocked and other bills bought, most of it regarding utilities. Osborne saw in Roosevelt the potential for an independent-minded Democrat, much like himself. It may be that, six years later, recalling that the young man from Dutchess County intended to enter politics someday, Osborne was the one who suggested that Mack and Sague seek him out.

No doubt every male relative of Theodore Roosevelt's was asked as a matter of course whether he would like to be president, too, someday. Friends of Franklin Roosevelt's remembered that he did indeed express an interest in following the path of his distant cousin and his wife's uncle. In that, he was not unusual; Theodore Roosevelt inspired energetic people to enter politics, then and ever afterward. Frances Perkins first noticed Franklin Roosevelt earlier in 1910 at a tea dance, hosted at a home in the sedate Gramercy Park section of New York City by a woman who tried to encourage intelligent young people to speak about important issues—and to socialize, as well. "There was nothing particularly interesting about the tall, thin young man with the high collar and pince-nez," recalled Perkins, "and I should not later have remembered this meeting except for the fact that in an interval between dances someone in the group I joined mentioned Theodore Roosevelt, speaking with some scorn of his 'progressive' ideas. The tall, young man named Roosevelt, I didn't catch his first name on introduction, made a spirited defense of Theodore Roosevelt, being careful to proclaim that he was not his kin except by marriage."[28]

Sometime in September, John Mack decided to speak to Franklin Roosevelt in New York City. He called at Carter, Ledyard and Milburn. Roosevelt was no doubt glad to see Mack: not only a friendly face, but a Democrat and a powerful figure from back home.

As of 1910, Roosevelt was three years into his legal career at the firm. He had entered into the life of New York City, but he still couldn't consider himself anything other than a temporary resident. For all of the enjoyment he received by joining the city's private clubs and attending parties, he knew he was going back to Dutchess County. He maintained Hyde Park as his legal address and, as often as possible, the family returned to the Spring-wood estate there. Roosevelt was enchanted by Dutchess County. He liked the trees. He studied the history. He trusted the people. In New York, he liked the clubs. It wasn't an even match.

CHAPTER FOUR

ANYTHING BUT TAMMANY

Franklin Roosevelt's fascination was politics, but he never expressed any interest in running for office in New York City. When he was asked repeatedly to run for mayor of the city, he would firmly decline, protesting that he was, on the contrary, "ever grateful that I have always been an upstate farmer."[1] He also stayed away because Tammany Hall guarded every route up or out for a Democrat in New York City.

Roosevelt harbored a longtime aversion to Tammany Hall, whether it was run honestly or not. He didn't trust what he called "the character of leadership" in the organization.[2] The ready opportunity for graft made him suspicious, as did a conviction that Tammany put unaffiliated individual candidates at a disadvantage, and it was those non-machine individuals whom Roosevelt believed were most likely to bring fresh thinking to government.

In the spring of 1910, when John Mack paid a visit to the offices of Carter, Ledyard and Milburn, he told Roosevelt that the Assembly seat centered in Dutchess County would be open that fall. It was already held by a Democrat, Lewis Stuyvesant Chanler, who had indicated that he would not run again. Roosevelt was enthusiastic about running for office in Dutchess County; he loved the place, despite its pronounced Republican leanings. He considered the possibility from every angle, including the potential for trouble from Eleanor's uncle Theodore (who sportingly gave his blessing to the idea of another Roosevelt, even a Democratic one, in politics). By early summer, Franklin had decided that the Assembly seat would make a fine opportunity. With that in mind, he went to Poughkeepsie and paid a visit to Edward Perkins (who bore no relation to Frances Perkins), the chairman of the Dutchess County Democratic Party.

One might expect that the chairman would be glad to see Roosevelt, or anyone else admitting to be a Democrat in such a heavily Republican part of the state, but Perkins was guarded, at best.

Perkins was an austere man, bald-headed and lean, meticulously correct in dress and manner. He was also a snob who looked down his nose at Franklin Roosevelt. A railroad investor and a banker, Perkins had an estate on the Hudson at least as large and even more impressive than that of the Roosevelts.[3] Three of his four children were married to titled Europeans, so he was not inclined to swoon just because a real, live Roosevelt walked into the room. Perkins probably saw Franklin Roosevelt the way many of his law colleagues had: as a callow young man, incidentally amusing.

As of 1910, prospects for local candidates in Dutchess County were rising, thanks in large measure to the efforts of Lewis Chanler and his brother Bob, who had devoted time and a great deal of their own money gathering new voters into the local Democratic ranks, often using baseball outings and clambakes as enticements. Lewis Chanler had been elected state assemblyman in 1908, and that constituted a foothold, one that the next Democratic candidate could stand to inherit. On top of that, Perkins had a plan to bring fresh money into the county's 1910 Democratic campaign. Perkins wasn't sure why the county's Democratic Party should put its new flutter of momentum behind a newcomer, but he said he would keep Roosevelt in mind. A few other local Democrats regarded Roosevelt highly and, besides, the inference was that his family would underwrite his campaign.

Perkins summoned Roosevelt and told him he could run for Chanler's Assembly seat, though the decision would ultimately rest with the full county committee. A close friend of Perkins later wrote to one of Perkins' daughters:

> Some time later Lewis Chanler changed his mind and decided to run again for the Assembly. When this decision by Chanler was made public, young Roosevelt stormed into your father's office and berated him for breaking his word or double-crossing, before your father could make any explanation of the change. Finally when he got Roosevelt cooled off he told him that he had planned to have him nominated for the State Senate which would be a greater honor than the Assemblyman.[4]

The use of the word "honor" was perhaps extravagant. According to common knowledge, the only distinction of running as a Democrat for state senator in the 13th District was that of joining a line of losers broken by only one winner over the previous fifty-four years. At first, Roosevelt was inclined to turn down the offer and wait for the more accessible Assembly seat to open up. Perkins, however, had a tempting proposition, even if he was still not sure Roosevelt deserved it. While the young scion would be expected to pay for his own campaign, Perkins had more than enough money to make the 1910 campaign a winning one, up and down the ballot. It wasn't his own money, though. He had made a deal with Charles Murphy.

Murphy, the saloon-keeper who had been at the head of Tammany Hall since 1905, had an ominous air about him, yet he was largely honest—which made him a refreshing change from his predecessors. In Murphy's ethic, accepting graft on city contracts was perfectly all right, but Tammany Hall would no longer involve itself with prostitution or gambling rings.[5] The club, in order to maintain its hold on newly arriving immigrants, had to lose its reputation for exploiting them.[6] Boss Murphy cut support of illegal activities and decided on a progressive political agenda. Some observers said that Murphy wanted to instill new principles in government; others thought he wanted only to impress the voters that Tammany was on their side.

"Mr. Charles F. Murphy was the type of person who, while he had a strategy board, he listened to them and made up his own mind," said Edward Flynn, another Tammany boss. "Neither the strategy board nor anyone else told Murphy what to do and what not to do."[7]

A man of very few words, Murphy was intent on bolstering pockets of influence throughout the state, not because of any ambition to control life and law in every corner, but because certain types of legislation were important to his most powerful supporters back in New York City. "I don't think Murphy had great concern about state politics as such," said Frances Perkins. "He just was concerned to see that his own people in his own bailiwick were protected and didn't get legislation they didn't want. I'm very sure that was it. He was not a broad, philosophical man. He was strictly a good operator of Tammany Hall."[8] Murphy needed loyal votes in the legislature. His door was open to upstaters who could provide them.

Edward Perkins liked Murphy and had been to see him with a proposition. If Tammany would advance enough money, then the Democrats of Dutchess County would lead the way in turning the eastern Hudson region into a Democratic enclave, electing, he promised, one congressman, two assemblymen, and a state senator. Murphy considered the offer. From anyone else, it would have been a laughable boast, but Perkins was reliable, and Murphy ambitious. He agreed to help, a fact of which Roosevelt was probably aware. There was nothing illegal about the shifting of funds, but it would have offended many of the local voters. Roosevelt, if he ran, would campaign on an anti-Tammany, good government platform. He wouldn't accept money from anyone—except his mother, of course. While he wouldn't have the use of Tammany money, he could be in a good position to be carried along with the good it did the rest of the local Democratic Party.

———◆———

In late summer, Roosevelt decided to take the long shot and run for the State Senate. His first move was to resign from Carter, Ledyard and Milburn. A more prudent move might have been to take a leave of absence, but Roosevelt was going into politics with all that he had. He apparently didn't want a backup plan. To that end, he moved to Hyde Park for a campaign of just over a month. Eleanor, who had given birth to a baby boy, Elliott, in September, stayed in New York. Franklin spent a hectic month campaigning through three counties from the back of a car. If he did nothing else by visiting every crossroads he could find, he let voters see how much he cared about the region.

In November, Roosevelt was elected as a state senator. True to Edward Perkins' prediction, so were two assemblymen and a congressman in the area, but none by a wider margin than the energetic Roosevelt. Across the state, the Democrats won a commanding margin in the legislature, as well as the governor's mansion. One veteran of the party recalled that the regulars came to Albany "with a feeling of hope":

> We felt that the eyes of Democrats not only in this State, but all over the country, were fixed on us, and that what we would do or leave undone here would be put down in the books and the Democratic Party would be judged according to the manner in which we conducted ourselves.[9]

Louis Howe took an interest in the Democratic victory, but only from afar. He was still living in Fall River, resting—or unemployed—and either way, saving his strength for the 1911 legislative season, when he was due to return to work for the *New York Herald* in Albany. Mainly, he and Grace were awaiting the birth of their second child and were thrilled by the birth of a son later in November. The baby, named Edward Hartley Howe, only lived for a week, though, the victim of meningitis. Louis couldn't express his grief, except to close a baby book purchased to record happy events by writing, "There are no records of the little brother's life set down within this book because they are written in our hearts and nothing can ever wipe them out."[10] The following month, the Howes—Louis, Grace, and ten-year-old Mary—moved into a furnished apartment in Albany.

— ◦ ◦ —

On New Year's Day in 1911, the Roosevelts moved to a large house in downtown Albany. That alone set them apart. Nearly every other representative looked upon the legislature as a part-time job, renting a room during the session and typically going home on weekends. Franklin and Eleanor rented a six-story house on State Street, one of the main avenues near the capitol, and took their children, as well as a staff of servants. Roosevelt didn't intend to treat the State Senate as a part-time job. The new place meant as much to Eleanor. At twenty-six, she had the first home she could call her own, a reflection of her tastes.

Two days after the move, Franklin was sworn into office: his second job, and the first one he cared deeply about. Both of the Roosevelts had waited a long time to start their lives on their own terms, and they were set on making good. Neither had been taken very seriously before. Eleanor was easily overlooked—by her own admission, the most assertive thing she did was sulk. At Harvard, Columbia, and at Carter, Ledyard, Franklin Roosevelt was looked on as a nice fellow, but not a leader. By the time the couple arrived in Albany, they had changed. Perhaps they were over-ripe to take charge of their own destiny. Eleanor recalled herself in transition and could have been speaking of Franklin as well:

> I wrote my mother-in-law almost every day, as I had for many years when away from her, but I had to stand on my own feet now, and I think I knew that it was good for me. I wanted to be independent. I was beginning to realize that something within me craved to be an individual. What kind of individual was still in the lap of the gods![11]

For Franklin, change emerged from the other direction, as well. He was greeted in Albany as a leader. The Roosevelt name helped. When the clerk at the State Senate called the roll on the first day of the 1911 session, he coughed before reading Roosevelt's name and the result was muffled. Those familiar with Theodore Roosevelt's energetic style braced themselves for a shout, but Franklin Roosevelt calmly said, "Here." That alone excited curiosity: a quiet Roosevelt was as much a surprise to a room full of politicians in 1911 as a Democratic one. For a few moments, capitol regulars took a look at the new senator and, according to a reporter for the *New York Times*, many of them took a second look, too: "Senator Roosevelt is less than 30. He is tall and lithe. With his handsome face and his form of supple strength, he could make a fortune on the stage and set the matinee girl's heart throbbing with subtle and happy emotion."[12]

Roosevelt was on a stage of sorts, and his appearance in an assembly of battle-weary politicians, most of whom had been fighting each other for years, naturally offered the hope that something fresh was arriving in their midst. Roosevelt thrived on such approval, as most people do. In fact, he was reared to live up to the high expectations of others. Welcomed by Osborne and the members of the Democratic League, he was more than capable of reflecting back in force the confidence suddenly shining upon him.

—◦ ◦ ◦—

Sooner than anyone might have thought possible, confidence in Roosevelt waned within the established Democratic circles. One of the first orders of business for the State Senate was the election of a U.S. senator. The Republican incumbent, Chauncey Depew, would have been happy to remain in office, but he had little hope of being reelected by the Democrats who controlled the legislature. As the new session opened in January 1911, there was no doubt as to whom the majority of Democrats would vote to elect: anyone that Boss Murphy told them to elect. He controlled the Democrats and they controlled the legislature. And for the time being, Thomas Fortune Ryan controlled Murphy. Ryan was one of the financial backers of Tammany Hall. No one controlled Ryan, but he owed William "Blue-eyed Billy" Sheehan, his partner in various utilities projects, a favor. Sheehan desperately wanted to cap his own checkered political career with a term in Washington, as a member of the U.S. Senate.

As a result, Murphy traveled north to Albany to meet with the full roster of legislative Democrats at the Ten Eyck, Albany's largest hotel. The Ten Eyck served as an auxiliary seat of the state government, improving on the capitol by providing drinks, steaks, and cigars to go with the deal making and debates. Murphy intended to call the Democrats into caucus there and oversee the nomination of his friend, everyone's friend, Blue-eyed Billy Sheehan. After that, Murphy could leave the formality of the election to the Democratic majority in the legislature (the final vote was to be taken in joint session). Sheehan and his wife traveled from New York, booked a suite of rooms at the Ten Eyck and prepared to celebrate the election with

Murphy. At the Ten Eyck on the night before the caucus, Murphy and Sheehan were trying to relax and save themselves for the big day to come, when they started hearing rumblings of dissent, which, to their utter astonishment, turned out to be true.

———————•◆•———————

Franklin Roosevelt, veteran of seventeen days in government, was leading an insurrection against the nomination of Sheehan, the election of whom, he said, "would mean disaster."[13] His immediate objection had to do with Sheehan's stand on the ownership of utilities. At first, he didn't know quite what to do about it, being new to government, and to politics. Roosevelt turned to the majority leader in the Assembly, thirty-eight year-old Alfred Smith—a Tammany man and moreover, a Sheehan man. As Roosevelt later wrote of his band of resolutely anti-Tammany, anti-Sheehan men:

> We were nearly all serving our first term, and knew little of procedure. A party caucus had been called. We expected to be defeated on the vote, and had been told that a caucus was in theory binding on those who took part in it. Some one said, "Ask Assemblyman Smith, the majority leader; he never tries to fool anybody."
>
> So we went to the leader of the forces opposed to us and got this answer. "Boys, I want you to go into the caucus, and if you go in, you're bound by the action of the majority. That's party law. But if you're serious about this fight, keep your hands clean and stay out."[14]

Spurred on by Thomas Osborne, Roosevelt and twenty other representatives refused to attend the caucus, pulling the majority out from under the Democrats. Without those twenty-one votes, Sheehan's hope of election to the Senate was quashed. More to the point, Tammany was stopped dead in its tracks.[15]

Louis Howe, caught up in the drama, filed a dispatch for the *New York Herald* that mentioned Roosevelt only by description, as the two had not yet met:

Twenty-one men, so little reckoned within politics that their very names, until yesterday, were practically unknown outside the limits of their home districts, these men successfully defying the weight of Tammany Hall, blocking the progress of one of the most carefully planned political moves in recent years, standing unterrified by threat and unmoved by the most cunning politicians, such is the amazing feature of the struggle at Albany today. All night and again today every known form of coercion and persuasion has been used to win these twenty-one novices over to the Sheehan camp in vain.

It is impossible to talk to one of them without feeling that they are terribly in earnest, that they have conceived something of the spirit of the old martyrs and are convinced that they must stand firm, even though the heavens fall. Led by a 'new Senator' without experience in the game, who looks like a boy, they have proved an ability to meet cunning with determination rarely shown by older men. Never in the history of Albany had twenty-one men threatened such total ruin of machine plans. It is the most humanly interesting political fight of many years.[16]

"There is nothing I love as much as a good fight," Roosevelt beamed as the siege took hold in late January.[17] Rooting Tammany out of the state capital and out of upstate New York had been Roosevelt's avowed goal since his campaign. It may have started as rhetoric, but the revolt he was leading in Albany was sure to have serious consequences. Tammany's friends had friends, and they could be ruthless. As the stalemate stretched out into months, most of the insurrectionists, as they came to be called, watched their political friends disappear. A few watched their careers or businesses fall, as well. One of the insurrectionists, an assemblyman, owned a small newspaper in his hometown. When he refused to attend the caucus and vote for Sheehan, the county government—his biggest advertiser—pulled its business and the paper was forced to close. He still wouldn't change his mind. Remarkably, Roosevelt kept his group together as a veritable fraternity. When they were not at the capitol, they were at the Roosevelts' house. And, in Eleanor's recollection, they were eating. One of her memories of the monumental battle was carrying trays laden with sandwiches and beer to the legislators. Another of her memories was trying to get them to go home.

"We made bossism the issue," Roosevelt declared to reporters. "I know this was the burning issue with the people who had suffered long under the dictation of bosses."[18] Roosevelt, of course, could get along without bosses and machines. He was born with most of what they offered, namely, money and connections.

Roosevelt's stand against bossism represented the stance of the voters who had elected him, but nonetheless, it came with the scent of elitism. It is true that Tammany had often delivered political hacks to Albany, men whose only qualification was the ability to control votes in their own neighborhood—or in their own saloon—while still obeying orders from above. Yet Tammany also stood as the only possible means for a New York Democrat without money or important connections or a rare sense of political savvy to embark on a career in government. Alfred E. Smith was just one example of a politician who would not have had a chance without the help of Tammany Hall.

A resident of lower Manhattan, Smith had left school when he was in the eighth grade to support his widowed mother. He sold newspapers on the street and peddled fish before finding a low-level job in city government, serving jury summons. At first, he was anti-Tammany, but he eventually found himself hanging around his local political headquarters simply because it didn't cost anything to enter and listen to the talk at meetings. Unimpressive in appearance, with average features and a prominent Irish nose, he exuded sincerity and a humble kind of intelligence. Smith impressed two Tammany bosses, who saw to it that he was nominated for the Assembly; he was duly elected in 1903. "I was diligent in my attendance at the meetings," he said of his first year as an Assemblyman. Then he continued with arresting candor, "but I did not at any time during the session really know what was going on. . . . In fact, I never knew there was so much law."[19]

Smith studied the complex rules of the legislature until they gradually began to make sense. Within five years he had earned a reputation for knowing more about New York State law than anyone else in or out of the legislature. Within another five, he was instrumental in the drafting of a new state constitution, earning the respect of Ivy League–trained lawyers such as Elihu Root Jr. and Henry L. Stimson. "He could read law as many a person today would read a detective story," said Jonah Goldstein, a lawyer and Smith's secretary in 1911.[20]

From an early stage, Boss Murphy recognized that Alfred Smith and others like him could be very effective for the state—and perhaps that would be a good reflection on Tammany Hall. Whatever his reasons, Murphy wanted Smith to reach his potential. Tammany Hall was involved in hundreds of deals, some all right, some tainted with dishonesty, and some downright dirty. Murphy couldn't stop it all, though he did distance himself from flagrant financial corruption, especially early in his career. More to his credit, he laid down the rule that the more promising Tammany politicians were not to be inveigled into anything unethical. Smith was among them. "Don't put Al's name on the list of people that do this," Murphy was quoted as saying in reference to corrupt dealing. "Don't you involve him in any way. He's got to be straight."[21] By every account, he was.

If Alfred Smith was incorruptible within the bounds of his office, he was the same outside of it, as well. It showed especially in his dealings with women. Smith would become known nationally for his recruitment of women for high-ranking posts; he launched many important careers (including that of Frances Perkins) and inspired others. Nonetheless, propriety was strictly observed, and Smith was careful to hold meetings with women in the open, or with a chaperone present to every extent possible, out of an old-fashioned respect for his female colleagues. He didn't want anyone to think that they had been promoted for reasons other than their ability. He was also mindful of his wife's position.

Since 1900, Smith had been married to a woman from the Bronx, Catherine "Katie" Dunn Smith, and they had five children. When they first met, Katie Dunn was slightly above Smith in station, a high school graduate from a family of smalltime merchants, enjoying a comfortable lower middle class lifestyle. That was a step up from Smith's genteel but lower-class background. As Smith rose in the political world, Katie Smith remained as she had been: a friendly woman from a New York neighborhood, a little garish, plump, and blithely unsophisticated.

Alfred Smith was majority leader for the Democrats in the Assembly in 1911, respected for his competence by members of both parties, upstaters as well as downstaters. "That Smith," admitted a Republican, "and the younger crowd with him represent a new spirit in Tammany Hall."[22]

In 1911, Smith and other veteran Democrats had been looking forward to passing a full slate of legislation, thanks to the large Democratic majority in both houses of the legislature and a pliable Democratic governor in John Dix, to boot. The conflict over Sheehan's nomination—with Roosevelt at its core—was not just an annoyance, but, to the party regulars such as Smith, an outrageous waste of an opportunity for Democratic progress.[23]

The standoff continued into February. The pressure mounted on the insurrectionists, but not one buckled. For Blue-eyed Billy, the winter that was to have been his triumph was a morass of daily disappointment and utter confusion as to why he, of all people, was singled out as the victim of the insurgents' wrath.

If Alfred Smith was, by his own admission, bewildered when he first arrived in Albany, Roosevelt was just the opposite: instantly dominating. Every reporter wanted to write a story about him, and he found time to accommodate all comers. For a man who had never been interviewed by a public newspaper—though he had worked for Harvard's college paper—he proved to be deft with his answers, giving the impression that he was speaking in a natural way, even as he controlled his words carefully. When Governor Dix wanted to influence Thomas Osborne into accepting a role in the new Democratic government, he arranged a luncheon for him at the mansion of a local Democrat; the Roosevelts were the only other guests. (Osborne accepted the job as Forest, Fish and Game Commissioner, but, as a man who abhorred hunting and fishing, he quit after two months.) Even Blue-eyed Billy Sheehan humbly requested an audience with Roosevelt, certain that they could emerge as friends. They did; Roosevelt had nothing against Sheehan personally—except his politics and his associates. Roosevelt was, as the *New York Times* called him, "the man of the Democratic hour."[24]

Starting a new life in Albany, Eleanor Roosevelt divided her days, spending time with her children at the house and with her husband at political gatherings or watching his work in the Senate from the gallery. She had a particularly stilted attitude at first. "I took an interest in politics," she recalled, "but I don't know whether I enjoyed it! It was a wife's duty to be interested in whatever interested her husband, whether it was politics, books, or a particular fish for dinner."[25]

The press loved Roosevelt, with his courageous—and newsworthy—stand. The Democratic regulars thought him "an awful arrogant fellow" and feared that he was breaking up the party.[26] But everyone in Albany in 1911 noticed him. "The first time I saw him," said Grace Howe, "was when we were coming out of St. Peter's Episcopal Church in Albany. Louis said, 'There's young Roosevelt—the man I was telling you about. A man of great promise.'"[27] Any such promise would have to be long-range; after a month or two in office, Roosevelt already had more enemies in the Democratic ranks than did the most noxious Republican. For the time being, Louis Howe wasn't worried about the new senator's prospects; he hated Tammany as much as Roosevelt did. "Keeping close tabs for my newspaper on every move made by the insurgents," recalled Louis Howe, "brought me into daily contact with Franklin Roosevelt. I had ample opportunity to study his potentialities as a leader."[28]

In late February, 1911, Howe was assigned to interview Roosevelt. He made an appointment to meet the senator in the evening. Most legislators lived in boarding houses and gave interviews at the capitol or in a quiet corner of the Ten Eyck. Howe knew them all well, the cramped offices, the nooks at the hotel. Roosevelt invited Howe over to his house, where the reporter was greeted by a servant and shown to the library. If Roosevelt meant himself for bigger jobs, he showed it by the way he lived. A few minutes later, he appeared and Howe only had to ask one question to receive a long and spirited oration on the prudence of the insurrection. "Oh, I know we are reading ourselves out of the party," Roosevelt acknowledged, before countering his own comment. "What party? The Tammany party?"[29] He went on at length, pacing around the room, as Howe sat in an armchair and took notes. Roosevelt wasn't saying anything that Howe hadn't said before, written before, dined on and drunk over, during his previous decades covering Albany politics. If anyone had earned the right to call Roosevelt a naive upstart, it was he. Instead, at their first meeting, Howe listened, if not to the words, if not to the tone, to the lively intelligence behind them.

Roosevelt did not record his impressions of the interview that marked the beginning of his long relationship with Howe, but to him, that evening, Howe must have looked like just another reporter. Dozens of them came to see Roosevelt during the standoff over Sheehan. Howe was one of the less powerful by reputation and he was even less imposing in person. For Roosevelt in those days, though, politics was a game and Howe was a veteran player, willing and able to talk about it on a level that was new to Roosevelt.

In a memoir written for a Democratic magazine twenty-one years later, Howe recalled the early days of their relationship. "During the talks Franklin Roosevelt and I had had together while the insurgent rumpus was in full swing," he wrote, "we had found that we thought alike on many questions and this had led to a warm friendship."[30]

Roosevelt was making some friends early in 1911, along with scores of enemies. As the pressure over the Sheehan standoff mounted, anyone who didn't tell Roosevelt to grow up, give up, and let Tammany have its way was not only a friend, but was probably invited over for supper.

———◆———

In New York City on March 25, a horrific fire took the lives of 146 garment workers—mostly young immigrant women—in the Triangle Shirtwaist Factory. The fire was caused by a cigarette, but the high number of deaths was attributed to unsafe working conditions. In the aftermath, emotions ran high, as an overflow crowd gathered at the Metropolitan Opera House and demanded protection for workers and called for the state government to take long overdue action. First, though, that government had another priority. It had to pick a senator.

CHAPTER FIVE

BATTLE ON
THE HUDSON

On March 27, 1911, the battle was finally over. Boss Murphy withdrew his support for William Sheehan. Blue-eyed Billy had to go home.

Other names were discussed, but Roosevelt and the insurgents insisted that the new senator come from their own list of eleven acceptable nominees. While conferences continued at the Ten Eyck and at the Roosevelt home, a few elected officials noticed that the legislative session was half over, with little of substance having been accomplished.

Alfred Smith, as majority leader, tried without success to bring the new standoff to an early end. He was presiding over a discussion about it in the assembly when one of his colleagues stood up in anger. "Why are we pursuing this aimless debate?" he demanded. "We are just drifting."[1] No one rose to argue the point.

On March 30, a fresh name for the Senate post floated from Murphy's office in Tammany Hall. Emissaries with polished diplomatic skills took the proposition to the Roosevelt house in Albany. The insurgents were ready to cooperate, but they had to be assured twice—on Murphy's solemn word of honor—that if they returned to the fold and voted for the new man, Tammany Hall would exact no revenge for their anti-Sheehan agitation.[2] Promises were made and on March 31, Murphy was back in Albany. When he looked out on the Democratic caucus at the Ten Eyck that afternoon, he was greeted by a sight he hadn't seen at any of the previous sixty-two caucuses since January 21: the insurgents. Murphy's new candidate, James A. O'Gorman, was declared the choice of the Democrats. Later the same day, O'Gorman, a state judge from New York City, was formally elected a U.S. senator by the legislature.[3]

Murphy claimed victory over Roosevelt. And Roosevelt claimed victory over Murphy. Murphy had exerted his Tammany-given right to make key Democratic appointments, but Roosevelt had forced the Tammany president to obey the legislature, at least for one brief span. When the siege was over, Roosevelt spoke out in favor of O'Gorman. "I think we have a man who will be dictated to by no one," Roosevelt said. "He is a man who satisfies me."[4] It was hard for other Tammany-haters to fathom why—James O'Gorman was Tammany through and through, having been active in the machine for twenty-nine years, even longer than had Sheehan.[5] Roosevelt had little choice; his insurgents had made their point and could not be unreasonable. It was worth wondering, and Blue-eyed Billy probably did wonder, what would have happened if O'Gorman had been Murphy's first pick. Sheehan might well have come through on the compromise.

Many veteran Democrats were openly disgusted with Roosevelt for placing a fight that they considered mere political gamesmanship ahead of the issues of the day. From the opposite point-of-view, many anti-Tammany Democratic Leaguers were just as annoyed, thinking that he had simply buckled under pressure at the end.

———— ·◆·· ————

Louis Howe was one of the very few people in Albany who wasn't disillusioned with Roosevelt at the end of the 1911 legislative session. If the new senator had made any mistakes, it only showed that he needed good advice, which happened to be Howe's stock-in-trade. Howe was dazzled by Roosevelt's youth, his honesty, and, inevitably, his independent fortune—but also by his dedication to the craft of politics. Most of the other legislators had careers outside of politics and full lives outside of Albany. Roosevelt didn't, which was why he had brought his family to the capital and then turned the bottom floor of his house into an extension of his office. By 1911, Louis Howe, on the other hand, was as dedicated as ever to the world of politics, but he had yet to successfully merge his family into it.

Grace and Mary Howe still counted their seasons according to the New York State legislative calendar. Generally, they spent winters in Albany, summers in Saratoga, and the rest of the time in Fall River.[6] They were with Louis in Albany in early 1911, living in a furnished apartment. One night, Louis and Grace went to the theater. Louis loved the stage from either side of the footlights, and Grace liked to mingle with society. From seats on the floor, the Howes spotted the Roosevelts in a box. Grace still remembered Eleanor thirty-five years later. "She was wearing blue that night," Grace said. "That pale blue she likes so well and wears most of the time."[7] Aside from evenings out, though, Grace was unhappy in Albany. She was living in an apartment far beneath anything to which she was accustomed in Fall River, watching Louis go out most of the days and many of the nights. When her husband was at home, he was in an unusually dark mood, having become aware of someone named "Willie," whom Grace knew in Fall River. Whether or not there was anything to his suspicions about Grace and the other man, his jealousy was real.

Howe was not a man with bland emotions. He exaggerated his affections, raised his love for Grace to something hallowed, and often dramatized his morbid forebodings, as well as the chronic ailments his friends dismissed as hypochondria. If Louis Howe were jealous, with or without cause, he would be relentless and exacting. So it was that Grace and Mary returned to Fall River early that winter, before the legislative session was half-over. Louis took a room at the Ten Eyck Hotel. Sometime later, probably in April or May, Louis wrote Grace a letter from the Ten Eyck:

Dearest Wife of Mine,

It is now 2:30 AM and I am forced to go to bed for lack of any one to sit up and keep me company. I must first dear write you a line, for I want to put something down on paper that you can have and keep and perhaps some time when what I say may make things easier, read. It is only this, dear.

You read my thoughts and my actions wrong, dear.

I trust you trust you trust you—Ever since that night dear when—for the sake of the little son that is gone and the little girl that is here we agreed to drop Willie out of our lives, I have felt that was over. Little girl I didn't want to see you go away because I was afraid—Just what I was afraid of I will tell you sometime but believe me, dear, that was not it. If I acted cross it was not that, it was because, when I realized all I had tried so hard to do to compensate for so much I had asked you to give up had been—like everything I had tried to do—a failure. That, if the doctors warnings came true—you would have no other recollection of our last winter than that I had taken you away from all that you cared for and given you in its place—"the worst winter you had ever had in your life"— oh little girl keep this letter from Sonny [Louis' name within the family] so that you can always know that no mean distrust of you was in his heart—only trust dear and a love that will never never die no matter what might happen to his body—Forgive me dear for the misery and sorrow I have caused you for the failure I have made of everything, for I can never forgive myself.

I love you I love you I love you
Your husband[8]

The salutation and signature were the same he used throughout most of their married life, whatever the subject of the letter. Some of the themes were perennial, as well. His sense of financial failure, as it affected Grace, was one. Another was his foreboding about his own death, which fueled his concern over his lack of professional success and resulted in the conclusion that he had little time left to provide her with a comfortable life. The letter was more significant than others, though, as it constituted Howe's first admission of the fear that he was losing her and losing his marriage. Previously, their separations had been tacitly heroic: the sacrifice he had to make in order to find success; the accommodation she had to make in support of his determination. In 1911, Grace's sudden return to Fall River was borne of her desire to escape from Howe and—for all of his denials—from his distrust. The winter's hard feelings were set aside in late 1911 when Grace announced that she was expecting another baby, but they weren't to be forgotten.

In the fall elections, Howe's work played to one of his strengths, making political predictions for the *Herald*, based on his own polling techniques. Generally, he took the time to go out into the hinterland as well as the cities in order to include a representative sampling of voter opinion. He had come to be regarded as one of the most accurate canvassers in the Capital district, on both issues and elections; in all, it was a type of work suited to his characteristic diligence and need for complexity.

In 1911, the key elections were those for the assembly. State senators, including Roosevelt, would not be up for reelection until 1912. Nonetheless, as the 1911 results came in, Franklin knew he was in serious trouble. Of the twenty-one original insurgents who stood with him the previous January, eighteen were assemblymen. With the weight of Tammany Hall against them all, only three were reelected.[9] Several from New York City had not even been renominated, in a clear mark of vengeance directly from the machine.[10] To the surprise of no one close to New York politics, Boss Murphy had abandoned his honor-bound promise to leave the former insurgents alone. He was expected to finish the job the following year and wipe the insurgent senators out of Albany.

A few weeks after the 1911 election, the Howes welcomed a baby boy, whom they named Hartley Edward. His name was an homage, through a reversal of the first and middle names, to the son they'd lost the year before, Edward Hartley Howe. Happily, the new infant was healthy and the family remained together in the capital as the legislative season began in January 1912. Howe was intent on making a steady living, mindful of the responsibility he held for his newly enlarged family. Nonetheless, he spent much of his free time with Franklin Roosevelt, a man who, according to the prevailing wisdom of Albany, had a very short future in politics.

———— • ◆ • ————

Howe and Roosevelt were well matched. Both were intelligent in a quick, rather than a contemplative, way. They thrived on analysis,

Howe being more calculating and Roosevelt more intuitive. In 1911 and 1912, though, Howe had more useful knowledge about politics. He was a frequent visitor at the Roosevelt house, although he was generally shown directly into the first-floor library that Franklin Roosevelt used for meetings, rather than the family quarters above.

"I hardly remember meeting him," Eleanor Roosevelt recalled of Howe in that period. "He was a newspaper correspondent, an old hand in the Albany political game. He lived in Albany with his wife and daughter, but his home for years had been in Saratoga, so he knew the countryside and had many old friends."[11] That was all she knew or wanted to know of Howe. At forty-one, he was no longer the smooth young tea-dancer of his youthful days in Saratoga Springs. He had, in the expression of the day, let himself go.

In an era when clothes were taken seriously as a sign of respect for others, and when grooming was indicative of self-respect, Howe was considered sloppy.[12] By modern standards, he doesn't look particularly disreputable in his dark suits. In his day, however, people could readily tell that they were cheap suits and that neither the clothes nor the man was as crisply clean as might be expected for someone in his position. In Howe's defense, he often couldn't spare the money for a new handkerchief, let alone a new suit. In addition, living alone in hotels or boardinghouses, he didn't always have his wife—or anyone—to tell him how he looked and why it mattered. It did matter, though, because the deterioration of his appearance, even the hollow cast settling into his face, paralleled the decline in his self-esteem. A man who spent a dozen years thinking of himself as a genius and simultaneously seeing himself as a failure could hardly help but betray the fact that in some way, he had already given up on himself.

Louis Howe only drank socially and was never known to be drunk, but many people were taken aback by his smoking. He smoked three packs a day and one might think that with all of that practice, he would be rather deft with smoking paraphernalia. He wasn't. Many complained that not only was he practically always smoking, but he managed to get ashes all over himself and everything nearby. Howe himself admitted that he should probably apologize to his wife, "for spilling ashes over everything."[13]

Franklin Roosevelt also smoked, but he made better use of ashtrays. Howe insisted that, in fact, the smoke itself helped cure his breathing problems. (If those problems were caused solely by nervousness, perhaps it did, up to a point.) Eleanor, who did not use cigarettes, tried to keep the smell of tobacco away from her young children and so the sight of Howe spewing smoke and ashes like a particularly rumpled volcano was bound to make a poor impression.

Eleanor wrote that while she was in Albany, she learned that "the first requisite of a politician's wife is always to be able to manage anything."[14] The politicians she entertained at a moment's notice were sometimes odd or coarse, brusque or cloying, and typically very distant from the people she'd been used to meeting in social situations. Louis Howe standing at the door was an amalgamation of all that she had seen of politics: the smudged, smoky, single-minded, loquacious, and inelegant world in which her husband moved. That was what Howe had become, the personification of politics, and she was uneasy around them both.

As the legislative session wound down in the spring of 1912, Howe was in better shape than Roosevelt. He had a good job lined up for the fall, producing canvasses, or polls, for the *Herald*. All that Roosevelt had lined up was a hard fight for reelection. Nineteen-twelve was a presidential year, of course, and that gave the two of them even more fodder for their discussions. As Republican William Taft prepared for a reelection bid, former president Theodore Roosevelt turned to a third party, trying to reclaim his mantle of power by way of the rapidly expanding Progressive Party.

Woodrow Wilson, the governor of New Jersey, was among the hopefuls for the Democratic nomination; Franklin Roosevelt came out early in support of him. Thomas Osborne was also enthusiastic about Wilson and he formed a committee, the New York State Wilson Conference, to promote his candidacy in the state.[15]

Roosevelt was to be the executive secretary of the Conference, a fact that influenced Howe's sense of initiative, as he allowed himself to be pulled into the cause. Howe had an uneasy history with Osborne, one in which he never quite reached the promised high points of seeing his boldest ideas put into action. He took an interest in the new organization, but it was doomed from the start. Boss Murphy, who was against Wilson, made all of the important decisions regarding the state's delegation to the Democratic National Convention—such as, which candidate the delegates would back. And it wasn't to be Wilson. Try as they might, in whatever guise, Osborne and Roosevelt had yet to get around Murphy.

In late June, the N.Y.S. Wilson Conference had a noisy one-day convention of its own in New York City. Roosevelt attended, in his role as executive secretary, but all the chants and cheers in the world couldn't change the fact that he, like the other Wilsonians, had been shunted to the side by the state party and Tammany Hall.[16] He planned to go to the national convention in Baltimore, not as a delegate or, indeed, in any formal capacity.

At the time, Louis Howe was at Horseneck Beach, expecting a visit from Roosevelt after the convention. While at the beach, he wrote Roosevelt a letter with a noteworthy salutation, one that may have been meant to bolster the non-delegate and non-entity on his way to the convention. "Beloved and Revered Future President," Howe began. "This is a line to remind you that you have a date with me to go in swimming. . . ."[17] Howe was nothing if not acutely aware of the feelings of those around him—those about whom he cared. Highly emotional inside and usually crusty outside, he knew when people were hurt and why, even if they didn't show it.

Roosevelt probably didn't make a fuss, if the other New Yorkers going to Baltimore made him feel unwanted—which is what he was. Mailed just before or during the convention, Howe's greeting might well have been a bit of encouragement, as if to keep Roosevelt looking forward to greater battles. But it was also an indication of how uninhibited he had become in his dealings with Roosevelt, addressing Roosevelt with the playful but serious praise he would use with one of his children.

The rest of the letter avoided all mention of politics, except in the last line, when he promised, "Every time I duck under the cool water this week I will think of you at Baltimore and regret (?) that I am not along."[18] The temperature in Baltimore was expected to reach the nineties.

Wilson had few friends among the New Yorkers at the convention, as the official (Tammany-driven) delegation was unified against him. Nonetheless, he won the nomination, with the help of some slick maneuvering by Osborne and Roosevelt to influence delegates from other states.[19] Roosevelt was ecstatic with the result and immediately joined Osborne in the formation of a new committee with a glorious name: the Empire State Democracy.[20] Roosevelt recommended that Howe manage it, for a salary, and Osborne agreed. Howe gladly accepted. His job polling upstaters each fall was no match for a chance to work under Osborne, with Roosevelt, and for Woodrow Wilson. He wrote to his boss at the *New York Herald* to say that he would not be available to cover the fall campaign, as he would be a *part* of the fall campaign.

Howe's boss was infuriated. The newspaper had its roster of reporters and canvassers in place for the important election, and Howe hadn't given the editors very much time to find a suitable replacement.

Another sort of history might be written about a man who, in Howe's position, would forsake the opportunity to join such a campaign—who would keep the reliable job for the sake of the family, gathering statistics behind the scenes, predicting trends and all the while predicting his own future down to its own last statistic. But Howe took a chance with the campaign job. Though he was working for the volatile Osborne, he was circling closer to Roosevelt's activities. The summer of 1912 marked a change in their relationship. Because Roosevelt was an executive in the group, Howe answered to him. He may have been older by eleven years and more experienced by far, but Roosevelt was the leader. Howe often called him "Boss" as a nickname. Roosevelt called him "Ludwig." According to Howe, they also called each other a great many other names when they disagreed.[21] Not long after they met, the two established a base of humor that entered into their conversations and most of their letters, which were rife with private jokes and sardonic commentary on the outside world.

———— ·•·•· ————

The Empire State Democracy started work in mid-July. Because Woodrow Wilson was against machine politics, the organization began by identifying ways to unite the anti-Tammany vote behind him. It was a reflex reaction. Wilson, however, was not interested in becoming a rallying cry in the New York State Democratic Party's ongoing civil war. In August, his camp made overtures to Tammany Hall and, indeed, indicated that Wilson would accept support anywhere he could find it in the state. Tom Osborne was aghast. In his view, the Empire State Democracy was not the kind of democracy that was supposed to include everyone. It was for people who hated Tammany Hall.

Leaving Wilson's fortunes largely to others, Roosevelt faced a challenge in his own re-election campaign. Edward Perkins, chairman of the Dutchess County Democratic Party, took his cue from Boss Murphy and pressed for another nominee to take Roosevelt's State Senate seat. Roosevelt had too much support, though, and Perkins abandoned his mischief. Roosevelt was further encouraged when the Progressive Party, of which Theodore Roosevelt was the standard-bearer, put a candidate in his State Senate race; that boded well for dividing the Republican vote. In late August, a month before the campaign started in earnest, Franklin and Eleanor went to Campobello with the children.

Osborne continued to promote the Empire State Democracy, but he was soon discouraged by the insistence of the Wilson camp that it favored party unity above all else. It soon became apparent that Wilson's managers in the state were working around the Empire State Democracy, rather than through it. Osborne was not only disgusted, he was running low on money, and he stopped underwriting the group.[22]

Louis Howe lost his job, once again, at the hands of Thomas Osborne. The same thing had happened so many times that it is remarkable to think that he never gave up and turned his back on Osborne. Either he was loyal in terms that had no selfish aims or else he couldn't afford to hold a grudge. In truth, Howe would not be able to abandon Osborne until someone else came along.

By September, Louis Howe was unemployed, through no fault of his own, and entirely without income. His old canvassing job at the *Herald* had been given to someone else and the paper was not inclined to fire that person just because Howe had changed his mind about quitting. He was lucky that the editors were still holding open his reporting job for the winter legislative season.

Grace and the children took shelter in Fall River, ever the symbol of Howe's failure to care for them financially. Meanwhile, Howe stayed in Albany and looked for work. In spite of the large number of campaigns in full swing, he couldn't find any sort of a position. Finally, he escaped to Horseneck Beach, where he lived inexpensively and wrote letters to people who might help. One of them was Franklin Roosevelt.

Roosevelt must have known it was coming, eventually: a request for a favor, in the form of a job. As Howe wrote:

> I notified the Herald as soon as Wilson was nominated and it made my boss very angry, as it upset his schedule. Now I am in a hole because there are five long months before Albany and the price of living has not gone down any. If you can connect me with a job during the campaign, for heaven's sake help me out, for this mess is a bad business for me.

Howe finished by reverting to that evergreen issue, the fight against Tammany Hall. "To my mind," he added, "now is the time to put that Young Men's Wilson Clubs idea through, using it as a blind to build up an anti-Murphy organization."[23]

Roosevelt read Howe's letter in Hyde Park, probably on his return from Campobello. Roosevelt couldn't fight Tammany statewide, though. He had his own troubles in the three counties he represented. He set Howe's letter aside, perhaps on the large pile of letters he regularly received from people asking for jobs in government.

After a few days in Hyde Park, Roosevelt noticed that he began to lose his energy. He and Eleanor left the children at the country house and went to New York City for a day or two of business. Franklin became feverish there, and felt much too ill even to get out of bed. Eleanor nursed him until Franklin's mother, Sara, visited and recognized at once that Eleanor, too, had a fever.[24] Bedridden, both Franklin and Eleanor were diagnosed with typhoid fever, a potentially deadly illness generally carried in unclean water. The Roosevelts recalled that they had been warned onboard the boat from Campobello not to drink the water provided in the cabins. They hadn't imbibed any, but they had made the mistake of using it as a rinse in brushing their teeth. Neither was gravely ill, but they were completely debilitated.

For over a week, Roosevelt was sick in bed when he ought to have been out greeting voters. The other candidates in his district were doing just that. Roosevelt tried to make plans for a return, but his illness lingered. Finally, the physician forbade him from leaving his bed for the duration of the campaign. What was more, he was not even to speak to anyone about it, for fear of tapping his energy.

Boss Murphy might as well have filled the pitchers on the ferry himself. For him, the news couldn't have been better. Even Roosevelt later admitted that at first he considered his Senate race lost. Lying in bed, he thought about it further and remembered Howe's letter. He called Eleanor to the bedside and asked her to contact Howe to see if he would be interested in running a surrogate campaign. Howe, vacationing at Horseneck Beach, was oblivious to Roosevelt's illness. On hearing from Eleanor, though, he rushed to New York and had his one and only meeting with the candidate, who could provide very little except a salary of fifty dollars a week, a liberal expense account, and permission to run the campaign without interference from anyone.[25]

"I accepted," Howe later wrote, "with enthusiasm."[26] He immediately moved his family to Poughkeepsie. Grace and the children took rooms at a boardinghouse. For Grace, a former student at Vassar, Poughkeepsie was a familiar place to live, with the added benefit of allowing her to introduce Mary, who was twelve, to the college. Louis, meanwhile, made his home at a local hotel, politics being a round-the-clock enterprise for him. From his point of view, he had more at stake in the campaign than Roosevelt did. If Roosevelt happened to lose, he could blame it on his illness and he would undoubtedly have other opportunities. Howe, on the other hand, would never have a better chance to show Roosevelt what he could do, and what a team they could make.

Going into the job, Howe had a number of weaknesses. He had never run a political campaign before. He was not from the mid-Hudson region and didn't know the geography. More important, the people didn't know him. He had never made a political speech before and, as anyone would admit (himself included), he wasn't known for his charisma. Quite the opposite. The final strike against Howe was that to win the election for his friend, he had only six weeks.

But Howe also had many years' worth of ideas that he had given to Osborne, usually without result: original thinking on campaign advertising, unifying themes, and untapped segments of the electorate. He had a well-honed understanding of the upstate voter, especially in small towns and farm districts. He was a facile writer. He knew the appeal of Franklin Roosevelt better than anyone. As to speech-making, he had theatrical experience and could even be a bit of a ham. And, finally, he had the help of many of Roosevelt's friends, including his neighbor, Jefferson Newbold Jr., the only other Democrat to hold the 13th District Senate seat within a half century or more. Newbold offered to escort Howe through the district and speak on Roosevelt's behalf.

"We went around Dutchess County together," Newbold later recalled to Roosevelt, "and I really got to know him and admire him."[27] The campaign of 1912 was one of the highlights of Louis Howe's life, and he described it in great detail in an article written twenty years later:

> I found myself a campaign manager with a candidate who could not lift a finger to win votes for himself. The doctors would not even let him speak to me over the telephone.
>
> In running that campaign I put to the test some theories that I had developed while acting as a political observer and commentator for my newspaper. Being in the enviable position of having no boss (for the first time in my life) I decided to carry out those ideas.
>
> While conducting straw votes for the *Herald* in rural counties, I had been impressed by the fact that politicians overlooked a bet in not making more of an effort to mobilize the force of the little fellows. There are "forgotten" voters as well as forgotten citizens.
>
> It was in what many campaign managers dismiss carelessly as "the sticks" that I concentrated my efforts. I stayed out of such centres as Poughkeepsie and Beacon, where the opposition was strongly entrenched. But I worked the rural districts night and day.
>
> I had faith in the knowledge I had gathered as a reporter; I took pride in its accuracy and decided to act upon it.
>
> Instead of mailing biographical sketches of the candidate to hostile newspapers and inserting small ads in their columns, I took full page space

in the smaller newspapers. Instead of trying to claim everything under the sun for Roosevelt in that space I ran ads that sometimes contained no more than a dozen words. If a political advertisement leaves one favorable idea in the reader's mind, it may be ranked a good ad.[28]

On election day, 1912, the results were bleak for the insurgents of 1911. Even with a Wilson victory and a strong Democratic showing throughout the state, Tammany Hall didn't forget. The only three assemblymen left from the bloodbath the year before were defeated. Among the three senators up for reelection, one from Buffalo lost his seat. Another from Schenectady hung on to keep his office. With Roosevelt's chances for survival uncertain at best, Howe watched the returns along the Hudson nervously. "When it was over," he recalled, "I telephoned Roosevelt's home, begged permission of the doctors to say one word to him, and when it was granted (for the first time since the beginning of the campaign), I was able to say: I just called up to congratulate you, Mr. Senator."

Roosevelt won by a wider margin than he had in his first race. As Howe predicted, the cities went to the other candidates, but the countryside surged for the man considered a good neighbor.

"One of the great pleasures of life," Howe wrote, "is to prove that you know what you are doing when you depart from precedent."

"That election," he wrote, "gave me that pleasure."[29] Roosevelt's victory was a triumph for Howe, with word circulating in political circles that he had masterminded the campaign. For the first time in his life, he could count on being in demand the next time he needed a job. Howe had to get used to looking at himself differently, too: still a genius, but for once, one not crowded by failure.

CHAPTER SIX

NAVY MEN

"I for one, was convinced that day," Louis Howe wrote of Roosevelt's reelection to the State Senate in 1912, "that Franklin Roosevelt was on the threshold of a brilliant public career."[1] Opinions differed on that particular point in Albany, where Roosevelt was a very lonesome insurgent at the start of his second term. He worked on bills pertaining to agricultural finance, but party leaders, including Alfred E. Smith, left him very much alone.

Smith, the new Assembly speaker, was in the midst of crucial legislative work—crucial in the history of the Democratic Party and in his own political development. He was vice chairman of the Factory Investigating Commission, the legislature's response to the horrors of the Triangle Shirtwaist Fire in 1911. Over the course of three years, the Commission, composed of elected officials as well as social workers and business leaders, would visit hundreds of factories all over the state. Smith took a leading hand in shepherding the resulting bills into law. With his combination of compassion and political practicality, he was becoming a hero among social reformers, a number of whom were strong-minded women. To their surprise and perhaps his own, Smith was entirely comfortable working with women on an equal basis. New York's state government, oscillating between corruption and dysfunction in the first decades of the twentieth century, became a model for other states in at least one respect: making strides in providing safe and fair working conditions. At the same time, Smith was fashioning a model for a modern politician.

Roosevelt wasn't involved in anything as influential as the Factory Investigating Committee when the 1913 legislative session began. Nor did he expect to be. Roosevelt had devoted a measure of his time ever since the election to making his second term as short as possible. As it began, he and Eleanor did not rent a house in Albany. She and the children remained in Hyde Park, while he took a couple of rooms at the Ten Eyck Hotel, from which he could check out at a moment's notice.

In truth, Roosevelt's reelection mattered more to Louis Howe than to the candidate himself. In terms of subsequent events, it probably didn't matter much whether Roosevelt had been reelected to his Senate seat or not. His reputation for reform and his early support of the new president put him in line for a position in Washington. In December, he had at least an indication that he would be named assistant secretary of the Navy. And the idea delighted him. He had been a serious student of the navy and its history since boyhood. "The Assistant Secretaryship is the one place, above all others, I would love to hold," Roosevelt said at the time.[2] In March, he received the appointment, packing up to make the move to Washington and leaving Albany to its latest losing battle with Boss Murphy (a struggle that would end with the impeachment of the new governor, William Sulzer, who dared fight Tammany Hall).

In early April, Roosevelt sent for Louis Howe, offering him, officially, the job of "clerk in the Secretary's Office, Navy Department (detailed for duty in the Office of the Assistant Secretary)."[3] Unofficially, he was Roosevelt's chief assistant. The annual salary, at $1,800, was better than any he'd ever earned and the work was certainly steadier.[4] Unlike Roosevelt, Howe had no particular love of the Navy or of ships; his primary credential along those lines was the time he put in looking at the ocean at Horseneck Beach. In that, he was one-up on the new Secretary of the Navy, Josephus Daniels, a former newspaper editor and senator from Raleigh, North Carolina. Aside from being a good administrator, Daniels had no particular ties to his new

work. Howe, who had been at the point of real destitution six months before, wired to Roosevelt, "I'm game" and within the month, he moved to
Washington to start his life over.[5]

—◆—

When Howe arrived at the Navy Department, he was aware that neither he nor Roosevelt knew what they were supposed to do or how
to pretend to be doing it. "I just stood by his desk," Howe recalled, speaking
of Roosevelt, "and when he signed a paper, I blotted it."[6]

The assistant secretary typically oversaw the business details of the
Navy, including procurement, contracts, and logistical issues. He wasn't directly involved in matters of deployment or strategy. Roosevelt had never
held an executive post before, but he proved to be a natural in managing a
staff that was productive and generally contented. Howe diligently studied
the matters put before him, no matter how arcane, until he was regarded as
an expert in the management of naval supply. "Howe was one of the
strangest men I ever met and one of the smartest," Daniels said much later.
"At first I thought Howe was just a Man Friday, enamored of his chief. But
he was a much abler man than that."[7]

With the help of Charles H. McCarthy, a civil service clerk assigned to
the office, Roosevelt and Howe learned the procedures and brought their
own influence to bear on the overriding goal of efficiency. The most ineffi-
cient aspect of the office, in fact, was the relationship between McCarthy
and Howe, who fought over the separation of duties and their respective
proximity to the assistant secretary. Howe was possessive and sometimes
petty where Roosevelt was concerned. He tried to set a rule that he had to
be apprised before anyone could enter Roosevelt's office. Not everyone respected his role as Roosevelt's keeper, though. McCarthy never did. He
was so bold as to step into his boss's office whenever he liked, without
Howe's explicit permission. Howe was driven to fury by McCarthy, but in
time the two learned to work together. Howe had no choice; he couldn't
quit, allow himself to be fired, or simply drift away—not if he wanted to
help Roosevelt in the long term.

For a man with Howe's job history and his temperament, an office such as that at the Navy Department offered strange and uncomfortable surroundings. He settled in, though, concentrating on the work before him, and made a remarkable record in fields about which he knew nothing before arriving: labor, contract law, logistics, and procurement, among them.

While Howe bristled at having colleagues at his elbow, he also had to adjust to working for Franklin Roosevelt. They had made a great many plans over the previous two years, but had never actually worked together, as boss and assistant, as partners with the same ambition, or as bureaucrats under pressure to produce actual results. From the moment Howe arrived at the Navy Department, they took on all of those relationships and others more subtle. Whether they were actually friends, though, or merely teammates with the same goal, was less apparent.

Whenever Roosevelt went away, on business or vacation, Howe sent him bundles of letters to sign, others to read, and miscellaneous papers reflecting the day's issues. The bundles, which went out almost daily, included memoranda from Howe that commented on each of the items included. The memos of June 28 and June 30, 1913—only about a month and a half after Howe started his job—run to a total of eight pages of single-spaced type. The tone of the memos, and their variety, would seem to echo the conversations between Roosevelt and Howe when they were together, as a small selection shows. Listing enclosures, Howe wrote:

- A letter gotten up by Admiral Griffen . . . in regard to the Fiske oil contract, which is so nicely put that I have added to it a note to Admiral Griffen expressing your pleasure in the way in which he handled the somewhat complicated reply. I think the way in which he frankly owns up to the Department being wrong is fine. It takes a real man to write a letter of that kind and my hat goes off to him.
- Memorandum in the case of the boy who is so seasick whenever he goes to sea and who wants to be a naval officer on shore for the rest of his life. I can't help chuckling over this every time it is mentioned.

- A little personal letter from Governor Sulzer which you can frame if you want to. I see he says the truth will prevail. Such being the case, Where would he get off?
- A catalogue of "Americana" from George D. Smith [rare-book dealers], in which I have marked various things which I thought might interest you. There are some charming little tidbits at from twelve hundred to three thousand dollars apiece, which I have not marked, but I call your attention to 217, which is an old Paul Jones piece at a comparatively reasonable price.[8]

Howe assumed quite naturally the quality that Eleanor Roosevelt had described as obligatory in herself, referring to a "duty to be interested in whatever interested her husband, whether it was politics, books, or a particular fish for dinner."[9] Roosevelt was interested in old navy prints, so Louis Howe scoured the catalogues of the antiquarian dealers. Eleanor Roosevelt had been speaking of a wife's role, according to her early perceptions. Howe wasn't seeking to replace Eleanor, but sublimating himself to please Roosevelt was something he seemed to need to do. At the same time, Eleanor had to accept that it was something she could not do. Early in her marriage, Franklin's strong personality had made her feel secure. "Gradually," she wrote, "I had to learn that to develop, one must have a certain freedom of thought and action." She then pointed to "the long and slow and sometimes painful process that I went through to attain that independence." Louis Howe went through a process equally as complex, but the result he craved was to curtail his independence.[10]

If Albany had once represented the first time that the Roosevelts set up their own household, Washington gave them their own identity entirely. Sara Roosevelt visited much less often than she had ever done before, in their other homes. The Roosevelts moved into a rented house and the Howes into an apartment a few blocks away. The two families sometimes spent holidays together. Eleanor appreciated that Howe was useful to her husband, but she remained notably unenthusiastic about him. She did come to have a warm regard for Grace, though. A day after Louis left on an official tour of the Caribbean, Franklin developed a high fever in conjunction with a severe sore throat. Eleanor contacted Grace and asked what she thought they should do, in terms of notifying Louis. "You'd better not let him know that Franklin is worse," Grace said, "unless you want him to jump right off that ship and swim ashore and rush back here to him."[11]

Howe was contented in his new Washington home, in large measure because of the fun he had with his children. As a teenager, Mary had outgrown some of his horseplay, but Hartley was delighted by his father's playful nature. When the boy was about seven (in about 1918), they produced a handmade magazine, the "Bubble News," with most of the drawings and the text by Louis. Eventually, the two of them played so much that it became a point of contention between Grace and her husband. "Dad liked to play and rough-house with Hartley after supper and then read to him, often rather exciting things," Mary recalled. "Mother felt this was very upsetting to his nerves and his sleep."[12] Finally, Grace approached the family physician, Dr. Adams, and convinced him to write out a prescription, addressed to no one in particular, but hand delivered to Louis. "Your boy must be put to bed immediately after dinner," it read, "and must not be played with or read to thereafter."[13]

"It always struck me that was unfair to Dad," Mary reflected, "since after supper was the only time he could see the child at all."[14] Howe curtailed his time with Hartley and brought home work to read, sitting in a chair in the living room of the apartment, a cigarette burning at his side. It was what he later called being "the prosaic old married man."[15] With the regular salary from the Navy Department, the Howes found a two-story cottage for sale at Horseneck Beach, near Fall River. It stood by itself, adding to the solitude that Louis Howe sought when he wanted to relax. They purchased the place, taking out a mortgage and paying it off in less than five years. Horseneck Beach was Louis' place, though; Grace was not fond of its rustic atmosphere. She and the children went back from Washington to Fall River every summer and Louis visited on many weekends, usually meeting them at the beach cottage.

Howe felt isolated from Grace whether they were together or apart. "I have felt so sure that I have lost your real love forever," he wrote in an undated letter of the Washington years, "that all life held was to try and make life just endurable for you, with no hope of making you really happy—that I have tried to bury my love for you deep in my heart—I thought that every time I kissed you I could feel you wince and draw back. . . ."[16] He was still concerned that there was someone else in his wife's life, and he even mentioned "Willie" again in his correspondence with her. In another letter written during the mid-teens from Washington, Louis was in a different mood: he thanked her profusely for writing a nice letter, sounding more like a person at the beginning of a courtship than in the fifteenth or sixteenth year of marriage.

During the summers Howe was in Washington, and, except for short breaks, he was alone there. Not only was his family away each year, but so was Franklin, taking long vacations to visit his family at Campobello whenever he could. By himself in the apartment, Howe once wrote to Grace that he pretended to check in on the children and then went in the master bedroom "and have sat here ever since smoking silently in the darkness." He described how he tried to persuade himself that he could hear "the rustle of your wrapper and the funny little pat, pat of your slippers."[17]

Howe circulated very little in Washington, aside from joining an Episcopal Church and a community theater group. Franklin Roosevelt, on the other hand, was far more social, though at first his invitations derived more from his family tree and school ties than from his official capacity. Most of the naval officers came to respect Franklin's knowledge, though at the same time, his ambition was hard to miss. "I don't remember talking to any naval officer around Washington when Roosevelt was Assistant Secretary," Admiral James Richardson recalled in the early 1950s, "who thought he was an honest man. Everyone considered him a slippery fellow."[18]

Both Roosevelt and Howe were active in using their ties to the Wilson administration to find jobs for once and future political supporters. They had particular success gaining appointments for postmasters. It was not so very different from the type of behavior for which they hated Boss Murphy, though on a minute scale, by comparison. On one occasion, they apparently shifted a contract for the manufacture of ship engines to a friend, in contradiction of the results of competitive bidding on the job— and were found out.

Politically, Roosevelt helped himself most by becoming a surrogate host for Democrats from around the country who wanted to see the president. With Wilson generally unable or unwilling to entertain mid-level politicians, Roosevelt was one of his favorite substitutes: a personable man who rarely disappointed his guests for good, "insider" Washington talk. Howe kept track of Roosevelt's new friends, and over the years, both he and Franklin carried on a correspondence with a large number of them as part of their effort to build a national following.

———— • • • ————

In late July, 1914, the First World War started with a formal declaration by Austria-Hungary against Serbia. Throughout the first week of August, other European countries entered into a state of war, and military action began with the invasion of Belgium by Germany. Uncertainty was universal, as hatred and fear burst forth from all quarters, ending in a flash what had been a calm or, at least, a controlled era. During early August, armies cheered their generals, diplomats fumbled with dwindling options, and ships of all types were sunk in the Pacific as well as the Atlantic. Nations at war wondered how long the fighting would last. Nations that had not yet taken sides wondered how long they could keep out of the fighting.

The specter of inevitable change and action was staunchly resisted by many Americans, who wanted no part of a foreign war. Franklin Roosevelt, however, may well have been stirred by the atmosphere of early August, with newspapers running out of room for all of the many dispatches from Europe. People were on the move and, in the spirit of the times, he apparently wanted to get out in front. Roosevelt wasn't focused on the new war, however, but rather, on an old and stubborn one. Two weeks after the outbreak of the World War, on August 13, Roosevelt suddenly decided that he was ready to leave the Navy Department—and that "one place, above all others" he had professed he wanted to be.

New York State politics was in a mess more crumpled than ever, with no leadership left in the anti-Tammany side of the Democratic Party. Thomas Osborne, having read a book about prison life, had abandoned politics and dedicated himself to prison reform. Being Thomas Osborne, with a notorious trunk of costumes, he wanted to enter the world of prison in disguise, but a rather more sensible prisoner at Auburn Penitentiary warned him against trying to fool the other prisoners. Instead, Osborne went into prison as he was, but with an assumed name, to live as an inmate for a week. He wrote a bestselling book about his experience and, as of 1914, was becoming a pioneering voice for prison reform.

Without consulting Howe, Roosevelt abruptly decided to fill the void for an anti-Tammany leader in New York State politics, announcing that he would run for the U.S. Senate there. Apparently, there were those in the Wilson administration, and possibly Wilson himself, who had encouraged Roosevelt to run for the seat. A small group of New Yorkers made an even more urgent pitch to Roosevelt. Vacationing at Horseneck Beach, Howe heard of Roosevelt's decision by way of a telegram in mid-August. By then, the course was irreversible; Roosevelt was in the race. It was the sort of baldly ambitious move that gave Roosevelt a reputation in some corners as an opportunist, short on dedication to anything other than his own advancement. Howe once said that his role in going to Washington with Roosevelt was "to provide the toe weights" to keep Roosevelt's feet on the ground and to keep him from making snap decisions—such as the one to run for Senate with no organization in place beforehand.[19] Howe might not have been happy about it, but nonetheless, he immediately left for New York to start a campaign. The first hurdle was securing the nomination in the first primary to be held for a Senate seat in New York State. By law, the legislature no longer selected senators.

Howe worked hard, pulling together contacts and sending out voluminous letters on Roosevelt's behalf. The candidate, meanwhile, was at Campobello during much of the campaign, in part because Eleanor was expecting their fifth child. When Roosevelt was available, he traveled the state in hopes of uniting the disparate factions in the party before Boss Murphy could weigh in with his preference for a nominee. Roosevelt and

Howe hoped that the Tammany choice would be the maverick publisher William Randolph Hearst, whom they considered an advantageous contrast to Roosevelt. Instead, Murphy chose the well-respected ambassador to Germany, James W. Gerard. If the Wilson administration had, in fact, pushed Roosevelt to run, then Murphy had brilliantly outmaneuvered him. Gerard was one of Woodrow Wilson's most generous supporters, which is largely why he received a plum foreign service appointment and why, in the upcoming primary, any Wilson support would quietly be pulled from Franklin Roosevelt. A solid candidate with a Tammany wind at his back, Gerard easily defeated Roosevelt in the primary, although he went on to lose in the general election. Franklin Roosevelt took his drubbing with a chipper outlook, though in truth, it had been an embarrassing setback. Fortunately, he still had plenty to do at the Navy Department.

As the war escalated, activity in the Navy Department took on a more urgent tone, especially since both Secretary Daniels and Roosevelt believed that the United States would eventually be pulled into the fighting and needed to prepare. They weren't the only ones. Congress continually increased funding for the Navy starting in 1914. The turning point came in 1915. After the British ocean liner *Lusitania* was torpedoed and sunk by the Germans on May 7, the Navy Department grew busier than it had ever been during peacetime. The following year, Congress authorized $312 million for the construction of 157 war vessels: another record, in war or peace. An hour after the appropriations bill was signed into law, the department had already placed advertisements soliciting bids for the three-year building program; both the ads and their alacrity emanated from Roosevelt's office.[20] "The Germans continued to talk peace," wrote Secretary Daniels of the year 1916, "but our navy continued to build ships, enlist men and accumulate reserves of guns, ammunition and war materials."[21]

When German aggression against American interests pulled the nation into the war in April 1917, the Navy Department burgeoned. Louis Howe absorbed extra duties and typically worked fourteen hours at a stretch. In a letter written to a friend in 1924, four years after he left his post at Navy, he boasted, "At this moment, thirty-two naval officers [are] doing the work which was my job with the old administration."[22]

One of the staffers hired to help with the increasing workload was R. H. Camalier, whom Roosevelt called "Camy." He also called him, "Rolly Polly Plump Boy."[23] Camalier was a heavyset man from the city of Washington and an ace in taking dictation and typing. "Mr. Roosevelt was a strict disciplinarian in his office," Camalier said, "but he was so congenial and so pleasant that it was not only a privilege and honor, but a pleasure to work for him."[24] If Camy or any of the others made a mistake, Roosevelt asked simply what caused it and whether it could ever happen again. He and Howe also made their own share of mistakes, but as Howe was relieved to report, none that endangered Navy personnel.

Camalier said that Howe was nothing like Roosevelt in terms of demeanor at the office. "As a negotiator," Camalier continued, "I don't think Louis Howe has had his equal. In handling contracts, he was the most meticulous man I've met in the Navy Department."[25] At the same time, Camalier thought Howe was a sinister presence in the office, making unnecessarily cruel comments, ignited by his jealousy of anyone who commanded too much of Roosevelt's attention. Many people commented on Howe's insulting nature, which reached a kind of peak at the Navy Department. He took special satisfaction in refusing to pay any attention to the rank of the people with whom he worked. He was as likely to be rude to an admiral as an ensign if he felt so inclined. Many officers were tough birds who took it in stride, but some took note and then bided their time. On those occasions when Howe did make a mistake, he found out exactly which were which, as those officers he had once insulted took pleasure in returning the favor. Roosevelt was much more popular with Navy personnel, but there were those who were lying in wait for him to stumble, as well.

Roosevelt and Howe discussed the 1918 election in New York, where the governor's seat looked tantalizing at first blush—just as the Senate seat had been all too tempting for Roosevelt in 1914. First, Howe contended that the assistant secretary of the Navy should remain in his post in wartime. Second, Howe believed that Roosevelt could not further his political career or goals by setting himself up in opposition to Tammany Hall, year in and year out. It was not only a futile pursuit, but it was doomed to leave Roosevelt in the wreckage of the past for New York politics. Meanwhile, in the present, Alfred Smith, a Tammany man, had accomplished practical and even heroic things for the people of the state while other politicians—including Roosevelt—had simply bashed away at Tammany. Unlike 1914, Roosevelt apparently listened to Howe's counsel and resisted all attempts to pull him into the race.

In mid-1918, New Yorkers began to call on Smith to run for governor. Among them was Franklin Roosevelt, but Smith's most ardent supporters were people who had worked with him in the aftermath of the Triangle Shirtwaist Company fire. One was Frances Perkins, who had been on the staff of the Factory Investigating Commission. Another was Belle Moskowitz, a social worker in New York who had helped to instigate the Commission. Moskowitz was one of the twenty-two women—one-third of the total roster—invited to serve on Smith's campaign committee, once he decided to enter the race. Inviting such a large proportion of women was smart politics on Smith's part. In 1918, women in New York State were to have the right to vote in state elections for the first time. The fight for the right to vote in national elections was still ongoing. Of all the many high-powered New Yorkers who rallied around Smith in 1918, as he began his rise through a decade of extraordinary influence, none was more critical to his success than Moskowitz.

Belle Lindner Israels Moskowitz was forty-one, a native New Yorker whose parents had come from East Prussia. Lithe and very pretty, Belle liked acting, and in her early twenties was a semiprofessional performer. She later turned to social work, as many ardent young women did at the turn of the twentieth century. After her first husband, an architect, died, she married Henry Moskowitz, a well-known social worker in New York. Both were inspired by Smith's actions after the Triangle fire to look on politics as a natural extension of social work: using government to improve the lives of people in need.

In working on the campaign, Mrs. Moskowitz quickly recognized that women were wary of Smith's ties to Tammany Hall, which many still associated with saloons, prostitution, and gambling. They had a different approach to the election than men, and so she suggested that the campaign committee organize a subsidiary women's campaign. The idea was accepted, and Mrs. Moskowitz was placed at the head. In that capacity, she came into contact with the candidate himself.

By 1918, Belle Moskowitz was no longer pretty or lithe; she was a rather nondescript and quite plump middle-aged woman. She didn't especially like to bring attention to herself. Nonetheless, Alfred Smith noticed her, and listened to her. "He was a keen judge of the credibility and the disinterestedness of people he talked with," recalled Frances Perkins. "He would ask the kind of question that required a clear answer; he could fairly dig information out of you."[26] As Smith met Mrs. Moskowitz in meetings during the fall campaign, he discovered a great deal that was worth listening to. He found that she was insightful, sharp, and articulate. On her part, she believed in Alfred Smith as she had never believed in any politician before. By the end of the campaign, the two had formed a bond that would have a permanent influence on New York State, the national Democratic Party, and on Franklin Roosevelt as well.

———◦•◦———

While Smith was waging his gubernatorial campaign in September 1918, Franklin Roosevelt was on his way home from an inspection tour in Europe. Rather susceptible to germs and illness for such a hale man, he contracted pneumonia en route and was bedridden on his return. While he was sick, Eleanor discovered evidence that he had been having an affair with her social secretary, Lucy Mercer. It was a shock at the time and apparently remained a source of pain to her for decades, perhaps for the rest of her life. According to close relatives, Eleanor offered him a divorce and he considered it. The effect a divorce would have on the children was a strong factor against it, as was Sara Roosevelt's word that she would cut him out of the Hyde Park estate if he broke up his marriage for another woman. The third factor—again, one based on the secondhand knowledge of cousins—was that Louis Howe was called into a family conference and asked what effect a divorce would have on Roosevelt's presidential chances. Howe didn't need to think about it, and neither would anyone else involved in politics in 1918: a divorce would effectively disqualify a candidate for any high office. Roosevelt agreed to stop seeing Miss Mercer. He tried to assuage Eleanor's pain, but the damage had been done.

The assumption on the part of some family members was that Eleanor stipulated in the new understanding—the replacement vows—that the romantic part of their marriage was to be over. "Through the rest of their lives," Elliott said in an interview, "they never did have a husband-and-wife relationship."[27] Certainly, they were never again to have the relationship with which they'd started out: that of a couple after the typical fashion, holding whole parts of their lives impervious to the outside world. To that extent, the marriage had been breeched, if not broken. Lucy Mercer, the specter of an outsider, was part of the Roosevelts permanantly. Nonetheless, they were agreed to move on as husband and wife. Even they couldn't have been certain what that meant, anymore.

Howe was aware that Roosevelt was more social than ever five years into his service in the capital; even Eleanor noted—and accepted—his ebullient flirtatiousness there.[28] That was part of his personality and he could use it as a blind, especially, it seems, in confusing those who knew him best.

For Louis Howe, the effect of the news of the affair and the near-end of Roosevelt's political plans could not have been easy to absorb. Howe may have known about the affair since it began (allegedly in 1917), but that is doubtful. Roosevelt tried to hide it in the open by taking Miss Mercer to various social events during Eleanor's absence from Washington.

Howe may have been a hardened reporter who knew every type of human foible as fodder for the daily news, but he was as serious about marriage as Eleanor had been. Even if he wasn't disappointed in Franklin, the man, he surely couldn't help but recognize how close Roosevelt had come to destroying the plans they had made for his career and the work they had both put into realizing them. Howe's loyalty was apparently shaken after the revelation of Roosevelt's affair. Colleagues who knew him at the Navy after the war reported that he went behind Roosevelt's back, helping others in the department, even at the expense of Roosevelt's interests. He also used Roo-

sevelt's name to solidify his own position in government circles. At that juncture, Roosevelt involved himself in the poorest decision of his career at the
Navy Department, in his response to the unraveling scandal at the Newport
Navy Yard. While every bad decision Roosevelt made can't be blamed on the
absence of Howe's counsel, he did, by his own admission, act alone in setting
a plan for Newport. He would have reason later to wish that that there had
been someone to talk him out of it—someone to hold his toes down.

During the war, operations at the Newport Navy Yard fell under the
purview of the assistant secretary. When recurring reports of coercive homosexual behavior at Newport reached Washington, Secretary Daniels
launched a general inquiry. Under Roosevelt, it developed into a secret investigation, which he assigned to a former detective from Connecticut and a
Navy lieutenant who was a physician as well. The methods the investigators
used for gathering facts in the case were, by any standard, shocking and ill-
advised: "enlisted men of the navy were improperly used as participants in
immoral practices," ran one undisputed description, "for the purpose of securing evidence on which to dismiss offenders from the navy."[29]

Enlisted men, a number of them not yet out of their teens, were assigned as special agents to become acquainted with suspected homosexuals
and accept their advances, if indeed there were any; the resulting sexual activity was described in court by the agent on whom it had been perpetrated,
resulting in a high number of convictions. When the method of using
sailors as bait became known, there were those, especially in the Newport
area, who demanded to know the extent of the Navy Department's complic-
ity in the sordid investigative technique. When Roosevelt's name was attached to the scandal, he emphatically denied knowing in advance what the
detectives had in mind.

Further criticism followed Roosevelt's close working relationship with
Thomas Mott Osborne, who was appointed warden of the Portsmouth
Naval Prison in Maine. Osborne, having dedicated himself to prison reform,
had served for a time as a warden at Sing Sing, in New York State. His enemies made accusations that he engaged in inappropriate relations with the
prisoners, charges that were never proven. When Secretary Daniels, encouraged by Roosevelt and Howe, appointed Osborne in 1917 to reform the

Portsmouth Naval Prison, the old insinuations eventually resurfaced. Among other actions, Osborne dismissed the guards from the prison and replaced them with "trustee" convicts, putting emphasis throughout on the honor system. Osborne was regarded by some Navy officers as having altogether too much sympathy for the men. Charges were made of "depravity" and "favoritism,"[30] on Osborne's part specifically, as well as generally, throughout the prison he administered. Both Daniels and Roosevelt were supposed by some to be complicit with the alleged activities.

The year following the war ought to have been easy, compared to the rigors and constant anxiety of maintaining the largest naval force in U.S. history. Instead, the flaws in the lives of the Roosevelts and the Howes were exposed and impossible to ignore.

Howe was living at the Hotel Harrington in Washington on the night in October 1919 that he wrote a letter to Grace, having had "plenty of time to lie still and think everything over." It was a low point, a turning point— or just another night when Howe's disappointments were too much to bear. "Forgive this scrawl but writing comes a bit hard yet," he told her. He meant physically. He'd been ill and his penmanship was strained. He also meant that it was hard to write. "Nothing seems to matter anymore," he told her. So it was that he was thinking of his son. "I wish Bub would write," Howe reflected.

> If he should forget [me], I think it would be the last straw. He's the only person in the world that cares for me and I'm afraid it wouldn't take him very long to forget. Everybody else is indifferent or hates me or is afraid of me or uses me to get what they want.[31]

In his mind, his wife was somewhere on that list and so, too, was his best friend.

CHAPTER SEVEN

THE EDGE
OF DECISION

In the spring of 1920, while still serving as assistant secretary of the Navy, Roosevelt took something of a leave of absence from Washington to present himself on various pretexts to New York State voters. After his clumsy try for a Senate nomination in 1914, he was ready for a more concerted move into statewide politics. At Howe's urging, he even courted the good will of Tammany boss Charles Murphy whenever possible, successfully relegating their old feud to the past.

The truce didn't exactly reflect hypocrisy on Roosevelt's part. The old game of attacking Tammany as a crooked protectorate and user of the common people had been seriously compromised by the honesty of Alfred Smith, who was elected governor in 1918. As Smith's first two-year term drew to a close in 1920, he was the leading light of the Democrats in the state, incorruptible and seemingly oblivious to the vested interests. Not only was Smith untarnished in political terms, he was revolutionary in his approach to government, as only a few in each generation might be.

Returning to New York State in the spring of 1920 to claim his political future, Franklin Roosevelt found himself listening to universal praise from fellow Democrats for Smith and the excitement he inspired in state government. In contrast to the Tammany-directed patronage expected of him, the first-term governor had developed his own approach, appointing authorities from any source, Democratic or Republican, male or female, and of a wider ethnic variety than any administration in the history of the state. His equanimity was not always reciprocated, though.

For all of his popularity, Smith, the veteran legislator, could accomplish little with the Republican-controlled legislature. "The Republican leaders regarded me as an accidental governor," he wrote, "and while governors come and go, legislative leaders apparently seem to go on forever; they were entirely content to bide their time and wait for me to return to New York City, when they might go on with the business of the state to suit themselves."[1] Belle Moskowitz, who had become one of Smith's closest advisors since the election, suggested another way to move the state forward, around the immutable legislature. Her idea was the formation of a Reconstruction Commission that would invite experts to study social problems in the state and to analyze the government itself.[2] "To the Reconstruction Commission," Smith wrote, "I recommended the study of practically every problem of the after-war period caused by the economic and political changes taking place."[3]

The Commission released reports throughout 1919–1920, covering housing, education, the unemployed, public health, and food supply, among other topics. The reports, Smith explained, "laid down a program which for the ten years following was the background of political platforms, the program of civic reorganizations and the basis of much remedial legislation."[4] The power of the independent study overwhelmed those who had long managed to remain aloof in the face of mere talk and opinion regarding problems in society. The recommendations presented in the Commission reports were founded on non-partisan research. The response may not have been uniform, but at least the reports demanded a response. They were a sensation when they were released, starting a debate that began to accomplish a dream for Smith, Roosevelt, and many other ambitious New York Democrats: the redrawing of party affiliations within the state on ideological terms rather than on the basis of organizational antagonisms and brittle loyalties dating from the Civil War era.

As Roosevelt made it clear that he was available for state office in the late spring and early summer of 1920, Tammany Hall was not only disarmed, but intrigued. Boss Murphy was only too glad to look at ways to use Roosevelt's formerly aggravating vote-getting ability to help sweep his own candidates into office. By June 1920, Roosevelt was Tammany's choice for the Senate.

At the same time, Smith was being discussed within the state as a potential presidential candidate, someone who could expand upon President Wilson's liberal initiative, limited as it had been in practice and much as it had been distracted, in any case, by the war. Belle Moskowitz, hearing about a plan to nominate Smith, was unfazed. "I never looked upon the proposal as more than a compliment," she wrote.[5] In the weeks leading up to the Democratic National Convention in San Francisco, Smith himself had no serious interest in promoting presidential aspirations. Wilson's eight years had ended badly, with the president debilitated from a stroke and the nation fragmented by economic and social unrest. The accepted wisdom was that the Republicans were going to win the White House no matter who headed their ticket—and that the Democrats were going to lose, no matter who headed theirs.

In the first week of July in 1920, Franklin Roosevelt traveled to San Francisco, aware that even he was mentioned in some quarters as a possible nominee. His own plan for the convention was to become better known for the sake of his future, and to acquit himself well enough within the delegation to angle toward a run for the Senate. He was not wholly enthusiastic about the Senate, since it was the governorship that led to the White House: two of the previous five presidents, Theodore Roosevelt and Grover Cleveland, had been New York governors. For the time being, though, Alfred Smith blocked that path—which may have explained the uninhibited gusto with which Roosevelt seconded Smith's name, when it was placed in nomination at the convention.

Smith was not seriously considered for the nomination, however. He hadn't prepared for it by organizing support in advance of the convention. Even if he had, the fact that he was a Roman Catholic undercut his chances. Prejudice against Catholics was widespread, and many party professionals were unwilling to back a candidate whom they considered a long shot from the start. When Roosevelt led a rousing tribute to Smith, though, the hall could hardly contain itself and the cheering of the delegates lasted a full half-hour. For Moskowitz, news of the reaction to Smith at the convention was revelatory, changing even her perception of Smith's future. When the very mention of his name brought down the house, he became a man to watch and with that, Moskowitz, along with others, began to plan in terms of a national campaign within four or eight years. Franklin Roosevelt, however, wouldn't have to wait quite that long.

The convention moved on to a struggle for the presidential nomination that ended with the selection of James M. Cox, the governor of Ohio. After that, the choice of a vice president was considered a "Wilson" slot, for someone openly associated with the president. The presence of a New Yorker on the ticket was regarded as advantageous, and several different camps came up with the idea of drafting Franklin Roosevelt. Boss Murphy was consulted, and in the aftermath of their truce, he agreed. With no opposition forming—and little interest in the decision, anyway—Roosevelt was nominated to run for vice president. "This certainly is a world full of surprises," Eleanor wrote to Sara from Campobello when she heard the news.[6]

Louis Howe was not in San Francisco for the convention, nor did he appear to have had any hand in promoting Roosevelt for the ticket. He probably wasn't expecting the news about the vice presidency, and that, alone, would have made him nervous. "I used to laugh at Louis and say one could not plan every move in this world," Eleanor recalled, "one had to accept circumstances as they developed. Louis hated to do that. He liked to feel that he dominated circumstances."[7] What may have concerned him most was that so much had happened without his guiding hand. But the vice presidential nomination was a step up for Roosevelt, even if there was not much optimism for a Democratic victory in 1920. His place on the ticket would introduce him to voters nationwide, and no matter the outcome, the exposure would leave him in line for future presidential consideration.

By July 16, Roosevelt was back in Washington, after a stop in Ohio to meet his new running mate. Governor Cox had stayed away from the convention, abiding to the tradition of feigned disinterest on the part of potential nominees. The day after Roosevelt arrived in Washington, he wrote to Eleanor: "All goes well, though of course very busily. On arrival yesterday I was met by Howe, McIntyre, Peoples, and lots of cameras and newspaper men. . . ."[8] (Marvin McIntyre was the publicity director of the Navy Department and Christian Peoples was a rear admiral, serving as a paymaster.) Howe was not used to being just one of the gang where Roosevelt's progress was concerned, yet he was distinctly detached as candidate Roosevelt came home. Indeed, what he saw was Roosevelt moving fast and in no need of help—greeting his three friends, and then hurrying off to the crowded day that continued, in the description he wrote to Eleanor: "lots of cameras and newspaper men, came home, bathed, breakfasted, again photographed and got to the Department at 10, to find things decorated with flags, flowers, Admirals, stenographers. . . ."[9]

Roosevelt resigned as assistant to the secretary of the Navy on July 24 and returned to Hyde Park before beginning the national campaign. Howe stayed behind, immersed in a campaign of his own. Having been named acting assistant secretary of the Navy in Roosevelt's stead, he wanted to make the appointment permanent. The increase in salary would be welcome. Moreover, the prestige associated with the title would enhance Howe's opportunities after he left government. And finally, he was doing the job, and that was reason enough to want the title. From the standpoint of the department, the move would ensure a smooth transition, since Howe, even under Roosevelt, had undertaken many of the details of the job. With the election certain to bring in a new administration, all of the appointed positions in Washington were in a lame-duck status, anyway. In pursuit of a few months of his own glory, Howe went after the job and even planted items in the papers indicating that he was under consideration for the appointment.[10]

R oosevelt left in mid-August to tour the West with a small entourage. He was spirited as a campaigner, visiting fifteen states in seventeen days, but he did little to anticipate the historical nature of the 1920 presidential election.[11] While he was away, in fact, the Nineteenth Amendment to the U.S. Constitution was adopted, granting women the right to vote in all elections. For former suffrage workers, the 1920 election was to be a hallowed reward—and their first taste of power in national politics.

In New York, Tammany Hall was never known to overlook a voter, and Charles Murphy gave immediate orders that committees in his machine grant half their seats to women, in keeping with the approximate proportion in the population. Alfred Smith, running for re-election as governor, had Belle Moskowitz to make sure that women were being addressed.

On the day that the Nineteenth Amendment was certified by the U.S. Attorney General, Eleanor Roosevelt was interviewed for a syndicated column, "With Women of Today." While expressing support for the League of Nations, which was one of the major themes of the Democratic ticket, she was noticeably reticent, saying that she was "no more interested in politics than other women." Based on the interview, the columnist wrote, "Her keen interest in her husband's career has never roused her to do anything active in politics herself and she has never campaigned for him as so many of the modern women have done."[12] While the sentence unintentionally implied that many of the modern women had campaigned for Eleanor's husband, the fact was that she was nonetheless about to join the ranks of the well-traveled political wife, on the campaign trail for the sake of her husband.

At the end of August, Louis Howe recognized that he was not going to be named permanent assistant secretary of the Navy, not even for the few remaining months of the administration. A well-connected, old-money Democrat from New Hampshire, Gordon Woodbury, received the job.[13] Howe had no political leverage to match. Naming him wouldn't bring Wilson or Daniels any good will in the party and on the contrary, it would antagonize certain Navy officers who regarded Roosevelt with very bad will. In the midst of the 1920 campaign, Roosevelt was once again targeted with attacks over the Newport accusations. Timed to embarrass the Democratic ticket, official investigations opened in the Senate to examine the conduct at the Navy Department. Roosevelt and his response to the situation at the base of it were a particular focus of the hearings. Because Howe had served under Roosevelt, his name would only have agitated the issue afresh and so, having no wish to serve Gordon Woodbury, Howe resigned from the Navy Department.

In late September, Franklin Roosevelt asked his wife to join him on his second campaign swing out West. He said he missed her and he certainly thought he needed her, in order to encourage the interest of female voters. Eleanor was expected to be seen at her husband's side at all the campaign stops, a role that political spouses have filled ever since: smiling through unceasing renditions of the same stump speech with, for those who look closely, a different backdrop for each. Eleanor wouldn't have much to do on the campaign, but she was dreading it, nonetheless, afraid that she had little to offer to a campaign steeped in international issues.

A little later, after Louis Howe had given himself a rest at Horseneck Beach, Roosevelt was glad to invite him to take part in the campaign. Catching up to the candidate in the Midwest, Howe joined those onboard the private railcar leased for Roosevelt's speech-making tour. The others were R. H. Camalier, the typist; another clerical worker named Anderson; Charles McCarthy, who worked in Roosevelt's office at the Navy; Marvin McIntyre, former publicity director of the Navy Department, who was in charge of travel arrangements; Thomas Lynch, a friend from Poughkeepsie, who handled expenses; and Stephen T. Early, another journalist who acted as advance man and organized publicity. In addition, one reporter was with the tour from beginning to end and others rode with the car for shorter spans of a day or two, making for a constant gaggle as the campaign moved forward.

When Howe boarded the campaign train, he was surprised to see Eleanor, and she was likewise unaware that he was to be a late addition to the tour. She was less than delighted. Though the families had become friends during the Washington years, spending many Christmases together, Eleanor admitted later that enduring Louis Howe was high on the list of things she did in the name of helping Franklin in his career. For more than ten years, beneath a veil of social necessity, she had accepted Howe as Franklin's friend, not hers. In fact, Eleanor and her daughter, Anna, made a game of finding new ways to express their dislike of Louis behind his back—and Franklin's. Sara Roosevelt was an enthusiastic participant in the game.

As far as Eleanor was concerned, Howe tried to cast too much influence over her husband, and she didn't understand what kind of man would take such a driving interest in the life and decisions of another. His presence gave her just one more reason to keep to herself, in the small stateroom reserved for her on the train-car.

The four-week campaign trip was unlike anything that Eleanor had experienced before, a traveling road show that made as many as six stops a day. Keeping to the message of the ticket, Franklin generally spoke in favor of the League of Nations as a means of avoiding another world war, but his favorite fodder was the Republican Party and its muddled message. In one stop, he described the ten types of voters who could and indeed should vote for the Republican ticket of Ohio senator Warren G. Harding and Massachusetts governor Calvin Coolidge. It was a list that became more brazen as it went on, finishing with:

- Those who expect to make large financial gain through the recognition of their special interests by a reactionary president.
- Those who want any old kind of a change, without stopping to observe whether they are jumping into the frying pan or into the fire.
- Those who believe we should at once start a war with Mexico in order to "civilize" it in the interests of American oil and mining companies.
- Those who read Republican papers only.
- Those who believe the flag is the personal property of Republicans and that no Democrat was ever a good American.[14]

Even in the role of vice-presidential candidate, Roosevelt wanted to reset the parties, reinforcing the impression that Cox was the "progressive" in the race, while continually painting Harding as a "reactionary" who wanted to take the country back in time.[15] In many gubernatorial races around the country during the previous dozen years, progressive Republican candidates had scared conservative party members into the ranks of the Democrats, distorting the presumed impetus for the Democratic Party to build on the traditions of Bryan and Wilson and occupy the liberal ground in politics. In pointedly disenfranchising conservative Republicans throughout the 1920 campaign, Roosevelt was pursuing a theme that interested him naturally, for 1920 and the future: the parties needed redefinition in a modern context.

Roosevelt proved to be a dedicated candidate, an overachiever working the crowd and making speeches wherever he was asked. In Fresno, he shrugged off a hard rain in the wake of a thunderstorm, speaking without so much as a hat to a field full of umbrellas. In Montana, he impressed the locals by crossing the Continental Divide by car three times in one day, ricocheting from one waiting crowd to another. To keep a tight schedule, he even took an airplane flight in Missouri; daring stuff for 1920. No one could keep up with him—at times, not even the audience. "It is becoming almost impossible to stop F. now when he begins to speak," Eleanor wrote to Sara. "10 minutes is always 20, 30 is always 45 & the evening speeches are now about two hours!"[16]

Members of the entourage tried to rein him in. "The men all get out & wave at him in front," Eleanor continued, "and when nothing succeeds I yank his coat tails! Everyone is getting tired but on the whole the car is still pretty good-natured!"[17] That apparently depended on the day. At one point, Howe lost his temper with Camalier and challenged him to a fistfight onboard the train. Camalier, who weighed at least twice as much as Howe, shouted for Franklin to call Howe off.[18] Roosevelt came running. On the same trip, Camalier did come to blows with press secretary Marvin McIntyre. The pressure of the appearance schedule contributed to the friction, but so did the atmosphere of the train car, where hard work alternated with an atmosphere of drinking and card games. The train trip with the boys, a fraternity in spirit, sometimes the sophomore spirit, would remain one of the high points of Roosevelt's life for many years afterward.

Eleanor found it less rewarding, since she was typically sitting by herself in her room on the train, when she wasn't at one of Franklin's speeches, serving as the onstage part of the audience. She didn't think there was much choice, in either case, and so she accepted the campaign junket for what it was, a rich opportunity for her husband. In truth, she wasn't doing as good a job as she might have. Her natural personality was appealing, but she wasn't comfortable showing it. A reporter from Iowa described her as, "modest, retiring and unassuming to a degree—backing as quickly and as far from the limelight as possible on all occasions."[19] According to her memoirs, during promotional interviews she reverted to her late grandmother's policy: tell members of the press as little as possible and, while being polite, keep to oneself. That wasn't quite the idea behind a publicity interview, however.

Louis Howe was having his own problems, of which challenging Camalier to fisticuffs was only one symptom. He had come late to a campaign planned by others who were working with Roosevelt. That made it a construct of personality, and not of method or projections of the type that were Howe's specialty. Preparation and strategy were not priorities on Roosevelt's campaign train. Logistics was a prime concern, and past that, Roosevelt relied on extemporaneous speaking. Steve Early called it Roosevelt's "playboy" campaign style.[20] On another occasion, he was more wistful: "We were all," he wrote, "young together then."[21] Howe's strengths had no real place in it. He could sit in on the poker games and laugh with Roosevelt and the crew at the end of each day, but he was as out of place as Eleanor was. Circumstances were controlling themselves, and nothing made Howe more uncomfortable than that. He soon turned to Eleanor.

When Louis first approached her, she was perfectly correct according to her grandmother's teaching: well-mannered, but self-contained. If the train tour had lasted only a day or two, that might have been the end of it. Instead, Louis had time to reach her. And he had the inclination, on a noisy train-car and a playboy campaign. Being pulled away from the brink of a fistfight cannot have been the image he cherished for himself in his first national campaign. Looking for something better, he was the one who had to seek out Eleanor, time and again, in order to introduce himself rightly for the first time in their lives. As Eleanor explained in the first volume of her memoirs, those few weeks reflected the turning point in her adult life.

> In later years I learned that he had always liked me and thought I was worth educating, and for that reason he made an effort on this trip to get to know me. He did it cleverly. He knew that I was bewildered by some of the things expected of me as a candidate's wife. I never before spent my days going on and off platforms, listening apparently with rapt attention to much the same speech, looking pleased at seeing people no matter how tired I was or greeting complete strangers with effusion.
>
> Being a sensitive person Louis knew that I was interested in the new sights and the new scenery, but that being the only woman was embarrassing. The newspaper fraternity was not so familiar to me as it was to become in later years, and I was a little afraid of it. Largely because of Louis' early interpretation of the standards and ethics of the newspaper business, I came to look with interest and confidence on the writing fraternity. . . .
>
> Louis Howe began to break down my antagonism by knocking at my stateroom door and asking if he might discuss a speech with me. I was flattered and before long I found myself discussing a wide range of subjects.

"I did receive an intensive education on this trip," she added, "and Louis Howe played a great part in this education from that time on."[22] When the tour arrived in western New York, she and Louis even played hooky together, leaving the campaign tour behind to take a day off and see Niagara Falls.

Eleanor Roosevelt later pointed to Howe's initial intervention on the campaign as the end of her years of shyness and the start of her self-confidence in public affairs. As important, Howe coached her in managing a partnership with news reporters, as a group. For a person who knew nothing about publicity before the trip, she would eventually stand equal to two towering experts, her husband and her late uncle Theodore, in the use of the media in molding and maintaining a public persona. The first lesson drawn from the campaign trip was to make an ally of the press corps and help them to do their job. Howe had more than there was time to do in the 1920 campaign in helping her to master the complexities of following the hardest advice of all, and yet the easiest to give: to just be herself.

Watching Eleanor moving gamely through the campaign trip, Howe recognized something familiar, something about being overlooked and judged on a less than dazzling first impression. Both Louis and Eleanor knew the good and bad of life around Franklin, of being in the role of care-takers, while others, as Eleanor once put it, "worshiped at his shrine."[23] It wasn't easy to fight for identity around Roosevelt, and Howe was deter-mined to give Eleanor the chance he didn't have and didn't want, to stand next to Franklin and not behind him in the public eye. He liked her and—uncharacteristically—wanted her to like him.

The suggestion is often made that on the train tour, Howe was only preparing Eleanor for an expanded role in subsequent campaigns, that his obsession with Franklin's success was the real motivation for his interest in befriending Eleanor. That is to paint Louis as an appliance, though, built for political calculation. Howe had powers in that regard, but they were bal-anced and indeed engendered by an extraordinarily emotional nature. At the time of the 1920 campaign, Howe had his own troubles—and there was no guarantee that there would be any subsequent campaigns, for him, anyway.

Howe was fighting for his place in the midst of the most important campaign of Roosevelt's career to date. Each of the other men on the trip was doing more than he to steer what was left of the trip. Howe's long-range plans were as dull as advice on safe investments whispered in the ear of a person holding hot dice at a gambling table. At times, Howe was as lonely as Eleanor, and sought out her company. He would undoubtedly rather talk about speeches than anything else in the middle of a campaign fight. If Eleanor, a bright neophyte, was the only one to engage on the sub-ject, then he had someone to talk to and laugh with.

———————

In November, the national election turned out as everyone predicted: Harding and Coolidge won a resounding victory over Cox and Roosevelt. Letters of condolence trickled into Hyde Park from supporters loyal enough to broach what they feared would be a sore subject. Roosevelt would have none of it. "Many thanks for your nice letter," he wrote to one such correspondent. "I feel though that you are a great deal more cast-down over the result of November than I am."[24] He attributed the loss to the fact that voters were weary of Democrats after the Wilson administration. He professed to feel sorry for the victorious Republicans, who were so certain to blunder, he felt, and thus leave an opening for defeat in the near future.

Alfred Smith, running for reelection as governor, also went down to defeat in the Republican landslide. He, too, attributed the outcome to public weariness with the Wilson administration, but he wasn't nearly as cheerful as Roosevelt about the whole experience. Turning his back on politics, he took a job as chairman of the United States Trucking Corporation at $50,000 per year. Mrs. Moskowitz opened a public relations firm.

Roosevelt, who was among those who considered that Smith was out of politics for good, started eyeing a run for the governorship in 1922. Smith, at the same time, considered that Roosevelt was through in politics after his loss in the national election. They made for an uncomfortable tandem, Smith and Roosevelt, friends in a limited sense, perennially quick to underestimate each other. As of 1920, though, they were, indeed, both temporarily out of politics and willing to give business a try. Roosevelt was grateful for a chance to make a good living. He accepted a position as a managing vice president with the Fidelity & Deposit Company, an insurance and bonding company based in Baltimore. He also formed a law firm in partnership with Grenville Emmet and Langdon Marvin. In addition to his two jobs, Roosevelt speculated in stocks and invested in a wide variety of business schemes. Planning ultimately to return to politics, he seemed to be in a hurry to expand his fortune for the sake of his family. By the end of the year, the Roosevelts were back at the house on East Sixty-Fifth Street with most of the children. James, the eldest boy, was away at Groton School, his father's well-loved alma mater.

"It is in many ways delightful to be back in New York again," Franklin wrote to a friend in January 1921, "and to be out of government employ. I am trying to carry on two jobs—practicing law in the afternoon and running the

New York office of the Fidelity & Deposit Company of Maryland in the morning. I know absolutely nothing about insurance as yet, but hope to learn."[25] The law practice was a partnership with two old friends, while the insurance job was a salaried position, courtesy of a new friend, the enormously wealthy Van Lear Black. The chairman of F & D, Black was a resident of Baltimore, where he owned, among other concerns, the storied *Sun* newspaper. At forty-six, Black was an adventurer by nature. In fact, he was a trailblazer in an underestimated form of derring-do: riding on record-breaking airplane flights. He couldn't pilot a plane, but as the Bleriot of airline passengers, he helped, in his way, to test the limits of aerial transportation. More important to Roosevelt, Black skipped around the eastern seaboard as though his private yacht were a water taxi, one that sometimes made a special trip up the Hudson to visit Hyde Park.

Black, who personally arranged for Roosevelt to serve as the executive in charge of the New York office of F & D, was far too smart a businessman to lose money on his investment in Roosevelt's salary. The Fidelity & Deposit Company specialized in underwriting surety and fidelity bonds, which guarantee the delivery of contracted services or manufactured goods. What Black understood was that many of the most lucrative bonds that F & D sold were related to large government projects. Roosevelt's name and the ability to reach ranking officials in the government—and corporations that did business with the government—could be crucial in bringing in new business. If Roosevelt made the difference in landing even one $1 million bond, he would earn his keep. In the meantime, he could oversee the office and, if he were so inclined—at some point along the way—he could even learn the insurance business.

———— ·◆· ————

Howe had the satisfaction of being asked to return to the Navy Department after the 1920 election at the request of Secretary Daniels. Howe was back without any particular title, but proved to be invaluable in helping the incoming assistant secretary, Theodore Roosevelt Jr., make a smooth transition in the job. At the time, Howe was holding a lucrative job offer from the New England Oil Company. The company's president wrote to Howe, saying that his outfit, "in its dealings with the Navy has been much impressed with the organization of the Bureau of Supplies and Accounts, particularly as regards the Purchase and Supply Divisions. It is our understanding that you have been responsible for much of this efficiency and we are prepared to make you a liberal offer to come over to our organization."[26] Franklin Roosevelt told Secretary Daniels that the offer was for $20,000 per year.

In July of 1921, Howe resigned from the Navy Department and went to Massachusetts to stay with Grace and Hartley. Mary was on a tour of Europe. Louis still had the offer from the oil company. And he was still trying to decide what to do.

For at least a year Howe had been trying to establish himself in a career apart from Franklin Roosevelt. But he was, all the while, the same man who had been fired at least four or five times before Thomas Osborne finally managed to part ways with him. Roosevelt wasn't anxious to rid himself of Howe's help, yet he couldn't promise much in the way of a paying job, other than a lowly post at F & D. For Howe, New England Oil was at the other end of the spectrum on both pay and prestige—but it lacked the excitement of a daily attachment to Franklin Roosevelt and the final, seemingly short hop in his journey to a presidential nomination. Howe had already invested ten years in that journey. Yet there were other considerations.

Howe's son, Hartley, who was about nine at the time, wrote an "Autobiography," of which a fragment survives:

> The story of my life might be told in these few words: Here today and gone tomorrow. I have spent a large part of my life moving out of one house and into another. However, to proceed.
>
> I was born at Saratoga Springs, N.Y., where my father was a member of the "fourth estate," a reporter.
>
> We moved to Washington, where I have spent the greater part of my life. Here I attended a private school which closed at one o'clock so that I had the afternoon free. Most of the time I spent in Dupont Circle near our apartment or else Dad took us . . . [27] [here it ended]

Hartley was probably entitled to command his father's attention, if the New England Oil Company would make that possible. Mary, who was twenty-one in 1921, was a student at Vassar College, majoring in astronomy. Like Hartley, she enjoyed her father's company, but both had been raised largely by Grace.

In thinking about the future, Louis weighed his financial situation, as well as the chance to mend or salvage relationships. He had not been able to save anything in 1910, when he only earned a couple of hundred dollars, and he hadn't done any better in 1920, when he'd earned a couple of thousand. Aside from the cottage at Horseneck Beach, the Howes did not own any major assets. They were even in debt, indicating that while eight years in Washington had certainly been a sojourn from the embarrassment of their poverty in Albany, it was not a guarantee against its return.

Howe's inclination was to find a solid, high-ranking position by which he could justify the previous twenty years of a "here-today-and-gone-to-morrow" attitude where his family's way of life was concerned. His marriage had been troubled for years, leaving him lonely and prone to dark thoughts. If, however, he could parlay some of his hard work as assistant to the assistant secretary into an executive position, he could start a new chapter on conventional terms—on Grace's terms. That was the original idea, but going home to Grace wasn't as simple as it had seemed in the planning.

As the Howes were summering in Massachusetts, preparing to leave for a few weeks with the Roosevelts at Campobello, Louis was optimistic. Since he was with his family for good, at long last, he cherished an idea that something might have changed for the better in his relationship with Grace. "A silly idea," he wrote, "that perhaps in a sensual way I might stir up a spark of the old flame for a moment led me to force myself on you until you told me before we went to Campo—that you hated my touch."

"So I gave up," he added.[28]

On July 13, Howe received word from contacts in Washington that the Senate Committee on Naval Affairs was on the verge of releasing a report in response to its investigation into the problems at the Newport Navy Yard. The report, according to Howe's sources, was going to be damning for Daniels and especially for Roosevelt. Howe wired Roosevelt at Campobello to give him advance warning.

Franklin Roosevelt was incensed that the Senate Committee was on the verge of releasing its report, despite the fact that he had not yet been asked to testify. At first, in high dudgeon, he decided to do absolutely nothing. Then, as he saw his political career in danger of disintegrating, he took what action he could, forcefully requesting a chance to testify before the committee in advance of the release of the report. Some arrangement was apparently made, by which he would have his chance to speak, and then he left Campobello for the long trip to Washington, stopping along the way to meet Louis and discuss the best strategy for controlling the damage. With that, the two parted company. Howe and his family went to Campobello, and Franklin went to Washington.

On Monday, July 19, Roosevelt presented himself on Capitol Hill. He was told that the committee did not need to hear from him because it had full transcripts of his testimony on the matter before another investigating board. Roosevelt demanded to be heard. The committee placated him by scheduling his testimony for 8 PM, without telling him that the report was to be released to the press at 4 PM. It was a cruel trick. Late in the afternoon, Roosevelt was trying to fight back, hastily preparing a typed rebuttal for distribution to the press.

"Lay Navy Scandal to F. D. Roosevelt," ran the headline in the *New York Times*.[29] Other papers named Daniels prominently, as well, but nearly all of them, throughout the country, quoted the committee's conclusion that Franklin D. Roosevelt was "morally responsible" for the travesty of using enlisted men, under orders, to attract and then consort with men in the course of the Navy investigation.[30] Roosevelt protested in his press release that "the insinuations that I must have known, that I supervised the operations, that I was morally responsible, are nowhere supported by the evidence, either directly or indirectly."[31]

Roosevelt was devastated by the broadside against his character. The emotional turmoil of seeing his career seemingly laid to waste took a toll.

He retreated to New York City, ostensibly to work, but also to await the fallout. Roosevelt was fortunate that the report was released in the dog days of summer, when interest in politics is at a low ebb, and also that the subject of the report was a remnant of the war effort, which many people found a wearisome topic. In 1921, the inclination on the part of the general public was to try to forget about the war and all of its ghastly aspects. Judging by the nation's major newspapers, which carried no further news on the report, the matter slid away. Nonetheless, Roosevelt's secretary, Marguerite Le-Hand, noted that as Franklin left the New York office to resume his vacation, "he looked quite tired."[32]

By August 5, when Roosevelt hitched a ride on Van Lear Black's yacht for a cruise up to Campobello, he was by all descriptions an exaggerated version even of his compulsively charming self. For the sake of his boss' boating party, he kept every conversation lively and even helped to steer the boat in the choppy waters of the Bay of Fundy. When he arrived at Campobello, he was still in high gear. Up to that point, Louis had been getting all of the attention at the Roosevelt camp, having suffered a fall on the tennis court and dramatizing it into a star turn as a wounded warrior. Once Franklin Roosevelt arrived, though, he took charge as entertainment director and, after a day or two, Louis left temporarily to look after his own business at home. Grace and Hartley continued their holiday on the island. Among other things, Howe had apparently made up his mind to send a letter to New England Oil, accepting the executive position that had been offered to him there. The job would start in autumn, when he would enjoy the comfort of family, such as it existed for him.

On the island, Franklin out-swam the children on August 10, a Wednesday, and then energetically put out a small forest fire before running two miles home with a plunge or two along the way. Arriving at the house dripping wet, he stayed wet and then damp for hours before changing into dry clothes. He went to bed with a chill and arose with a fever the next day.

He shaved and came out of the bathroom with a limp, his left leg growing numb. Lying down for a rest, his muscles became weaker.

Eleanor called a local doctor, E. H. Bennett, who believed Roosevelt was suffering from a very bad cold. It was at that point that Grace sent a telegram to Louis from Campobello, telling him that Franklin was seriously ill. As she had joked with Eleanor, years before in Washington, her husband would swim the ocean to be near Roosevelt in times of illness. And so he would have.

At the end of the week of August 8, 1921, with a blanket of steamy hot air hanging over the Northeast, Louis Howe was sweating out a train ride of twelve hours, heading north through New England toward Campobello Island. All that he knew from Grace's telegram was that Franklin Roosevelt was bedridden and that his illness was not only serious, but baffling to the local doctor.

Louis McHenry Howe (1871–1936) as a boy in Saratoga, New York. Courtesy of the Franklin D. Roosevelt Library.

Howe, sitting in the front row at center, was an active teen in Saratoga. He liked bicycling, hiking, and tennis, a game he would continue to play through most of his life. Courtesy of the Franklin D. Roosevelt Library.

(above) *The Roosevelts at Campobello, about 1913. Franklin and Eleanor watch as three of their children (left to right), James, Elliott, and Anna, cavort with a friend, Norris Brunnell Jr. Courtesy of the Franklin D. Roosevelt Library.*

The Howes at a gathering, circa 1918 and probably in Washington. Standing, left to right: Grace Howe, Huibertje Pruyn Hamlin, Louis Howe. Seated: unidentified man, Franklin D. Roosevelt. Courtesy of the Franklin D. Roosevelt Library.

A homemade magazine, produced by Howe with his eight year-old son, Hartley, and dated May 2, 1920. Howe, who listed himself as the assistant editor, painted the cover in watercolor and bound the magazine with a ribbon. Courtesy of the Franklin D. Roosevelt Library.

At a stop during the 1920 campaign. Left to right: Louis Howe, Tom Lynch, Franklin and Eleanor Roosevelt. To Eleanor's surprise, she and Howe formed a deep friendship during the course of the campaign. Courtesy of the Franklin D. Roosevelt Library.

COPYRIGHT 1906
BY ALVA E. STERN.

HEARST IN WAR.

HEARST IN PEACE

HEARST IN THE HEARTS
OF HIS COUNTRYMEN.

William Randolph Hearst (1863–1951) was an intimidating presence in national and New York politics in 1906, when this postcard was circulated. He was an unpredictable force for years afterward. Roosevelt was opposed to him in any capacity, especially that of leader of the evolving Democratic party, but ultimately benefitted from his support. Courtesy of the Library of Congress.

Governor Alfred E. Smith (1873–1944) of New York in 1923. Smith's political ambitions gave impetus to the Roosevelts' return to public life in the early 1920s. Courtesy of the Library of Congress.

*Belle Moskowitz (1877–1933),
standing at right, in about 1914.
Moskowitz, a former entertainer
and social worker, became a
political advisor of lasting
influence over the Democratic
Party. She was as loyal to Al
Smith as Howe was to the
Roosevelts. Image reproduced
courtesy of the Lear Center for
Special Collections and Archives,
Connecticut College.*

*"Springwood," the Roosevelt home
at Hyde Park, New York.
Courtesy of the Franklin D.
Roosevelt Library.*

Franklin and Eleanor Roosevelt on the south porch of the house in Hyde Park. This picture, taken in 1922, was part of the first set released to the public following Franklin's paralysis the year before. Courtesy of the Franklin D. Roosevelt Library.

TWO PLACES ON TICKET WANTED BY NEW VOTERS

Mrs. F. D. Roosevelt Suggested for Comptroller.

MISS MILLS SECRETARY

Women Say Smith Is "First, Last and Only Candidate.

Fighting to place two women on the state ticket in the face of determined opposition and for official recognition on the state committee, Democratic

At the 1922 New York State Democratic Convention, Eleanor was the Roosevelt touted as a candidate for elected office. From the Syracuse Post-Standard, *September 29, 1922.*

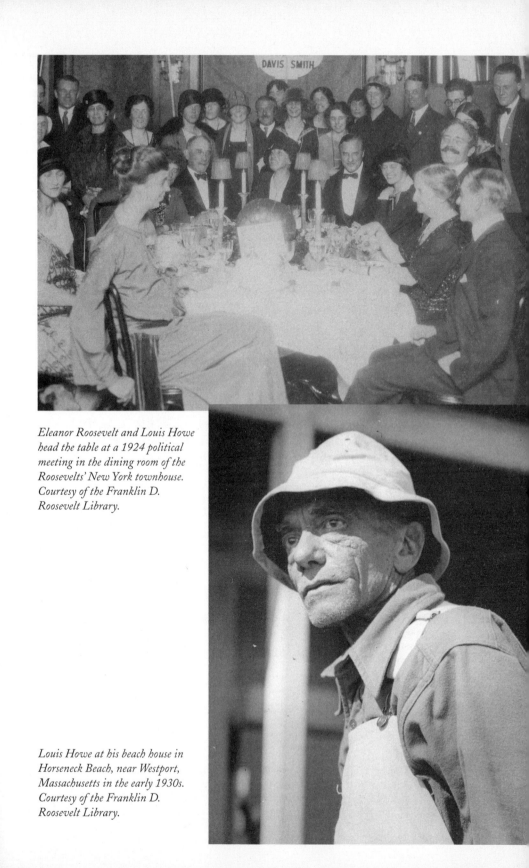

Eleanor Roosevelt and Louis Howe
head the table at a 1924 political
meeting in the dining room of the
Roosevelts' New York townhouse.
Courtesy of the Franklin D.
Roosevelt Library.

Louis Howe at his beach house in
Horseneck Beach, near Westport,
Massachusetts in the early 1930s.
Courtesy of the Franklin D.
Roosevelt Library.

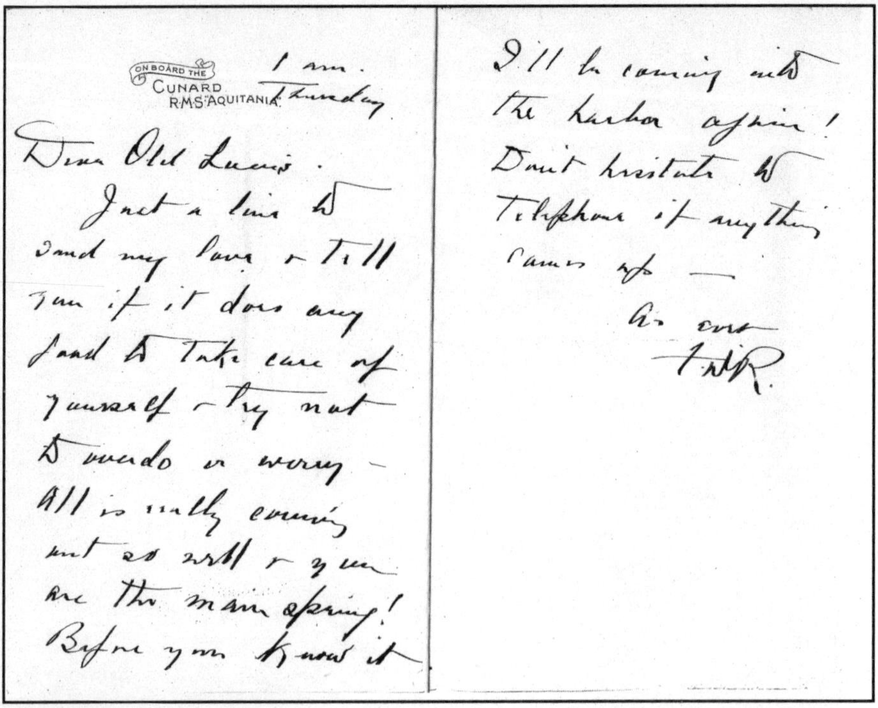

ON BOARD THE
CUNARD
R.M.S. AQUITANIA

1 am.
Thursday

Dear Old Louis:

Just a line to send my love & tell you if it does any good to take care of yourself & try not to overdo or worry — All is really coming out so well & you are the main spring! Before you know it I'll be coming into the harbor again! Don't hesitate to telephone if anything comes up —

As ever
FDR.

Franklin Roosevelt, preparing to sail to Europe in 1931, wrote a note to Howe, affirming their friendship in unguarded terms. Courtesy of the Franklin D. Roosevelt Library.

Howe, looking dapper, was disarmed by a momentous day: Roosevelt's Inauguration as President, March 4, 1933. Courtesy of the Franklin D. Roosevelt Library.

CHAPTER EIGHT

A COUPLE OF THREE

On Friday, the twelfth of August in 1921, Louis Howe was ferried to the Roosevelts' dock at Campobello. The children in the house remember the sight of him rushing through the living room with a grim expression, not stopping to say hello to anyone, as he bolted up the staircase. He found Franklin in bed, unable by then to move his lower legs. "That," Howe said to an interviewer years later, "changed everything."[1] It was a week that did change everything. Franklin Roosevelt would never walk unassisted again. Louis Howe would never again live with his family, except as a visitor.

The following day, Saturday, Eleanor wrote to Franklin's half brother, James, known in the family as "Rosy."

> We have had a very anxious few days as on Wed. evening Franklin was taken ill. It seemed a chill but Thursday he had so much pain in his back and legs that I sent for the doctor, by Friday evening he lost the ability to walk or move his legs but though they felt numb he can still feel in them. Yesterday AM Dr. Bennett decided he wanted the best opinion we could get quickly so Louis Howe (who, thank heavens, is here, for he has been the greatest help) went with Dr. Bennett to Lubec [Maine] & they canvassed the nearby resorts and decided that the best available diagnostician

was the famous old Dr. W. H. Keen of Philadelphia who agreed to motor up and spend the night. He arrived about 7:30 & made a most careful, thorough examination and the same this evening & he thinks a clot of blood from a sudden congestion has settled in the lower spinal cord temporarily removing the power to move though not to feel. . . . Louis and I are rubbing him as well as we can. The doctor feels sure he will get well but it may take some months. . . . I am writing the family that he is ill from the effects of a chill. . . .[2]

Rosy wrote back a few days later offering to help in any way that he could, including by making a trip to New York, where Sara was scheduled to arrive from Europe on August 24.[3] Whoever met her at the dock would have to break the news about Franklin's mysterious illness.

On August 15, both Eleanor and Louis wrote letters to Frederic Delano, Franklin's uncle and a businessman with connections up and down the East Coast. By then, Franklin was worse than ever, paralyzed from the chest down, with his arms and hands growing weak, and his face showing signs of paralysis. The imperative was no longer simply to know what was gripping Roosevelt, but when it would stop progressing. The real concern over the first weekend was that the paralysis would not stop until the muscles controlling his vital functions were as still as his legs.

Frederic Delano lived in New York, but happened to be in Washington when the letters reached him. He later said that Howe's description, "gave me the data I required to present the matter to the Doctors . . . that letter was most helpful in getting a grasp of the situation."[4] Delano consulted with a physician who suggested that the mysterious illness might be infantile paralysis, or poliomyelitis (polio), common enough in children in those days, but known to occur in adults, as well. Eleanor had already suspected that Franklin might be suffering from infantile paralysis, a virus that often started with a chill and the symptoms of a bad cold. Delano immediately took a train to Boston "in order to be near the scene of action and perhaps consult a doctor who could go to Campobello."[5]

In Boston, Delano spoke with Samuel A. Levine of Peter Bent Brigham Hospital, a thirty-year-old internist and an authority on infantile paralysis.[6] After reading the reports from Campobello, Dr. Levine named it as the cause of Franklin's condition. Delano relayed Levine's message and emphasized his strong recommendation that Louis and Eleanor stop massaging Franklin's legs, as pressure on the nerves would cause more harm than good. Ever afterward, Franklin had to reconcile himself to the lingering theory that their well-meaning rubbing had exacerbated his paralysis.

R oosevelt's fever continued during the week, but the progress of the paralysis stopped, just as he was about to lose the use of his hands entirely. As it was, he couldn't write or hold a fork. Eleanor and Louis tended him around the clock, Eleanor sleeping on a couch in his bedroom and Louis using a cot. The children were kept away. Some of them had already exhibited slight symptoms, such as a runny nose and a stiff neck, which could have been related to Franklin's illness. The hope was that by keeping them isolated, the chances for a household epidemic were reduced.

Grace Howe remembered that each of the adults took turns reading to Franklin. Eleanor was especially fond of reading aloud. In fact, before Franklin arrived for his visit, she had written him a letter admitting that when she read aloud after dinner, Grace would be snoring, Louis sleeping soundly, and another guest, Mrs. Shepherdson, holding her eyelids open with her fingertips. Franklin, however, was a more grateful audience. "One day," Grace recalled in a newspaper interview, "I happened to read a small item about an infantile paralysis epidemic in Upper New York State. He said, 'Grace, read that story about the epidemic again.' I did—and I've often thought that that was the first time he realized himself what he had."[7]

On Wednesday, August 17, Franklin's fever began to recede, the first sign that the illness, still unidentified, might be in abeyance. As usual, letters awaited his attention and Eleanor turned to the chore of answering them. Howe advised her to be careful. "If the public heard the words, 'infantile paralysis,'" he told her, "it might think that Franklin's mind had been affected. . . . The wrong thing at this time might wreck his political career."[8]

Eleanor was taken aback. With the illness as yet uncontrolled, and her husband lying in misery on a rugged island, she had not been thinking about possible long-range ramifications. Howe, on the other hand, couldn't help it.

Marguerite "Missy" LeHand, Roosevelt's secretary at his law firm in New York, was among those who had written. Unaware of the trouble at the camp, she had sent a letter asking quite boldly for a raise. One week after the onset of the illness, Eleanor read the letter aloud to Franklin. Still unable to move from the waist down, with his legs hypersensitive to the lightest touch, he summarized his response to her request for a raise. When Eleanor wrote to Missy LeHand that day, she gave a glimpse into Franklin's own state of mind. With all that was happening to him, he was back to business and the secretary's concerns were his.

"He asked me to write to you," Eleanor responded in the letter to Missy, "that his impression is that you are now getting $30 a week and he fears neither the F&D nor Emmet, Marvin and Roosevelt would be willing to jump to $40 but he feels sure he can get you $35 now and hopes that will be satisfactory for the present."[9] LeHand would later be one of Roosevelt's closest companions, but at the time, she was fairly new to his employ. It was not the identity of the correspondent that made him insist upon delivering a personal reply, when nearly anyone else would have ignored all such mundane matters to concentrate on a crisis of life and death. Reading mail and answering letters was essential to Roosevelt—a matter of life, indeed—and it was that to which he reverted comfortably, when nothing else about him was comfortable. He wasn't capable of dictating his own replies, but he could respond to the main points of a letter and let Louis or Eleanor compose a reply. Taking a cue from Louis, Eleanor wasn't specific in describing Franklin's illness to Missy, noting only that he "had a severe chill . . . which has resulted in fever & much congestion."[10]

Roosevelt needed help with much more than just reading and correspondence. The muscles controlling elimination were not functioning, and he needed enemas and bladder catheterizations in order to remain alive. In the absence of any other nursing care, Dr. Keen had instructed Eleanor in the methods required. He advised her to engage a nurse as soon as possible, but she had a harder time finding a nurse willing to relocate to Campobello

Island than physicians willing to call there. For two weeks, Eleanor and Louis filled the gap, their lives revolving around the drama of managing and augmenting Roosevelt's abilities.

For nine years, Howe had been Roosevelt's political advisor and assistant, and for longer than that, he had been a friend—but to a man who had hundreds of friends. On that basis, Howe could have left with Grace and Hartley on the pretext of getting out of the family's way at a trying time, or he might have remained to lend moral support, staying downstairs and answering letters. Instead, Louis was in the sickroom with Eleanor, changing sheets and bedpans, and sleeping on a cot just outside the room as she slept on a sofa inside. They were not merely nursing Franklin, but guarding him. He had never known paralysis and they couldn't spare him from that affliction, but he had never known despair, either, and they could do something about that.

In reply to Franklin's note, Missy LeHand sent two letters, one chipper and a bit gossipy addressed to Franklin, and one friendly but more sober for Eleanor in which she said that, while she was trying not to tell anyone about Roosevelt's illness, "it apparently is known."[11]

Frederic Delano secured the services of Dr. Robert Lovett of Boston, who was in fact the chair of the Harvard Medical School Infantile Paralysis Commission. Lovett agreed to take almost a week out of his own practice and make the journey to Campobello. He wanted a colleague, a Dr. Jameson of Bar Harbor, Maine, to assist him. Huybertie Pruyn Hamlin, a native of Albany, who had grown up knowing the Roosevelts and had known Franklin since childhood, happened to be visiting Bar Harbor, about seventy miles down the coast from Campobello. She and her husband had a daughter who had taken ill with a different malady in Bar Harbor that week, and Dr. Jameson was tending her. "After the danger was over," Mrs. Hamlin later recalled, "the assistant, Dr. Jameson, called me into the hall and asked me if I would object to his leaving the hospital for several days as Dr. Lovett of Boston had telephoned him to ask him to meet him at Bangor and go down to Campobello where one of the Roosevelt family was ill. . . . The fact of having Dr. Lovett summoned to the Roosevelts could mean only one thing and that was infantile paralysis. He said it was just that but he did not know who had it. When he returned he told us the tragic news that it was Franklin himself who had it."[12]

Dr. Lovett arrived on the island August 25. Roosevelt was still unable to move from the waist down, and his face was sagging on one side. His nerves were so raw on his lower legs that even the weight of the bed sheets made them hurt. Lovett conducted his examination and gave a diagnosis of infantile paralysis. He said that Roosevelt would probably recover in a half year, though the prognosis was not definite, by any means.

The day after Lovett left, Roosevelt regained the use of the muscles controlling elimination. A nurse arrived later that day. With Roosevelt slowly gaining strength, the priority shifted to moving him off the island and back to New York. Howe left to arrange the transportation and hospitalization.[13]

Sara Roosevelt arrived in New York on a liner from Europe at the end of August. She was met at the dock by Frederic Delano, who informed her that her son had become ill and was paralyzed. On September 1, Sara was on Campobello Island. "I got here yesterday at 1:30," she wrote to Fred,

> and at once . . . came up to a brave, smiling, & beautiful son, who said, "Well, I'm glad you are back Mummy & I got up this party for you!" He had shaved himself and seems very bright and very keen. Below his waist he cannot move at all. His legs (that I have always been proud of) have to be moved often as they ache when long in one position. He & Eleanor decided at once to be cheerful & the atmosphere of the house is all happiness, so I have fallen in and follow their glorious example.
>
> Thus far, dear Eleanor is not tired, but there is much writing to do & Mr. Howe will attend to much of it, as he returns on Saturday (tomorrow). . . . Dr. Bennett just came & said "This boy is going to get all right." They went in to his room & I hear them all laughing, Eleanor in the lead![14]

Even while Louis was away, he still contributed to the determined merriment. Eleanor had asked him to buy a watch at Tiffany & Company in New York as a memento for the local boatman who had been a great help in the family's crisis. Faced with a wide array of watches at the jewelry store, Howe wrote to Franklin, and tacitly to Eleanor, complaining about the difficulty of selecting the right watch out of so many. He described some possibilities in the letter and finished by insisting that "Lord knows I have acted as your alter ego on many weird commissions, but I must positively and firmly refuse to risk my judgment on neckties, watches or pyjamas."[15] While Howe was away, he also sent a message to the New England Oil Company, turning down the job he'd been offered. "The doctors," he later recalled of Roosevelt, "said if he were ever fully to recover he must continue active. Accordingly, I put my other plans aside and went to live in his house and do what I could to help him keep on with his career."[16]

In early September, Howe was back on Campobello with a detailed plan for moving Franklin to New York safely and somewhat comfortably—and without anyone from the press seeing him. It involved secrecy, subterfuge, and perfect timing. While Howe was in New York, he may also have arranged for Roosevelt to receive an invitation to join the Executive Committee of the New York State Democratic Committee. In any case, the invitation was delivered to Campobello and Howe encouraged Roosevelt to accept. The reply they sent to the committee explained, however, that Roosevelt would be convalescent for some time.

A few days later, Grace and Hartley left Campobello for Fall River. Louis couldn't think of leaving the Roosevelts. Grace did not record her feelings regarding her husband's decision to stay with Franklin and Eleanor. Instead of starting a new phase, with a full-time husband and money to spare in Boston, she was returning to the nomadic life, and so was Hartley. According to the new plan, Grace was to rent an apartment in Poughkeepsie, where she and Hartley would live, while Mary was in college nearby. Louis would come up from New York on weekends, when he could. After twenty-one years of marriage, Grace may not have been surprised. She may not have been disappointed, either, except that Hartley had to stand by and watch his father choose another family and someone who needed him more.

If Howe was going with the Roosevelts to help Franklin with his career, it shouldn't have been necessary for him to live under the same roof. He might have found an apartment of his own. No one recorded who it was that made the offer of a place in the household—and in the family. It might have been Franklin. Eleanor reported to Missy at the end of August that he was able to offer opinions on any matters she brought to his attention; he was feeling better "and quite able to attend to things."[17] If Franklin made the offer to Howe, he may have had finances in mind, in addition to the comfort of having Howe's company at all hours.

If it were Eleanor who made the offer, or request, for Howe to join the family, it was reflected in the section title she chose for the part of her 1938 memoir, *This Is My Story,* covering the transition after the distressing summer at Campobello: "Louis Howe Takes Charge." She had learned over the previous year, starting on the campaign train, to trust him. While both were deeply involved in Franklin's recovery after his paralysis, Howe was already, as of late August, taking responsibility for the details of his everyday life. He was also quietly insistent that the presidential dream must not be allowed to wither.

The idea of joining the Roosevelts may originally have been Howe's. Frances Perkins had known Howe since the Albany days when he was a reporter and, starting in the early 1920s, she would see him frequently. She had her own theory about him: "I always thought that Louis wanted above everything to be loved," she said. [18] As Perkins pointed out in the oral history she recorded for Columbia University in the mid-1960s, Howe came from a loving, supportive, sometimes unorthodox family that doted on him. For some reason, he hadn't found the same warm embrace in his family with Grace. Perhaps he hadn't allowed it. To judge by letters, he loved each member of his family with a varying mixture of delight and disappointment; perhaps no one could return his love, alternating between desperate need and oblivious detachment. The record of more than two decades of disjointed home life reflects the fact that in his own place in the world, Howe was not happy or was not made happy.

"The Roosevelt family," Perkins said, "including Mrs. Sara Roosevelt and Mrs. Eleanor Roosevelt, were all nice and kind to him, and sweet to him. He just basked in the sunshine of their smiles and friendship. It was interesting to see him just loosen up."[19]

The idea of a grown man with a family of his own impressing himself in the marriage of two other people was unusual and practically unprecedented. Part of the reason that it worked is that Franklin and Eleanor needed Louis equally. The question may be debated as to which Roosevelt he most had in mind to help, to save, to reclaim. Of course, history and many acquaintances acknowledged that he was "the Man Behind Franklin Roosevelt" at the time of the presidency. But Howe was also the Man Behind Eleanor Roosevelt. Both reached out to him in 1921, and that was the place that made him happiest: within arms' length of the Roosevelts.

In September 1921, Louis Howe took on the responsibility he craved: "to help" Roosevelt, as he had put it, "keep on with his career."[20] That job started with purely practical arrangements as Roosevelt was belted onto a stretcher and passed through the windows of train cars like cargo in order to get to New York on September 15. A few friends were at the freight station in New York to see Roosevelt arrive, and as he was carried from the train to a waiting car, he cheerfully called out to each and handed out open dates for lunch. One turned away in tears.

While Howe would never have wished for Roosevelt to be debilitated in any way, he may have found satisfaction in the very stark prospects that faced him. If a person is inclined toward being a savior, it is better to start with deconstruction, whether that which is to be saved is a town, a company, or a person's future. At times in the past, Roosevelt needed someone to occasionally say "no" to him, as when he jumped into the 1914 Senate primary, but no one had the proximity to his every decision then. In Roosevelt's new political universe, Louis Howe was planted at the hub. Doctors had warned that a lack of mental activity could result in a reduction of Roosevelt's faculties, a concern during the recovery stage from any traumatic illness. They needn't have worried. Franklin's mind wasn't likely to atrophy when he arrived in New York. He had a wide circle of friends there who could be counted upon for visits, once his strength permitted. He had his business interests, and Missy LeHand could be counted on to visit him on a regular basis to work through his correspondence. Sara and the children would be around to talk and laugh with him. And Eleanor would be there. She had proven to be a superb nurse—even Dr. Lovett had commented on it. Surrounded by a large family and loyal friends in business and politics, Roosevelt would not be alone or neglected. Nonetheless, Louis was aware that Roosevelt would also need fresh faces—the sort of new acquaintances he would be meeting if he were in circulation in the city.

As soon as Franklin Roosevelt was admitted to the New York Presbyterian Hospital, then located on Madison Avenue at Seventeenth Street in Manhattan, Howe released a statement announcing his condition and the diagnosis. Carried in newspapers around the country, the piece intimated that special treatments at the hospital were certain to restore the use of Roosevelt's legs. The news brought a stream of letters from well-wishers around the country. Marvin McIntyre, the veteran of the 1920 presidential campaign, had returned to Washington to run his own press agency. He supplied the former candidate with news on the rising careers, and the expanding waistlines, of various members of Roosevelt's campaign team. "Wish the old crowd could get together again for a day or so," he added.[21] Josephus Daniels wrote to his former assistant and so did Woodrow Wilson. Many of the well-wishers expressed relief that, according to the newspaper report, he would regain the use of his legs in a short time.

In truth, Roosevelt's new physician, Dr. George Draper, held out little hope, writing in the case record after his initial examination, "The lower extremities present a most depressing picture."[22] Draper and the other doctors told Franklin that they couldn't predict with certainty whether he would walk again or not. All the while, they were careful not to discourage his optimism.

In October, the chairman of the Executive Committee of the State Democratic Party, Herbert Pell, sent Roosevelt a note, reminding him to be at a meeting in midtown Manhattan on the eleventh. He also invited Roosevelt for lunch beforehand. The same letter probably went out to all of the committee members, but Howe couldn't resist attaching a note to the letter, for Franklin's benefit, "Mr. Pell should wake up and hear the birdies."

In mid-October, Roosevelt's medical progress reached an important milestone in his return to business. Writing to a retired sailor who had sent a letter of good wishes in mid-September, he said, "A long time has elapsed since your nice letter reached me, but I refused to have it replied to until the doctors were willing to let me dictate something myself." He then went on with a long and detailed response.[23]

Other correspondence filled his days, especially after he could dictate his own letters in his own style. The New York *Daily News* wrote to him that month requesting his motto in less than thirty-five words. His first choice was, "I'd rather be right than vice-president," and his more serious entry was, "Never remember an injury or forget a favor."[24]

After about six weeks, Roosevelt had regained much of his old energy and overcome the weakness or paralysis in his face, arms, and upper back. On October 28 he was discharged from New York Presbyterian with no improvement in the strength of his legs. Dr. Draper prescribed braces and crutches, which were ordered, though a course of rehabilitation of the back muscles would still be needed before they could be used. The Roosevelts also bought a wheelchair. Franklin refused to believe that he would have to use it for long.

When Roosevelt was nominated for the vice presidency in 1920, he and his running mate, James Cox, had visited Woodrow Wilson at the White House. As they both knew, the president was suffering from the effects of a serious stroke. Cox and Roosevelt approached the portico where the meeting was to take place. "We saw the president in a wheel chair," Roosevelt said, according to a friend, who recorded his description, "his left shoulder covered with a shawl which concealed his left arm, which was paralyzed, and the Governor said to me, 'He is a very sick man.' The Governor went up to the President and warmly greeted him. Wilson looked up and in a very low, weak voice, said, 'Thank you for coming. I am very glad you came.' His utter weakness was startling and I noticed tears in the eyes of Cox."[25]

Roosevelt knew what the wheelchair represented to most people at that time. Stephen Early recalled that when he heard the news of his friend's paralysis, he was reminded of seeing Roosevelt at the 1920 Democratic National

Convention in San Francisco the year before, carrying a Wilson banner straight through pockets of anti-Wilson delegates: "A big, young, wide-shouldered, powerful figure, he shook off interferers without deigning them notice. And now he was stricken, doomed it must be to look out on the rush and hurry of the political life he loved above all things from a wheel chair. It brought a queer, tense feeling in the throat to think of it."[26] Roosevelt knew that feeling; it may well have been the same one he felt seeing Woodrow Wilson on the portico of the White House.

On October 28, Roosevelt was taken to his home on East Sixty-Fifth Street, determined, no matter what the doctors said, that he would walk again. It was apparently the only goal he had—that, and to refuse anyone a reason to pity him.

CHAPTER NINE

ELEANOR AND LOUIS

"**A**fter he was paralyzed, of course, life changed greatly," Anna, the eldest of the Roosevelt children later recalled of her father. "There had to be so many different people around him. Louis Howe was around practically all the time."[1]

When the Roosevelt family returned to New York with Franklin in mid-September 1921, Howe occupied a large room on the third floor of their house on East Sixty-Fifth Street. The room was next to the one that would be used by Franklin when he returned home from the hospital. James was away at Groton School and the other four children often visited Hyde Park with Sara. At fifteen and a nature-lover, Anna far preferred Hyde Park to Sixty-Fifth Street. In late September, she wrote a cheery letter to her mother from the Springwood estate, asking if she could stay longer, sending her love to her father and adding a postscript, "Remember me to Mr. 'owe."[2]

There were weeks in early autumn, with Franklin still in the hospital, when Louis Howe left each morning to attend to Roosevelt's business, generally at the F & D, and came home to Eleanor: a household of two, aside from the servants. To anyone watching from down the street, they would have looked like an ordinary couple, rather than two troubled individuals, each married to someone else, in the process of forging an extraordinary alliance. Eleanor looked back on the early days after the onset of her husband's illness and said that she "simply lived from day to day" and got through as best she could.[3] Howe was made of different stuff. He had to plan, but he soon realized he had a serious adversary in Sara Roosevelt, one of the thousands of people who presumed that Roosevelt was permanently out of politics.

Sara briefly discussed what she called her "quiet ideas for his future existence" in her book, *My Boy Franklin* (1933). Of course, she wanted Franklin to return to Hyde Park where, she wrote, "I hoped he would devote himself to his restoration to health and to the writing perhaps of the book he had always longed to get on paper."[4]

Roosevelt would need time to recover from the shock to his health, as Sara believed. Even aside from the paralysis of his legs, his body was exhausted. And there was no guarantee that he couldn't suffer a setback. All of that being the case, it was only natural that a caring mother would argue for her child to ease off and adopt the least taxing lifestyle possible. Even at thirty-nine, a son is still a child to his mother. Sara received criticism through the years for what was seen as her attempt to squelch Franklin's political ambition in the wake of his paralysis, yet it would have been more shocking (and less sympathetic) by far if she had taken any other position: playing the Hollywood stage mother, for example, and pushing her kid back into the limelight before he was ready.

The question is whether Sara intended that Franklin should retire to Springwood and never return to public life, or use the house for a completely unrushed recovery. She may not have thought that far ahead. For the time being, Sara advocated a long sojourn, without the strain of politics, at Hyde Park. Louis Howe was nonetheless adamant that Roosevelt had to make a return to public life, or better yet, signal somehow that he had never left it. Indeed, with Howe's intervention, Roosevelt was already back, through the letters going out under his name.

"I am convinced he would have dropped from public life completely," wrote James Roosevelt of his father, "had it not been for Louis Howe. Father was too busy with his fight for his life to think of his political future."[5]

Franklin Roosevelt had his own strong will, of course, and an outsized degree of ambition, but his illness and its aftermath would have been capable of robbing at least some of his determination to win high office: just enough to ensure that he might not try. Howe, as James said, does deserve a large share of the credit for preserving all of Roosevelt's ambitions and at least some of his opportunities, but then, the best proof that Roosevelt's intent never really wavered is that he didn't send Howe away—Howe with his long-range plans and stubborn belief in his "Beloved and Revered Future President." Roosevelt pulled him closer.

Howe surely cared about Franklin's physical recovery and well-being, yet he assumed that Franklin would be the best judge of his own progress in that regard. Howe gave more thought to his mental and emotional recovery, topics he discussed with Eleanor. Among his concerns was that Franklin was living under a delusion. Neither Eleanor nor Louis believed that he was truly going to have the use of his legs again.

Howe was thinking ahead to the moment when Franklin ultimately accepted that fact: then he would need politics in a profound way, in order to replace the ambition to walk again.[6] Howe maintained that Roosevelt needed the mental stimulation of political strategy, and he argued that if Roosevelt abandoned his political ambitions, the paralysis would eventually reach his ambition and his spirit. Howe made those arguments, and they each reflected an understanding of Roosevelt. Ultimately, though, Howe was a man of political calculation. The reason why he couldn't be a party to the surrender of Roosevelt's career was that it wasn't necessary. Howe saw a route forward. If he didn't—if, in his unsentimental analysis, he considered that Roosevelt could not attain high public office—he would not have encouraged that hope, first in Eleanor and then Franklin.

Much later, Howe confided in Roosevelt's son James that he had worked out a schedule for Franklin's political career. "I'll tell you, Jim," he said, "It would make a marvelous primer on politics, on how you can maneuver the right man to the top if you plan properly."[7]

As of 1921, though, Howe might easily have been wrong, and the course he pressed might have ruined Roosevelt's health for good. Howe's solution to balance the two priorities—Roosevelt's physical well-being and the resumption of his public life—was to lift one of them off of his shoulders. Howe assumed all of the taxing aspects of Roosevelt's career, from meeting with potential political supporters up and down the East Coast to writing reports and editorials to attending the meetings and conventions of the party as a surrogate. For Roosevelt, the years 1921 and 1922 offered the unreality of political life without any strain. Howe took that burden, and left Roosevelt with the toy of politics: the opportunity to offer opinions, advice, and cheerful letters to old friends and new.

Howe's point of view was that his plan couldn't hurt. Sara's was that it certainly could. Eleanor agreed with Howe, believing that the greatest danger was that her husband should lose interest in life, and life as he had known it was not a quiet state of retirement. The ultimate decision would be Roosevelt's, of course, but the household would have an influence, which was one reason why by the time Franklin moved home from New York Presbyterian Hospital on October 28, the atmosphere within the family was not quite the "all happiness" that had prevailed as though by edict at Campobello.

In fact, the house was overcrowded, with Eleanor sleeping on a cot in the room used by her youngest sons. Anna, among others, thought it was bizarre for Howe to have the second-best room in the house, after Franklin's, while the rest of them were squeezed in together. Eleanor believed that Howe had to have close proximity to Franklin in order to assist him at all hours, but she nonetheless offered the room used by Howe to Anna, on the condition that she would have to vacate it in the afternoon when the nurse needed a sitting area within earshot of Franklin. Anna rejected the offer, remaining in a small back room that at least offered complete privacy, and with that, Eleanor was satisfied that she had tried to appease her daughter. The tensions didn't diminish, though. Anna regularly lost her temper, believing that her mother was more devoted to Howe than to anyone else. "Anna accused him of stealing mother's attentions from her. He did," James wrote in his memoir. "And he didn't care. He felt mother was needed more in public than in her private life, that she had a higher destiny than merely being a mother."[8]

The children were taught to keep quiet in deference to their father's condition, as Anna explained in an interview many years later. "What happens to the nerve centers is very traumatic," she said, referring to her father's condition. "It's a very difficult thing to—not to be upset by a sudden horrible noise—not horrible noise, big noise."[9] Franklin, largely bedridden during his first months at home, tried to lessen the shock of his paralysis for the children by teaching them about it and enlisting them early in the battle to overcome it.

At the same time, Eleanor and Louis were active in bringing guests to visit Franklin. They encouraged his reading, which occupied much of his time, but they didn't want him to lose his rare, finely tuned social skills, or worse, to feel isolated. They even invited authors whose works had piqued his interest. As a result, as Anna had described it, there were often "many different people around him."[10] The notion of the house as a refuge mainly for the family eroded over a very short time, causing more arguments.

"My mother-in-law," Eleanor later wrote, recalling her efforts with Howe to bring in visitors, "thought we were tiring my husband and that he should be kept completely quiet, which made the discussions as to his care somewhat acrimonious on occasion."[11] Sara Roosevelt, quite a formidable personage herself, had never met a force quite like Louis Howe before. He had walked into a home—which she owned and in which she had always dominated—and recast it according to what he thought was best for her son and daughter-in-law.

Sara Roosevelt was intimidating, in part because she didn't stray far from her conservative, old-fashioned manners. She didn't try to accommodate herself to a more modern age, but stayed within the mores and habits that suited her strengths, tried and proven as they were. "I remember old Mrs. [Sara] Roosevelt in the townhouse," said Joan Morgenthau Hirschorn, the daughter of the Roosevelts' friends, Elinor and Henry Morgenthau Jr., "because I remember how scared I was when I had to go visit her, how I had to be so polite, and how my mother instructed me on how I should be and all."[12] That was Sara's style, not that she didn't have a bright sense of humor and an affectionate personality around her family. She did like to get her way, though.

As of 1921, Eleanor had been married to Franklin for sixteen years. She seemed to enjoy her mother-in-law during the first eight years, being generally grateful for her advice, but the subsequent eight years had been harder, as she outgrew her proscribed role and resented the need to fight for status within her own home. Howe was aware of Eleanor's situation, including her complicated relationship with Franklin, and recognized that she was long overdue to find a way to stand on equal ground with her mother-in-law.

Sara had a history of controlling Franklin, too, though he could stand up to her. Her method of coercion of him was through financial support. She not only earned more than six times as much as he, but owned all three of the houses that he counted as home. Her brother Frederic oversaw her investments, with help from professional advisers, but she was a responsible manager in her own right and, overall, a much better businessperson than her son.

Franklin Roosevelt earned a gross income of $38,502, according to his handwritten income tax filing for 1921. He received $16,129 in interest and dividends, largely from the trust fund he had inherited from his father (who died in 1900). He lost $172 on two stock transactions. His farm land in Hyde Park lost $93. The most surprising figure, though, was that he only took in $250 in his law practice, and spent almost ten times that in expenses at the firm, making for a loss of $2,469.[13] He hadn't been at the firm the whole year, but even so, it wasn't an auspicious record. Franklin's main source of income was his $25,000 salary at the Fidelity & Deposit Company. Van Lear Black continued the salary despite Roosevelt's absence for five months at the end of 1921.

While Roosevelt was supposed to be overseeing the New York F & D office, he didn't know nearly enough about insurance to guide the veteran staff members who worked there. For that reason, Howe (who was not known for his understanding of insurance, either) could easily substitute, and manage the office on a day-to-day basis, mainly by letting the experienced employees get on with their work.

Howe worked on potential business for the F & D and, even in that, tried to find something that would cheer and bolster Roosevelt's spirits. In December, when the firm sold construction bonds to the Newport News Shipbuilding Company, Howe wrote to the president, Homer Ferguson, with whom he and Roosevelt had worked on major projects during the war. "If by any chance," Howe wrote, "the fact that this was Mr. Roosevelt's company, influenced you in making this award, it would cheer Mr. Roosevelt tremendously if you could write him a little line to that effect."[14] Whether or not such a note would cheer Roosevelt, it would certainly interest Van Lear Black. Howe did learn the bonding business, but typically spent the greater part of the day assisting Roosevelt in his ventures in politics and investment.

Through Howe, Roosevelt maintained his most public post, as executive chairman of the Woodrow Wilson Foundation, which was in the formative stage. The concept was that the foundation would bestow annual awards in the encouragement of peace, and so fundraising was practically its sole occupation during the first years of its existence. Howe was given a place on the executive committee. He also pursued a long-standing invitation from Harper & Brothers publishers for Roosevelt to write a book on any topic he chose, though nothing came of it.[15]

Not all of Howe's time was taken up by business. One day, he stopped by the Ritz-Carlton Hotel to visit John B. Shearer, a friend from the New England Oil Company—which was having a banner year. Had Howe chosen to join the company the year before, he might have been able to live at the Ritz-Carlton, too. As it was, Shearer did live there; he recalled an afternoon with Howe in a letter to Roosevelt many years later:

> Louis McHenry Howe, Esquire, garbed in his raincoat and a hat that no tardy bird would own, drifted in to my not too modest flat at the Ritz-Carlton, N.Y. one late afternoon in quest of some Navy A. gasoline with cracked ice. He got it.
>
> Some one suggested the bones—produced after a hard search, we tossed them for an hour and Louis began to find himself behind the crimson sphere . . . the sweat poured from Louis' brow, wilted his famous collar, blackheads popped on the floor and his morale was lower than a snake's belly!
>
> And then we told him—loaded dice! Talk about a mad wet hen—he cut me dead for two weeks.[16]

In the meantime, Franklin Roosevelt continued his correspondence, with help from Louis Howe and Missy LeHand, and reveled in the wide variety of topics about which people wrote. A woman named Ellen E. McCormick of Binghamton, New York, picked up her pen to remind him that in a speech in her city, he had advocated action in matters of government. "When anything was wanted," she recalled him saying, "write letters and keep on writing letters and eventually you would obtain your end."[17] On that score, he was taking his own advice. When Caroline O'Day, the vice-chairman of the state Democratic Party, asked a favor, he leapt to respond. O'Day, then about fifty-two years old (she did not reveal her exact birthdate), had spent her twenties in Europe, making her way as an artist. At thirty, she married a successful oilman and settled in Westchester County in New York State. A friend described her "mental strength and firm adherence to her convictions."[18] She was involved with the New York State Democratic Committee and wrote to Roosevelt in January 1922 to ask for two suggestions on organizing an effort to put at least one woman in a leadership position in each election district, of which there were thousands. He wrote a long letter in reply; his suggestions were not entirely original (he recommended that they find the right leaders for each district and said that social gatherings staged by prominent Democrats presented a good recruitment opportunity), but every line evinced his interest in rebuilding "what might be called the prestige of the party."[19]

When asked, Roosevelt consistently assured people that his recovery was proceeding ahead of all expectations and would be complete quite soon. "I am afraid you will look in the papers in vain for any particular news," he wrote to an acquaintance in upstate New York. "I am proceeding to recover in such an orderly and respectable manner as to be absolutely un-interesting from a newspaperman's standpoint. You know the old saying—'Happy is the country which has no history'—I have always felt that it might be amplified by adding 'and a man who has no news value to the papers.'"[20]

His recovery was not orderly, however. His energy had yet to return completely as of the winter of 1921–22. Over that winter, he worked on learning to convey himself up and down the stairs. His legs, despite his continual assurances that real change was imminent, were not responding. He was right about one thing: he had no news value to the papers. He was a former vice-presidential candidate, which is, by and large, not a celebrated category. Roosevelt was forgotten as quickly as any of his predecessors. Aside from being listed in occasional reports on the fund-raising progress of the Wilson Foundation, with which he wasn't even actively involved, he didn't receive much attention in the newspapers.

As the household became a battleground that winter, even Franklin was losing his temper, which he didn't often do. Anna goaded him into it, pestering him at the dinner table with complaints over the living arrangements, until he would finally snap and tell her in a harsh tone to leave the room. Eleanor once described her response to the crisis of Franklin's polio by saying that she lived from day to day. That may have been true at first, during the stark transition forced upon the family in Campobello. In New York, however, it wasn't possible. Pressures built up and stayed with her. When her son James discovered her crying uncontrollably in one of the bedrooms one day during that winter, his first reaction was not to tell Franklin, or Sara, or even to go to her himself. He immediately ran to find Louis.

At the time, Howe was the only person to whom Eleanor could turn, but even he couldn't help her that day, as her emotions completely broke down. He could only stay near, until she calmed down by herself. On another occasion that winter, Anna found them alone in the bedroom her mother had been using—it wouldn't be accurate to say "her bedroom" because she only had a corner in John's room. Howe was sitting on the bed and Eleanor was sitting on the floor next to him as he stroked her hair. The image is evocative. That a quality of love had developed between them was certain. The scene that Anna reported, as intimate a moment as it was, didn't suggest an affair. What is quite certain from letters and family accounts is that neither of them was bolstered by that sort of comforting acceptance in their own marriages. What Anna saw reflects the frailty of even the strong ones, and the want inside of Eleanor Roosevelt and Louis Howe.

More confused than ever, Anna took out her wrath on Howe. Though the exact sequence of the events cannot be determined, it was during that same winter that Eleanor caught her daughter writing a letter to a cousin lambasting Howe. Eleanor ripped up the pages and tried to make Anna remorseful for what she'd written, but the episode only widened the breech between mother and daughter.

Anna was encouraged in her attitude toward Howe by Sara, who had her own reasons to feel threatened by him and his assumption of a central place in the household. Factions developed within the family and ensured more ill will over the winter and early spring of 1922. Sara and the children had every reason to react, though. As admirable as Howe's support for the Roosevelts was, in view of the rubble in which he found them, he was not rebuilding what had been there before. He was building something new. The pattern of the family's very home life was changing, and not just because of Franklin's paralysis. Howe was the architect of the changes. But neither Franklin nor Eleanor, each for their own reasons, could revert to life as it was before. Howe had plans to lift each of them up and move them forward; and the rest of the family would have to follow.

In the early spring, Howe convinced Eleanor to enter into political work. She had been an officer in the League of Women Voters for a year or two and had attended the annual meeting of the state organization in January.[21] The League was scrupulously nonpartisan, though. Howe wanted her to join the Democratic side. In her first memoir, written in 1938, she described the circumstances: "Mr. Howe," she wrote, "felt that the one way to get my husband's interest aroused was to keep him as much as possible in contact with politics. This seemed to me an almost hopeless task. However, in order to accomplish his ends, Mr. Howe began to urge me to do some political work again."[22] In her second memoir, written in 1947, she was more blunt about the way she entered politics under Howe's direction. "I was pushed," she said. She added her impression that it was "not because Louis cared so much about my activities, but because he felt that they would make it possible for me to bring into the house people who would keep Franklin interested in state politics."[23]

Howe didn't need help with that, though. He could bring home—by the busload—people who were in state politics. He knew them all. He didn't have to press Eleanor into service as a procurer. As she had noted, though, he was a remarkably sensitive person. After spending the winter with the Roosevelts on East Sixty-Fifth Street, even an automaton could see that Eleanor was miserable with herself, sometimes crying, sometimes "clamming up," as she put it. "In many ways," she reflected, "this was the most trying winter of my entire life. It was the petty irritations, as I look back on them now, which made life so difficult. My mother-in-law . . ."[24] She wouldn't even have had to finish the sentence, had Howe been listening. He obviously cared about her and would have been callous not to try and get her out of the house to lead something of her own life.

Howe was fascinated with the involvement of women in politics, after the extension of universal suffrage in 1920. He resented the prevailing opinion that most women who voted would do nothing more than follow the inclinations of their husbands or fathers. After the results of the 1920 election, though, he had to admit that in ninety-five percent of the cases, that was just what had happened, according to studies of the new electorate. To Howe, that only showed that women voters had to be treated differently. While he understood the argument that women and men as voters should be treated in exactly the same way, he had found that it didn't work: issues were not of equal interest and, moreover, the means of persuasion were not equally effective. For example, women, he found, wanted facts, not catch-phrases. They thought in the short term and were more impatient for a schedule with every promise. They tended, he felt, to give up too easily, and lose interest in a fight, unless an issue was so critical to their way of thinking that they couldn't let go.

Louis Howe had harbored an obsession regarding Franklin's future in politics for a long time, but over the winter of 1921–22, he had another to add to it. The people who commented on Howe after that juncture usually spoke about his unequaled loyalty in the plural, where before it was focused only on Franklin. "He was so intent on what he knew these two great people could do," remarked Anne Gilbert, who met the Roosevelts and Louis Howe in the late 1920s, "and he tried in every way he could to bring out what was the best in both of them. He really did. He was a great person, never interested in anybody but them."[25] Almost any friend of the Roosevelts would express much the same opinion, referring to a humanitarian impulse of a rare order. It was people who worked with Howe in other capacities who were more likely to see him as a crusty sourpuss—with wrinkled clothes.

In the spring of 1922, Howe arranged for a woman named Marion Dickerman to dine with the Roosevelts. Dickerman had grown up in Chautauqua, New York, and graduated from Syracuse University, intending to become an educator. In 1919, she ran for the State Senate from Oswego County, on the southeast shore of Lake Ontario. Running against a powerful Republican, a man with his eye on the governor's chair, she didn't have a campaign machine, but she was a sober and likable woman with an able campaign manager in her energetic friend Nancy Cook. The two had met at college and they neither promoted nor hid the fact that they were a couple in private life. In November, they made a horse race of the election for State Senate and, although Dickerman didn't win, she did garner a lasting claim to fame as the first woman in the state to run on a major party ticket for an influential office.

"Eleanor and Louis knew that he had been cut down physically," Dickerman said of Franklin in a 1973 interview, "but his mind and his spirit were almost more vital than his body and that was what they felt should be fed, nourished and kept alive." She credited Louis with bringing in "all sorts of people"—and she found herself among them, being asked to dine on East Sixty-Fifth Street one evening. "The reason why they invited me to dinner that first time," Dickerman continued, "was that they had heard about my campaign and Franklin became interested in me from that point-of-view."[26] At dinner, Marion spoke of her interest in improving working conditions for women, which reminded Eleanor of the strong feelings that she'd had on that issue, even as a child. The two met a few more times, as Eleanor started to take her first steps—with Howe pushing—into politics. She met Dickerman's friend Nancy Cook, who invited her to a meeting of the Women's Division of the New York State Democratic Committee.

The Women's Division was the natural place for Eleanor. While women had positions in the overall party, the Women's Division was more active in bringing new blood into Democratic politics. It was dominated, logically enough, by those who had led the fight for female suffrage. Having won that fight, they were ready for new ones. They were a formidable group, with personalities both strong and well mannered: in other words, people with whom Eleanor could easily identify. Frances Perkins, who was part of the same circle at the time, described that pioneering generation:

> They were not the wives and sisters of Tammany Hall politicians; these were ladies who had education, sometimes fortunes, or at least a modest access to the world's goods and position in the world. . . . They weren't afraid of anything. They had something back of them, nobody would arrest them, nobody would cry them down if they undertook to speak on street corners. They were ladylike people. They were polite people.[27]

Caroline O'Day, Harriet May Mills, and Elinor Morgenthau were prominent examples. Another was Marion Dickerman. Eleanor immediately liked both Dickerman and Cook, as well as O'Day, whom she also met early on, and the decision was quite natural to join the Women's Division. She had no particular leadership experience and was loath to speak in public, but Howe assured her that he would help her create, or carve out, the persona expected of the latest Roosevelt to enter the political world. For the time being, she clung to the motivation that Howe had given her: that the whole effort was for Franklin. "I don't want him forgotten," Eleanor told Frances Perkins.[28]

CHAPTER TEN

MR. 'OWE
AT HYDE PARK

I n early spring of 1922, Sara Roosevelt sent her chauffeur to pick up Franklin Roosevelt in New York and take him with his nurses on a short visit to Springwood so that he could see the place, but also so that he could give it a test run in view of his new needs.[1] In May, Franklin came back to take up residence at the estate with Eleanor and all of the children. He didn't hide the fact that he was thrilled to get back home, both because it *was* home, as New York City never was, and because in the open space and fresh air of the estate he could pursue a new regimen of exercises.

Sara Roosevelt was delighted, of course, postponing her regular European summer trip so that she could be with them. She might have felt vindicated, recalling those who had crossed her when she said she knew that her son would be more comfortable at the big house, but she could only take so much solace in his move, since he was only going to stay for the summer. That was the plan, anyway; she was aware that it could change. Another part of the plan called for Howe to spend weekends at the house with the Roosevelts, after working at the Fidelity & Deposit Company all week.

Since September, Louis had spent most weekends in Poughkeepsie with Grace and Hartley. Without resentment, but indeed sympathy, Grace recalled that he typically came home on a Friday evening and slept or dozed straight through until Sunday morning. He didn't have a chance for that kind of rest and renewal at the Roosevelt house. Yet when Franklin and Eleanor moved up to Hyde Park, he used his weekends to see them. For Howe, the routine—even the train schedule—would barely change, except that he wouldn't get off the train in Poughkeepsie where his family lived; he'd take it to the next stop near Hyde Park.

In 1922, the Roosevelt estate comprised approximately 750 acres, stretching along almost a half mile of land overlooking the Hudson River. Properties of similar size dotted the heights between the river and the Albany Post Road, which ran parallel to it. The driveway on the Roosevelts' property was a quarter mile long, turning off the Post Road toward the river. Sara had lived there since her marriage and continued to operate it in the manner laid down by her late husband, James. She wasn't so rigid, however, that she hadn't felt free to renovate the house with Franklin in 1915—to the point that James Roosevelt probably couldn't have recognized the place.[2]

The renovation had transformed the house from a large Italianate house into a Georgian-style mansion. The expansion included bedrooms and servants' quarters, along with two rooms on the first floor that would reflect Franklin's taste and meet his needs. The first was the library, a great room that ran the depth of the house on the south end. Lined with bookcases, it offered comfortable chairs for reading and ample tables and desks for hobbies. The second was a study on the north end of the house, with easy access to an outside porch.

"The Roosevelts certainly lived well," observed a neighbor, Olin Dows, "but quietly—simply, except for politics. Their life wasn't jet set at all. It was high society wherever they went, but it was very quiet and stylish."[3] Some of the houses along the river were ostentatious in the manner of Newport, Rhode Island, or Palm Beach, Florida, with architecture consistent with castles or state capitols. The Vanderbilt house, about five miles north on the other side of the town of Hyde Park, was practically a duchy on its 660-acre tract overlooking a bend in the river. The house cost $660,000 and the furnishings twice that. The Astor place in Rhinebeck, farther up the river, encompassed 500 acres with more than ten miles of private roads, one of which was treated as a public road by residents in the area, to the annoyance of the owner. "Mrs. Vincent Astor Closes Highway to All Except Friends,"[4] ran a headline in a local newspaper.

The Roosevelt estate didn't seek to inspire headlines or to strike passersby with awe. It was in keeping with the less boastful style of upstate New York. Inside, the family wanted for very little. Sara Roosevelt relied on a full staff of servants; approximately eight, depending on the season: a cook, butler, footman, parlor maid, kitchen maid, laundress, chambermaid, and personal maid.[5] Sara managed the estate, hiring the servants, maintaining the property, and planning the meals. Both Franklin and Eleanor chafed under her control of the household, but it had the benefit of freeing them from the pressures of running a house—especially one with eight servants.

———◆———

By summer, Franklin was working on two different regimens of exercise, one to help him become more mobile, and the other to renew the use of his leg muscles. With the first set of exercises he had to rely on the wheelchair or his leg braces and crutches, or else crawl on the floor. To help, Sara had footpaths on the estate graded with firm gravel so that Franklin could go to the gardens, the barns, the playhouse, and even the home of his half-brother, Rosy, about a quarter mile away. "He would be pushed in his wheel chair around the grounds," recalled Olin Dows, "usually by Robert McGaughey, for many years his mother's house man and butler. Often he'd go to see the 'Rosy' Roosevelts, passing the children's playhouse along the way."[6] The wheelchair was only supposed to be a temporary expediency, however.

"When he first came up here," said Louis Depew, who would serve as Sara's chauffeur for twenty-three years, "he would walk around on crutches first, then there were bars to exercise on."[7] The bars, set up on the south lawn, were a twin set, with one double row at waist height and one at eye level. By the hour, Roosevelt made progress back and forth, using his hands on the lower bars for support. Each step was demanding. The crutches were just as exhausting to use, since he had to move his whole body along with the weight of the braces, using, effectively, just his arms, shoulders, and upper back. In the house, Roosevelt also practiced a kind of crab walk on the floor, which could be performed with or without his braces.

In the hopes of strengthening his legs so that he could toss aside the braces someday, Roosevelt exercised in bed; his efforts didn't look like much: just a man concentrating hard and occasionally seeing one of his toes move. The second aspect of his program without braces was hydrotherapy, which started when the Astors offered him the use of their indoor swimming pool. He went to their estate at least twice a week and found the water very satisfying, measuring his progress by how deep the water had to be in order for him to stand or walk without holding the side of the pool. The water was such a boon that eventually Sara had an outdoor pool built at Hyde Park.

The various aspects of Franklin's exercise regimen accounted for about five hours each day. That left some time for recreation, into which he delved with the same dedication. Nearly every day he went for a ride with his nurse in Sara's Lincoln, with Louis Depew driving, to look at the land and to stop and chat with friends. He often made it a point to visit Moses Smith, the straight-talking farmer who rented about fifty acres from Roosevelt, growing mainly vegetables. Smith also cooperated with Roosevelt on his favorite endeavor, tree farming.[8]

Another person who might be included in his rounds was Thomas Leonard, a contractor whom Roosevelt had known for about a dozen years. Leonard noticed that Roosevelt, always an amiable person, was reaching out more in that summer of 1922 than he ever had before. "He found time to spend a little more time with his friends when he had occasions to meet them," Leonard said. "He cultivated a greater admiration—I'd say affection for the people generally."[9] Roosevelt was in every way slipping into the role with the pleasant name and, from Louis Howe's viewpoint, the ghastly implications, of country squire. Lily Norton, a guest who had visited Sara at Springwood before Franklin's arrival there, wrote a kind of epitaph for him in a letter home. "I am staying up here with a dear friend, Mrs. James Roosevelt," she reported. "It's a lovely region, but tragedy rather over shadows this once so happy & prosperous family for Mrs. R's only son, Franklin Roosevelt was struck down in August with a terribly serious case of infantile paralysis. . . . Now he is a cripple—will he ever be anything else?"[10]

<hr />

Inside the family, Roosevelt was never looked upon as a cripple, that is, as a person whose main identity was expressed by what he could not do. Eleanor avoided that attitude entirely and so did the children. And they all took their cue from Franklin. He would speak freely about the events on Campobello that had paralyzed his legs, and everyone who spent time with him, especially during the first few years afterward, knew that he could speak endlessly about the physiology and treatment of the condition. Only rarely, however, did he refer to his condition in negative terms.

In 1921, before Roosevelt was stricken, he had agreed to fill an upcoming vacancy on the board of trustees of Vassar College. During the summer of 1922, Henry Noble MacCracken, the president of Vassar, visited Roosevelt and reiterated the invitation. "He told me that my board would not want a cripple," MacCracken recalled. "It was the only time I ever heard him refer to his suffering."[11] MacCracken assured Roosevelt that he was very much wanted, and Roosevelt said he'd think it over. The following year, he joined the board, serving productively for his full term of ten years.

MacCracken made a surprising comment about Franklin Roosevelt, especially as it came from a college educator. "From Groton, Harvard, and Columbia Law School he seemed to have learned nothing," MacCracken said, "so far as my contacts evidenced."

"From the woods, the sea, birds, horses, people," MacCracken continued, "he learned and continued learning."[12] That was undoubtedly true, but Roosevelt also had a lively interest in books. "During his convalescence he read a lot," Howe remarked in an interview. "History has always been his favorite subject: I do not think there is a man in the country who knows more of our history up to 1830 than Franklin Roosevelt. He is the only man I know who has read all the numbers of *The Federalist Papers* for pleasure."[13]

━━━━◆◆◆━━━━

In that first summer of change, Hyde Park was given its chance to comfort the Roosevelts, troubled not only by Franklin's illness, but by an acrimonious winter on Sixty-Fifth Street. Franklin made no secret of the fact that he needed the place. "Life here had always a healing quality for him," Eleanor said.[14] Their son, Elliott, later pointed out that the region had the same effect on her. "It was very, very important," he said, "not this particular area here at the main house, but the Hudson River Valley was extremely important to her . . . to my mother's 'psyche.'"[15] Eleanor had grown up spending summers at her grandmother's house along the Hudson. Not all of her memories from that gloomy house were as enviable as Franklin's at Hyde Park, but then, for both of them the Hudson was home. He must have had some unhappy experiences there that he didn't talk about, having been trained, perhaps, in his mother's rigid edict: that life at James Roosevelt's Springwood had been perfect. But by all accounts, it had a kind of serenity, and as the Roosevelts settled into Springwood in the summer of 1922, they forgot the fighting over whether or not to bring Franklin back and waited for the place to stake its own claim on his future.

"Franklin is very well," wrote one houseguest in a letter not long after they were settled. "It is good for him to be up here for he is very fond of the place—and is out-doors more."[16]

Louis Howe not only followed Roosevelt to Hyde Park for long weekends, but he entered wholeheartedly into the life of a country gentleman. Franklin was already referring to himself, humorously, as "the squire of Crum Elbow."[17] Being a squire, he naturally used the anachronistic, original name for the Hyde Park area: Crum Elbow. "Louis Howe would come here," Depew remembered, "and he and Louis used to sit on the porch making models. They made different models and they'd take them down to the river sailing them like that."[18] Louis poured through rare-book catalogues with Franklin, took rides in the car with him and patiently listened to his explanations of the latest developments with his legs, but it was the model boats that took up the greater part of their time, as they designed them, built them, and then raced them on the Hudson.

The races had entered the big league the year before, raised to a level just below an Olympic sport in an effort that hinted of a Louis Howe theatrical production. First, someone convinced Eleanor to donate a challenge cup to the winner of a model-boat race across the Hudson. Then someone planted a long story about the race in the *New York Evening Post*.[19] As described in the article, the Roosevelt Cup sounded like the sort of thing Louis liked to organize, for merriment. It had the Howe hallmarks of an endeavor with detailed regulations, taken very seriously within its own world and, at the same time, tinged with mockery for anything taken seriously anywhere. In 1922, the races were staged on a daily basis, as Franklin and Louis made sailboats and continually improved them, abiding by the rule that the hull could not measure more than thirty-eight inches long. Roosevelt and Howe devoted almost as much time to thinking of names as to building the boats. Roosevelt tended to either borrow names from naval history, such as *Resolute,* or to rely on *Crum Elbow*. Howe used *Shamrock* for a while and when that wore out, he settled on *Horse's Neck,* a reworking of the name of his favorite beach into an expression of the day (used in polite company to replace another one involving horse anatomy).

Whenever the two commodores were ready, Depew drove them down to the riverside and then helped Franklin into the back of a rowboat. Once Franklin had set his boat in the water, Howe would launch his entry and climb into the front of the boat. Depew then rowed them away in pursuit of the toy boats. "They'd be down there sometimes two and a half or three hours, sailing those boats," Depew said.[20] Franklin Roosevelt apparently held the record at fifteen minutes for a one-way crossing. As a pursuit for grown men, it was probably regarded as a silly waste of time by some of the strangers who stopped to watch, but then tennis and golf—or any sport, for that matter—could have been seen as just as silly. The incongruity was that at the ages of forty and fifty-one, respectively, a couple of otherwise hard-charging men had three hours per day to devote to anything involving toys and challenge cups and being rowed around in a river. The hours spent with the boats, on the porch or on the river, were invaluable, though, returning another kind of strength to Roosevelt after his illness and giving the friendship of Roosevelt and Howe a respite from business, politics, and all other pursuits in which they lived up to the expectations of strangers.

Roosevelt's physician in New York, Dr. George Draper, had encouraged him to walk as far as he could each day, using braces and crutches. The advice may have been to try and go a little further each day. However Draper worded it, Roosevelt turned his walk into a challenge to go under his own power all the way from the front door to the Albany Post Road—the full quarter-mile. It was the most strenuous exercise in his self-imposed regimen and he never did attain his goal. He usually went by himself, because the exertion made it impossible to carry on a conversation. If he fell, though, he had to wait for someone to come and help him to his feet.

When Roosevelt used the parallel bars, on the other hand, he enjoyed company in the form of friends staying at the house or members of his family. As the host, he steered the conversation, entertained with anecdotes, and made the time lively with the party of bright banter that he could bring with him anywhere. That wasn't unusual by itself, but the houseguests often commented on the fact that while he was holding forth amid the laughter, sweat was pouring down his face and the muscles in his arms were twitching from the effort to budge his body forward. Huybertie Pruyn Hamlin, his childhood friend, was part of the coterie one day at Springwood. "One of his knees had locked," she wrote in a memoir in the *New Republic*, "and he was carrying through a program of very rigid exercises trying to improve the condition. I watched as he made his endless rounds, for two or three hours a day, holding on to the wooden railing of a rectangular walk. Usually, several of his friends were sitting around, and he talked and laughed cheerfully as he circled the platform, holding himself up by the railing and dragging his almost useless legs after him."[21]

If anything, Eleanor and Louis redoubled their efforts to bring visitors into the house to lessen Roosevelt's feeling of isolation. Political figures, of course, were at a premium on their list. Roosevelt himself often concluded letters to friends or intriguing acquaintances by inviting them to stop at the house for lunch. The location of the estate could not have been better for attracting visitors if it had been built as a rest stop, being just about midway on the main road between New York and Albany, without the necessity for even a slight detour.

With the summer of 1922, the nature of the house at Springwood changed significantly. Having long been a private refuge, it slowly took on the purpose and pace of a hotel. Not only was it a memorable backdrop in which to meet Franklin Roosevelt, it was blatantly used as a lure, being such an appealing setting. Another politician trying to make a comeback and living in an average house couldn't expect party leaders to visit. Howe knew that Roosevelt could—and that Springwood would be an asset in the renewal of Roosevelt's career, and then in its escalation. Long after it was necessary to stir Franklin's thinking with new faces and fresh conversation, the place would be an unending open house. But its status as a private family home would have to be sacrificed.

The cohesion of Franklin Roosevelt's family was changing, along with the atmosphere in the house. Anna Roosevelt commented on it later. "The children," she said in an interview, "I think without a doubt, to a certain extent fell in between, because there were other goals which didn't include the children."[22] While Howe can't be accused of setting out to place the children in a secondary position, he was the one who set the goals to which Anna referred, for both Franklin and for Eleanor. He was the one whose life, as of 1922, was devoted to making sure that nothing blocked those goals. And, most damningly, he was the one who had let his own children "fall in between" in deference to those same all-important political goals.

Howe was trying to re-instill ambition in the Roosevelt house. Little by little, it took hold on a scale even more intensive than it had been before. His intervention, the continual stream of guests, and the blatant effort at redirection for the two heads of the family, all may have seemed to Franklin and Eleanor at the time to cover more gaps, emotionally, than they created.

———◆———

Grace Howe was biding her time in Poughkeepsie, seeing Louis when he had an extra day—which was not often. On one such occasion, he made an elaborate plan to take Mary and her friends out on a midnight picnic after a college prom. Mary told biographer Lela Stiles, "He rented cars and took seven or eight couples out into the back country near [the town of] Fishkill, where he cooked and served, at the end of long sticks, succulent steaks three inches thick."[23]

Grace sometimes visited Hyde Park with Louis, but overall, through most of 1922, they lived lives that were more separate than ever, despite being only about fifteen minutes apart by automobile. When Hartley was home and he knew his father was coming for a visit, he sat by the window and watched down the road with binoculars. At Horseneck Beach, the two of them built toy boats with enthusiasm. In fact, in his fascination with ships and the navy, Hartley was more like Franklin than Franklin's own boys. Elliott Roosevelt tried to build a toy boat one year, but lost interest. His father, as he said, was not a very good teacher. The wonder is that Howe didn't invite his own son to help him and Franklin build the boats and race them. Hartley would have reveled in the chance to make the boats and to be with his father.

Howe couldn't take Hartley along, though. As he and Franklin built boats, they talked. They talked away whole afternoons, sitting on the porch. No one knows anymore what was said, but while Roosevelt may have been playing, Howe was working. He had Roosevelt talking. All that he needed next was something for Roosevelt to do—or, more important, a battle he could win, and an adversary more worthy than the latest version of the *Horse's Neck*.

CHAPTER ELEVEN

ANYBODY BUT HEARST

Fingy Conners was back in New York City in 1922, and back in politics. The Buffalo magnate had changed in some ways since his last foray, when he led the aborted effort to make William Randolph Hearst governor. That was 1906. Sixteen years later, he was much richer; no longer a mere millionaire, he was a multimillionaire. Among other things, he'd entered farming in a big way, buying a 5,000-acre spread in Florida and 11,000 more acres there for other projects, including a toll highway that was in the planning stages. He was more refined in his deportment than he once was and usually managed to keep himself in check when he was speaking for the record. Perhaps that was because he was sixty-five and no longer a newcomer, fighting his way upward. Or because he had a son who had graduated from Yale with a degree in French, and so at long last Fingy had a family reputation to uphold.

In early June, Conners came out of political retirement and treated New York to a true déjà vu, as he was once more in a reception room at a New York hotel, standing before a gaggle of reporters and speaking for William Randolph Hearst, who was, just as before, in Europe. And, of course, Conners was assuring the reporters that beyond doubt, the next governor of New York State would be William R. Hearst.

"The booming of Hearst has solidified the opposition," observed the *New York Tribune* afterward, "making it practically certain that his nomination would split the party."[1] The state elections of 1922, which had been looking fairly dull, were suddenly full of drama for the Democrats. They, too, were having flashbacks of '06. The New York State Democratic Party, squandering the positive influence it could exert nationally, was unable to unite around issues and so it drifted with seeming relief into something much more familiar: anguish over William Hearst.

Tammany Hall, still dominated by Charles Murphy, had yet to take a stand in the jostling for the nomination. In the interim, as in 1906, Conners made sure that his man jumped to an early lead, encouraging "William R. Hearst Associations" to sprout up, county by county, throughout the state. Hearst returned from Europe on June 21 and was forced at dockside to say a few words about his political future. He was either garbled as usual or purposely vague—but in any case, Fingy had to step in the following day to translate. "He'll run if he's nominated," he said bluntly. Someone asked what Hearst himself had to say on the topic, and Fingy sounded almost like his old self, with the truncated phrasing of a man with a fist in his pocket. "When you hear me, you hear Hearst," he said.[2]

Hearst had said at dockside that he was back from Europe on a sad mission, to accompany the body and the widow of one of his traveling companions, who had died as soon as the party reached England. Hearst intended to return to Europe after three days to rejoin his wife, who would be in Paris. The part about his friend's unfortunate death was true, but Hearst was glad to be in the United States, anyway, to check on one of his investments, the movie *When Knighthood Was in Flower*, into which he had poured millions of dollars. The historical drama was in production in California, scheduled for a September release. One of the stars was Hearst's mistress, Marion Davies.[3] The fact that Hearst was having an affair was well known in Hollywood and in some quarters in New York. The Hearsts had already discussed divorce several times in light of it, and Tammany Hall, to which Mrs. Hearst had longtime family connections, undoubtedly knew all about it. Mr. Hearst apparently presumed that he could keep news of the affair out of the campaign; he had never had a problem shielding his private life from the public, even as he sold other people's scandals by the column inch in his papers.

Another question was whether Hearst would muster enough interest to run a successful campaign. Previously, his commitment to his own political fortunes had wavered at critical junctures. In 1922, he might not be inclined to fight very hard for the chance to live alone in Albany for months at a time, when he could be in Hollywood with Miss Davies. According to Fingy, though, Hearst needed to win the governorship, because he was headed for the presidency in 1924.

Hearst didn't get off to a good start as a modern candidate. When he was interviewed at shipside in New York he was asked how he would court the women's vote. He responded that he "had little interest in the attitude of the women."[4] He ought to have reconsidered. In New York, Belle Moskowitz was already forming the Women's Democratic Union in opposition to Hearst.[5] Caroline O'Day helped to turn a breakfast meeting of the Westchester County Democratic Women's Organization into an anti-Hearst rally.[6]

In Poughkeepsie on June 22, the day after Hearst returned to the United States, Eleanor Roosevelt was presiding over a meeting of the Dutchess County Women's Democratic Club. With only days to prepare since Conners' announcement, she had coauthored a resolution with Elinor Morgenthau, a new friend in political work. It was simple enough:

> Resolved: That we urge in the state convention, the nomination of such candidates as are truly representative of the principles of the Democratic Party, who supported the Democratic national and state tickets in 1920, and who are honorable and honored members of the communities in which they live.[7]

The resolution didn't exclude many people, but Hearst was one of them, since he had supported the Harding-Coolidge ticket in 1920 over that of Cox-Roosevelt. Some other candidate might have been welcomed back into the fold. Franklin Roosevelt, for example, had voted Republican on occasion before he entered his own race in 1910. Political infidelity, however, was as good an excuse as any on which to base the newest effort to block William Hearst. In addition, women who were ambitious in Democratic politics had a special reason to resist him on that point.

As newly enfranchised voters in the national elections, women were trying to stake a claim to power and responsibility in their political parties, and they were overtly loyal to them. Those who feared or reviled Hearst in 1922 pointed to his abandonment of the party in the last presidential election as an unforgivable act of treason. Women active in the party were quick to take up that argument, as it strengthened their own credentials as both independent thinkers, resistant to heavily publicized "booms," and as party loyalists, leading the way in closing ranks against a bad Democrat. Hearst certainly hadn't endeared himself to female voters with his impromptu comments in New York, but the leaders of the Women's Division, Eleanor among them, took an even longer view in opposing him.

When Eleanor Roosevelt presented the resolution at her Poughkeepsie meeting, it passed unanimously. "Eleanor is spending her spare time in the business of organizing the Democratic women of Dutchess Co.," wrote a friend early that summer.[8] The activity in her political circles in both New York City and Dutchess County was increasing with the excitement over the state election, and she was called upon to perform jobs from the most basic—such as canvassing Democratic women at their addresses—to speaking and running meetings, as she did in Poughkeepsie. At first, she was invited to speak primarily because of the drawing power of her name. To her credit, though, that didn't make her think herself above the minor jobs that often mean even more to the organization of probable voters.

"Louis was constantly encouraging Eleanor," remembered Marion Dickerman. "Franklin," she added, "was pleased with what she was doing and joked with her a little bit."[9] The role reversal of staying home while Eleanor went out politicking was entirely new for Franklin. He might easily respond to it with humor, which was typically part of his language. He undoubtedly knew that her work was intended to be helpful to him, and anyone could see that it was positive for her. Once when Gabrielle For-bush, a writer who worked on Democratic campaigns, had dinner with the Roosevelts at Hyde Park, Eleanor had to leave early to go into New York. "I could see they had a good understanding," Forbush noted. "It showed in the way FDR looked at her and she at him, as they said good-bye. He was really proud of her and said something in her praise as she went out. His mother said, with a stiff little smile, 'Yes, my daughter-in-law is *so* busy.' [Roosevelt] came back with something appreciative that was very good."[10]

Speaking in public, however, had never been Eleanor's strong suit. She could remember watching her husband's speeches as a first-time candidate for State Senate, as he fell into the habit of taking long pauses in the midst of a thought. To her, each pause lasted a lifetime, as she waited in the fear that he might never start talking again. Her own tendency was just the op-posite. She spoke in a monotonous stream, punctuated by nervous laughter, rather than pauses. At her earlier speeches, she was accepted by audiences apparently because they were friendly and she presented the very picture of a nice person, trying hard to get through her speech. That did not, however, make her convincing or her points memorable. As she took a greater role in politics at Howe's urging in 1922, trying hard wasn't enough to win over a tough audience.

Starting with Eleanor's serious entry into political work in the spring, Howe had taken it upon himself to transform her into a strong speaker. "Louis used to go to meetings where she spoke," Dickerman recalled. "She had then an unfortunate habit, for when she became nervous her voice would go up and she had a funny little giggle. Louis was most severe— 'Nothing to laugh at, stop that.'"[11] For months, Howe trained Eleanor at home, in the living room either at Springwood or Sixty-Fifth Street. Ac-cording to James, she gave more than a hundred speeches with an audience of exactly one person: Louis, who would coach her through each effort, giv-ing her advice and notes afterward.

Howe was well suited to his role as director. He had been interested in theater all of his life and had learned something about the stage assets of timing, vocal inflection, attitude, and the one that kept people from gig-gling: concentration. Moreover, Howe had sat through many hundreds of political speeches in his earlier years as a reporter. He had become aware of those techniques that were effective, both at the time and in the long run of winning elections. Further, he knew Eleanor's capabilities and she trusted him, even to the extent that they developed a system of hand signals, which they used during her public appearances. If she were falling into a bad habit, she would see him raise his hand from his post in the back row. After each speech, they critiqued her performance together.

Howe was not a man to sugarcoat his comments; he didn't bother doing that with Franklin and he was just as blunt with Eleanor. At that time, she might have been sensitive to criticism. She was troubled with doubts about the role she had always expected to fill as a wife, insecure about her place in her own household, and growing more resentful of Sara's control over the family. Howe's well-intentioned coaching could have been disturbing to Eleanor. Apparently, though, it had just the opposite effect, especially as the audiences grew more attentive and she was able to pinpoint exactly why.[12]

"It was not very obvious to me at that time," Eleanor later wrote, "why making speeches was necessary, and at first it was the most painful thing I had to do. Now I can see that Louis felt that unless I learned to be useful to the party in this way, I would not get much consideration from any of the leaders."[13] Howe recognized her gifts of intelligence and compassion, and he wanted the leaders to see them, too. They wouldn't if she didn't present herself and her positive attributes clearly.

In the process of helping Eleanor with her speeches, Howe also drew out and helped define the persona that Eleanor projected through the rest of her life in the public eye. At the least, he showed her the possibilities for emphasizing one's strong points. Franklin had come by his expertise in self-presentation naturally—after he learned to stop pausing to the point of inducing panic in the audience. Eleanor learned it, with Howe as a tutor, but she learned it well. Howe gave her the tools of style, but it helped that in the contentious summer of 1922, she had something important to say.

———— ·◆· ————

Through the summer, the only one who was content to be quiet on the subject of the return of William Hearst was Charles Murphy. He had supported Hearst as he would have a brother in 1906. The second time around, he was inscrutable. Fingy Conners, whom Murphy had personally recruited as the chairman of the state party in the old days, was in the position of having to call on Murphy repeatedly to solicit his endorsement. Murphy refused even to see him.[14] Hearst, for his part, purchased his first upstate newspaper, the Albany *Times-Union*.[15] As an indication of his intentions, the transaction was clearer than anything he might have said—and he still wasn't saying much. He bought the paper from a previous governor, who had found it useful for political ends. By buying the Albany paper, Hearst sent a signal to his potential supporters that he was in earnest about taking the governorship.

Upstate Democratic leaders who were against Hearst decided that they had better have a meeting. They chose Syracuse as the place and July 7 as the date. The organizers invited Franklin Roosevelt to attend, in the confidence that he couldn't support Hearst, if only because the publisher had refused to support him when he ran for vice-president with Governor Cox. "I am glad to have the notice of the Meeting," Roosevelt replied, "and only sorry that I cannot get up to Syracuse for it."[16] Knowing that the letter might well be read at the meeting, he did not dwell on his paralysis, the description of which would serve no useful purpose. Instead, he wrote a letter well suited to a public gathering: a speech by remote.

During the week before the meeting was to take place, Grace and Hartley were staying at Hyde Park, while Louis spent most of the week in New York. Grace had packed up her Poughkeepsie apartment, seeing no reason to pay rent on it all summer while she and Hartley were to be in Massachusetts. The plan was to move her belongings to Springwood for storage until autumn, but that was taking longer than she thought, due to movers who wouldn't drive in the rain.

Sara had already left on her summer trip to Europe, taking Anna and James with her, but the other Roosevelts were home and looking forward to fireworks at Springwood on the Fourth of July, which fell on Tuesday.[17] The Fourth, however, turned out to be much quieter than anyone anticipated. The rockets had been ordered well in advance, but they didn't arrive until after the holiday. Grace wrote to her mother, capturing a weekend in the life of Springwood, starting with the fireworks:

Louis put them off when he got up here Friday evening. All the people in the place gathered for the fireworks and ice cream in the kitchen afterwards—and most of Hyde Park village came down and sat on the edges of the lawn to view them—in fact we saw a sign [in town] which said the movies would begin early "on account of the fireworks."

The Adolph Caspar Millers were here over the 4th and are very delightful.

Now Mr. Van Lear Black of Baltimore is expected on his yacht, bringing the Gov. of Maryland, so Franklin wanted to put out a Maryland flag for his arrival. None could be bought, so the Women's Exchange at Rhinebeck is making it in great haste.

Later

The yacht arrived and they all came up for tea and tennis and a swim and then stayed to dinner so we were twelve to dinner. . . .

I think I shall be ready to take to my bed for a couple of days, when I get to the Beach.[18]

Through the Grand Hotel pace of life at Springwood, Grace could not help but notice that Louis and Eleanor had changed. For years, she had seen them in a stiff relationship, interacting for Franklin's sake. That was no longer the case; it was well-known throughout the family that they had been a masterful team at Campobello. Grace could plainly see that they had only grown closer since.

———— ·•· ————

On Saturday, July 7—while the Maryland flag was flying at Springwood—two hundred upstate Democratic leaders, male and female, met in Syracuse, the most centrally located city in the state. Before they actually met, however, they argued. Because of dissent over the approach to the problem of attacking Hearst without personally abusing him, the meeting was delayed for two hours. By the time the two chairmen called it to order, they had decided how to move past the discord, beginning the proceedings by reading Franklin Roosevelt's letter, which hit the note they required. It didn't reflect anything in the way of original thinking; the party didn't need anything like that, or another point of view at that juncture.

Roosevelt's message was more valuable on a practical basis, reflecting a sense of the trends in the party and just exactly where to place himself so that he would pull them together and let the momentum collect.

Roosevelt started the letter with the inarguable fact that the party's candidates should "represent the best thought of the Party." He pointed out, with only slight exaggeration, that the Republicans' failure on the state and national level had caused "a tremendous drift" back to the Democrats. His only reference to Hearst was the dagger some Democrats wanted, but it was heavily veiled, as others would want. "It would be unfortunate," he wrote, "for us to go out in search of false gods, and political nostrums which, though making appeal to the unthinking, are fundamentally unsound."[19] The part about the "false gods and political nostrums" hinted of Louis Howe's sweeping style, though there is no reason to believe that Roosevelt would not have written the letter himself, possibly with editorial input from Howe.

After dismissing false gods who appeal to the unthinking, the letter described the candidate the party should nominate, carefully maintaining the suspense of attaching a name to the ideal until the very last line. Roosevelt and Howe knew that the letter, if properly executed, would be read at the meeting, and it turned out to be the only letter that was. With that goal in mind, they timed the suspense and then advanced the name of Alfred E. Smith. At the sound of the name, the meeting burst into cheering that lasted well over a minute.[20]

The trouble was that Alfred Smith wasn't sure he wanted to be governor again. Smith loved his family circle most of all. In his autobiography, he told the story of a summer at the beach when the children were given two goats. When the summer ended, the children couldn't bear to part with them, despite the fact that it just wasn't practical to bring goats back to a small house in Manhattan. But the goats were, by then, part of the family. "I suppose I was just as insistent as the children that we keep them," Smith admitted, and so he rushed back to reconstruct his back yard on Oliver Street to make room for the goats.[21] That was one side of Smith, and although the story pertains to animals, he was not any different about people. It was his hallmark to try and find a way. His closest colleagues—and many voters—were deeply affected by his guiding sense of empathy.

There was another side to Alfred Smith, though. He'd spent many years as the man in the horsehair robe, living on a paltry government wage while circulating among the very rich. Van Lear Black didn't visit Oliver Street in his yacht. And yet Smith was invited to yachts and penthouses and mansions on Long Island. For a long time, he'd had power as an elected official, but practically no money. His job at the United States Trucking Corporation gave him a taste of the reverse. There could be no doubt that after two years at the trucking company, he liked feeling rich.

Smith was aware that some Democrats in the state were looking to him to fend off the Hearst offensive, but no one could be sure that he intended to run. Fingy Conners was spreading the word that he was not running. Mrs. Moskowitz, however, was actively promoting his candidacy through the Women's Democratic Union, and if anyone knew what Smith was thinking, it was Belle Moskowitz.

Many people who knew them both well presumed that Mrs. Moskowitz did his thinking for him, anyway. They pointed to the fact that while he had forged his own career as a legislative leader in the New York State Assembly, in which a group mentality is intrinsic, he thrived as governor with her advice and ideas. She did have natural executive ability, defining problems and bringing the right people together to find solutions. "She was a great combination of femininity and masculinity," said Samuel Rosenman, an active Smith supporter at the time. "She had a masculine mind, in the sense of being aggressive, forceful, sound and persuasive. At the same time she was—we knew her family and we knew her well—she was a very devoted mother to a daughter and to two boys, and a very devoted wife to Dr. Moskowitz."

"She was also a sound politician, in the true sense of the word," Rosenman added. "She knew how to handle people, and she had a great sense of public relations."[22]

As with Louis Howe, Mrs. Moskowitz exhibited no inclination to run for office herself. She would have had the opportunity; a number of the women with whom she was working regularly in politics had run for office, or would eventually. To an even greater extent than Howe, she preferred to remain in the background, never seeking publicity, giving interviews, or writing letters referring to her own activities. Alfred Smith reflected her viewpoint and was receptive to her specific ideas. She and Howe were both content to make a good candidate great, if they could.

A typical impression of Howe was that he was veritably smitten with Franklin Roosevelt and wanted nothing more than to live, homely as he was, through the handsome aristocrat with the friendly charm. That version of their relationship, though, smacks of a fairy tale and overlooks the fact that Howe had a vision for American society. Had the Roosevelts not shared that vision, or had they turned away from it, Howe would not necessarily have followed them—or convinced them to follow him, as the case may have been. Nonetheless, his sense of imperative on issues was not as pronounced as that of Belle Moskowitz. In a 1960 interview, Rosenman recalled:

> She, I'm sure, had more to do than anyone with providing Smith with his great social outlook towards matters of state. She herself had been a social worker, but she was a practical kind of social worker. She wasn't what we'd call today a "Do-gooder," as that term is used in a sense of derision. On the contrary, she was a very sound, liberal, progressive thinker, and I think she had a great deal to do with keeping Smith on the liberal side of matters.[23]

Upon receiving news of the Syracuse conference, Smith listened politely to the Democrats who wanted to vanquish Hearst, but he was still noncommittal about running for governor. The Syracuse conference had failed to draw a statement out of him.

———◦•◦———

On Sunday, Louis prepared to leave Hyde Park to spend the week in New York. Later that week, the Howes intended to drive to Massachusetts, where Grace typically divided her time between the cottage and her mother's home in Fall River, while Louis and Hartley could think of nowhere else they'd rather be than Horseneck Beach. The two of them looked forward to a summer of swimming, sleeping, and naval architecture, building boats to sail in the calm waters that nosed into the marshlands from the beach.

Grace was on edge, as the time drew near for Louis to leave. Just as Anna had become angry when she perceived Louis' place in her mother's life, Grace, for the first time, had seen Eleanor's new place in Louis' life, and she was shocked.

Louis and Grace were in the front hall at the house as he was about to go, when Eleanor came downstairs, as Louis described it, "to give me Franklin's last messages and errands."[24] When Grace saw Eleanor, she left the room abruptly. She refused to come back or say good-bye to Louis.

The next night, Louis wrote a letter to Grace at Hyde Park, reflecting that he was every bit as wounded by marriage as was Eleanor, even after so many years and a life of outward civility. He was not a man to abandon hope, but the position in which he found himself was nearly unbearable.

For more than ten years, Louis had been tormented by jealousy toward a person whose very name, "Willie," grew into a kind of code word. By 1922, that name and the spectre of a man Grace once knew, or still knew, filled the gap between the two Howes. "Willie" evoked what was gone, the relationship that Louis knew he and Grace had lost. And "Willie" was emblematic of all that Howe, in his own mind, was not.

Howe's version of Willie (who is mentioned only in his letters, not in Grace's) may have been intended to hurt himself, far more than Grace. He had always been prone to self-pity, in reconciling himself to the frustrations of his life. In that, he was not unlike Eleanor. She "clammed up," as she put it. Howe had a greater sense of the dramatic, where his illnesses or his career disappointments were concerned. His recriminations, so satisfying in his own exaggeration, were grounded in the truth. There had been a man named Willie known to Grace. Whatever he had meant to her, he remained in their life. Of Lucy Mercer, Eleanor Roosevelt made a remark often quoted in biographies to describe her pain: "I am like an elephant; I can forgive, but never forget." Whether she did indeed forgive is questionable; perhaps she tried. Howe, in his own case, was more helpless.

Even if "Willie" hadn't existed, Howe would have had to make him up. He wrote to Grace:

I have given all my life to try and make you happy but I only make you more unhappy. When you told me four years ago that you hated me I tried to make myself believe you didn't mean it. When you told me two years ago that you loathed the touch of my body that it made you crawl and feel sick to have my arms around you I knew that I had lost out and that all hope that the love which Willie took away would come back was gone. It was all there was in life that mattered to me except Kiddens and Bub and there has been no real fun for me ever since. I just took it that God didn't want me to have any real happiness and tried to readjust my life. . . . You told me last July—just a year ago—before we went to Campo—that you hated my touch. So I gave up that also and from that time on have kept my vow never to ask it of you again unless you asked first.

Howe then reiterated his conviction that poor health could bring about his death at any time, a notion with which he had lived since his earliest childhood. He then turned to the situation with Eleanor.

I have said nothing of Eleanor for I know that in your heart you know that there is not, nor ever could be anything to which you really could object. She has been dear and kind to Mary and Bub and you and she has done much to make what was a very hard place for me to be in endurable. Can you blame me if in my utter loneliness I have found her friendship a very pleasant thing.

Do you want me give that up too?[25]

CHAPTER TWELVE

MINOR TRIUMPHS
OF A MAJOR TYPE

In late July 1922, Alfred Smith wasn't saying anything. Belle Moskowitz was waiting. Tammany's Charles Murphy wouldn't answer any questions, and Hearst was in California.[1]

Something would have to end the indecision on Smith's part, eventually, but he'd already received letters from a roster of influential Democrats without budging. With or without Smith, September promised dates from which there was no turning back. The State Democratic Convention in Syracuse was due to start September 27. Even more important, at least in certain circles, *When Knighthood Was in Flower* was to premier at the Criterion Theater in New York September 21. Crews were redecorating the movie palace for the gala.

Franklin Roosevelt was among the many who corresponded with Alfred Smith that summer; they discussed the letter that Roosevelt had sent to the Syracuse conference. Roosevelt pointed out that in it he had stopped short of asking Smith for a statement, because that would have put the former governor on the spot. Roosevelt was breezy, but deferential; Smith was brief and duly grateful. The ex-governor was inundated with letters and other communiqués asking him to step in and turn away Hearst. "They were all unanimous that the fight would not be effective unless I was willing to become a candidate myself," Smith later wrote. "This I was reluctant to do. Having had a long and stormy political career, I was content to stay in business."[2]

For the time being in late July, the stage was left to Hearst, which is to say, Fingy Conners, chomping a thick cigar and slamming the table, as a reporter noted, "with his jeweled fist." The same reporter, D. T. Lynch of the *New York Tribune*, took note of the appearance of the colorful magnate at one press conference. Actually, he was not colorful at all that day, but was, rather, "a symphony of silver and black, wearing a shepherd's plaid suit, [and] a black cravat which fell gracefully over a shirt of soft white linen."[3] The papers had little choice but to run descriptions of Fingy's fashion sense. The Democrats were stalled, and the cut of Fingy's suits passed for news.

Franklin Roosevelt continued with his regimen of exercise and the banter that went with it when friends were on hand. Using crutches, he went into New York every few weeks to call on the Fidelity & Deposit office "to see that it is still chained down," as he put it.[4] Every so often, he received a letter encouraging him to run for governor, senator, or president—or anything—but he had to shrug that kind of talk away. In truth, he might have had a hard time winning a major election, even if he hadn't been recently ill.

Roosevelt's former boss at the Navy Department, Josephus Daniels, thought his old friend's future in politics was uncertain at best. He later looked back on Roosevelt in the span following his illness and listed his political liabilities—the paralysis didn't even make the top three. First was his graduation from the elite Groton School ("one of the worst things that could happen to a man who wants to be a Democratic candidate"); second was his graduation from Harvard (a bastion of "conservative and Republican ideas"); third was his pathetic loss in the 1914 senatorial primary ("Everyone said that was the end of Franklin Roosevelt"), and then, Daniels added, there was the paralysis.[5]

Joseph M. Proskauer was a flinty lawyer who was second only to Mrs. Moskowitz as an adviser to Alfred Smith. He was never enthusiastic about

Roosevelt, and recalled that in the very early 1920s the feeling was shared by others. "During those years," Proskauer said, "Roosevelt was not very prominent in politics, despite his nomination in San Francisco for the Vice Presidency, and none of us took him very seriously. At that time, there was a tendency to laugh at Roosevelt a little for that performance about the sena- torship." Proskauer was referring to the state legislature's standoff in 1911. "He opposed Sheehan's candidacy for the Senate and according to the gospel won a great victory. The victory was that instead of getting Sheehan, who was a pretty good upstate lawyer, they withdrew him and nominated a Tammany Hall judge, O'Gorman, that they would much rather have nomi- nated in the first place. And that was generally known in politics in those days. It accounted a little bit for the lack of seriousness with which Mr. Roosevelt was regarded in those days."[6] Proskauer asserted that Alfred Smith shared that attitude. "Smith," he said, "did not believe that Roosevelt had real ability."[7]

Roosevelt never expressed anything but friendly admiration for Smith. If he and Howe had wanted to topple or at least undercut him, they could have ignited the old upstate argument against Tammany Hall, of which Smith was a product. But Smith had managed to rise above that fray. And anyway, as of 1922, what was good for Alfred Smith was good for Franklin Roosevelt. Smith had charted the liberal path for New York that Roosevelt meant to follow for himself someday. The best possible scenario for Roo- sevelt was the reestablishment of that path by Smith. He could follow on its firm footing later. In terms of party organization, Franklin dared not think what wreckage Hearst might leave for those who followed him.

On the last day of July, writing to a woman who had sent him a story of Hearstian treachery in Painted Post, New York, Roosevelt reflected on the Hearst methods, as he had heard about them in his own neighborhood. "About ten days ago," he told her, "Mr. Connors [sic] stopped off in Pough- keepsie for a few minutes, sent for a certain disgruntled member of the County Committee and promised him all sorts of money said to be any- where from four to twenty thousand dollars to get the delegate to the con- vention from this County." Roosevelt promised that if Hearst were the nominee, he would exercise his right to write in Smith's name.[8]

Harriet May Mills also contacted Roosevelt, asking for money to help the women of the Democratic State Committee buy a car—just an inexpensive Model T—for her and her coworker, Marion Dickerman, to use in campaigning all over the state. She didn't mention Eleanor, who was, after all, a member of her Finance Committee, but then, it was just a form letter sent to "a few of our leading Democratic men." His reply didn't mention Eleanor, either. After committing to a fifty-dollar donation toward the car, he brought up the Hearst question, which had completely captured his fighting spirit. "I know you must be getting some information in regard to the Hearst efforts upstate," he wrote. "I hope you will feel free to write me confidentially in regard to them at anytime."[9] Mills was Eleanor's friend, and the work of the women in the party was Eleanor's growing occupation that summer. As Franklin made clear in his letter to Mills, though, he was independent of his wife in his own political pursuits, just as he always had been.

Louis Howe, having postponed his vacation to Horseneck Beach, had taken care at the beginning of August to attend a Boy Scout reception on Bear Mountain, a state park about twenty miles north of New York City. Hartley was a Scout in Fall River, but that had nothing to do with why Howe attended the gathering at Bear Mountain. Alfred Smith was going to be there, and Howe managed to run into him. A few days later, a Buffalo politician traveled to New York City to see Smith. No letters, no telegrams: he showed up in Smith's office at the trucking company and told him bluntly that his county, Erie, was going to choose Hearst delegates, if there was no one else in the running. After that point, as they both knew perfectly well, it wouldn't matter what Smith decided. The delegates would be locked in.

———————

Smith harbored personal animosity for Hearst because of a series of particularly offensive lies about him published in Hearst newspapers when he was governor. There was one about killing babies by keeping the price of milk high that was unfounded and apparently unforgettable. In his memoirs, Smith referred to it as part of his motivation for coming to a decision about the race of 1922. He imagined Erie County sending Hearst delegates to the convention and he saw events unfolding after that to make Hearst governor.

Roosevelt chose that moment to write Smith a letter, doing just what he had not done in the letter to the Syracuse meeting in July: he requested that Smith make an announcement of his plans. The letter was released to newspapers as soon as it was delivered to Smith's home and it was published all over the state on August 15. Howe had probably gotten wind of Smith's thinking, or at least he had laid the groundwork for some participation by Roosevelt when he met Smith at the Boy Scout reception. If the letter was actually sent without any advance planning, it represented a risky move on Roosevelt's part because the content was patently well considered. Had Roosevelt's dramatic gesture, his call to arms, been ignored by Smith, it would look as though Roosevelt were sadly out of touch or simply out of favor. Joseph Proskauer would have one more false step to snigger about.

"I am taking it upon myself," Roosevelt wrote, placing his reputation on the line, "to appeal to you in the name of countless citizens of upstate New York, Democrats, Republicans, Independents, men and women—to ask you to say now not later that if nominated for Governor you will accept."[10]

The letter was either going to be very big news or a fizzle in the 1922 campaign. The *New York Times* wasn't sure which and printed it on page 13, while everyone waited to see what happened next. The following day, the *Times* printed Smith's reply on page one. "Dear Frank," it began, "I have your letter of August 13th and I have carefully read it. I appreciate your kindly sentiments and they compel me to talk to you straight from my heart." After describing his sense of obligation to the party, Smith affirmed that he would "answer the call."[11]

Ultimately, Roosevelt's letter received as much publicity as Smith's. The two together were referred to as the "Dear Al–Dear Frank correspondence." On the whole, the party was relieved that the suspense was over. But it was far from healed. A reporter found the mayor of New York, Mike Hylan—a Hearst supporter—reading the two letters together: "'I can't figure out who Frank Roosevelt represents,' the mayor murmured with a puzzled frown," ran the reporter's account.[12] The bad news for the party was that even Roosevelt's straightforward endorsement was run through a filter of suspicion and paranoia by a party veteran such as Hylan. The good news for Louis Howe and for Eleanor Roosevelt was that "Frank" was representing himself again in the political world.

Roosevelt was given credit for taking charge of the situation when it seemed to be adrift and for acting the elder statesman in bringing it to a conclusion. George Foster Peabody, an investment banker from Saratoga Springs, was among the many who wrote with gratitude to Roosevelt in August. "You did a high public service," Peabody wrote. "I am glad to express my sense of indebtedness to you."[13] It was a minor victory, but a buoyant one for Roosevelt, who had after all had gone to Groton, graduated from Harvard, lost in 1914, and faced down a paralyzing illness in 1921. In fact, his letter to Smith was written a year and a day after he lay in bed at Campobello, unable to move from the chest down.

———◆———

The year had brought Roosevelt's physical recovery a long way. The strength in his upper body was good—he could beat his teenage sons at either arm-wrestling or real wrestling, whichever they preferred. His energy, however, had not returned to its peak, in his own opinion. The paralysis itself was not perceptibly better than it had been when he left New York Presbyterian Hospital ten months before.[14]

After a year, the effects of the illness were becoming part of his personality. Remarkably, those effects were not perceived to have been negative by anyone close to him. Bitterness, regret, and disappointment bypassed him. "Not once during the critical part of his illness," said Howe in a later interview, "did he show any signs of discouragement or despair."[15] There were sporadic reports that in the morning he was sometimes blue, but he seemed to be able to snap himself out of it when someone entered the room. Those near to him found that the lasting changes in Roosevelt were positive ones.

Eleanor drew criticism for remarking in her second memoir that "Franklin's illness ... proved to be a blessing in disguise."[16] She was thought to be callous in finding something to celebrate in paralysis—as long as it was someone else's. Eleanor and Louis had given something of themselves to sustain him during the first year after he was stricken. They were each in a good position to note the changes that year brought. "He had to think out the fundamentals of living," she wrote, "and learn the greatest of all lessons—infinite patience and never-ending persistence."[17]

Howe's opinion, expressed to Lela Stiles, was quite similar in spirit. "You see, he had a thousand interests," Howe said of Roosevelt. "You couldn't pin him down. He rode, he swam, he played golf, tennis, he sailed, he collected stamps, he politicked, he did about every damn thing under the sun a man could think of doing. Then suddenly there he was flat on his back, with nothing to do but think. He began to read, he began to think, he talked, he gathered people around him—his thoughts expanded, his horizon widened. He began to see the other fellow's point of view. He thought of others who were ill and affected and in want. He dwelt on things which had not bothered him much before. Lying there, he grew bigger day by day."[18]

Roosevelt still had a kaleidoscope of hobbies and interests, but more of them, as Howe noted, tended toward a contemplative side that he had not allowed himself to explore before.

With the letter to Al Smith and the swell of respect it inspired, the Roosevelt comeback had begun. He would still be referring to it months later, as though Smith would never have found a way into the election without him. And perhaps he wouldn't.

Once Smith had announced himself as a candidate, "the war began," as one newspaper noted gleefully. The rush for delegates was the first battle. About 730 were expected at the convention in Syracuse. Though Smith's forces were vocal about courting the women's vote, only about 110 of the delegates chosen in the scramble of late August were women. In Dutchess County, where Eleanor was leading the Women's Committee with her friend Elinor Morgenthau, the proportion was much better. Four of the eight delegates were female. Eleanor was one of them; Franklin was accorded the honor of selection as an alternate.[19]

At the end of August, Marion Dickerman and Nancy Cook were driving on a short vacation upstate and stopped to see a friend near Hyde Park.

She commented to them that she'd heard they were staying at the Roosevelts' house for the weekend. They didn't know anything about it and so the friend called Eleanor, who said that her invitation to the two women must not have arrived in time—but it still stood. The chance to snag Dickerman and Cook, two Democrats connected to high-level state party activities, was too good to miss in the strategy long since established by Eleanor and Louis. Franklin, in particular, was a glutton for news, tidbits, confidences, and plain political gossip. Dickerman and Cook were sure to bring it.

"He could never just go about," Dickerman later explained. "That's where Louis filled in. But there were many, many evenings that that man was alone."[20] For that August weekend, at least, Eleanor had just the kind of guests she and Howe looked for: two women who knew all the latest news—and didn't want anything from Roosevelt.

Dickerman and Cook drove to Hyde Park, met the Roosevelt family, and were a hit with both Franklin and Eleanor. "There were so many interests, ambitions, desires that we shared," Dickerman said, "that we all became close friends."[21] Franklin enjoyed them both and, in fact, would remain friends with them for the rest of his life. They met Howe soon after. While he was delighted to have fresh faces and lively conversation brought to Roosevelt, he was known to become jealous when someone presumed to occupy his territory as best friend and chief protector. Dickerman easily sidestepped that problem; she looked past Howe's gruff manner and adored him.

———— •◆•· ————

The timing of the visit by Dickerman and Cook was propitious for Eleanor. Howe wrote that Grace's reaction to the depth of his relationship with Eleanor had been impossible for Eleanor to ignore, that "it hurt her very much."[22] Eleanor couldn't distance herself from Howe, but an emotional year with him, punctuated by the upset over Grace near the end of that year, had probably made the opportunity for new friends and new fields appealing to her. Eleanor was coming into her own as a leader in the

state Democratic Party and so, as Dickerman observed, their interests coincided. They were upstaters, as were all the people closest to the Roosevelts.
Marion told her biographer, Kenneth S. Davis, in speaking of her immediate acceptance by the Roosevelts, that "at the time it seemed perfectly natural, as everything about the Roosevelts seemed always natural, never
artificial or pretentious."[23]

As the convention approached in late September, Hearst was still a serious contender, though the question of the day was which elected office interested him most. In the interest of peace in the party, his representatives,
including Fingy Conners, suggested that Hearst would run for governor,
while Smith could run for the open seat in the U.S. Senate.[24] Smith did not
take the offer. Then Hearst's forces suggested that Smith could run for governor and Hearst would run for Senate. The assumption was that anyone
who could do one job could do the other, which overlooked the fact that the
two offices have practically nothing in common.

Five other slots on the statewide ticket were open, including comptroller and lieutenant governor. Harriet May Mills had run for secretary of state
in 1920, losing by a wider margin than the others on the Democratic ticket.
In 1922, as delegates arrived in Syracuse, four women were being cited as
potential candidates for state office: Mills, who was the most powerful
woman in the state's Democratic politics; Marion Dickerman, still remembered for her valiant run for state Senate in 1919; and Caroline O'Day,
known among the enlightened as an eloquent speaker and among the practical as "the wife of a Standard oil millionaire." (Actually, her father-in-law
had been the Standard Oil man; her late husband, Daniel O'Day, had been
an independent oil king.)

The fourth woman being touted for a nomination was Eleanor Roosevelt.[25]

Eleanor had dozens of good friends at the convention, including Louis
Howe, who was on the ground as Franklin's representative. Howe was
equally devoted to Eleanor. He may even have been more devoted to
Eleanor on a personal basis, but if she was going to be a candidate for
statewide office, he had to run it through his instinctive analysis, the one
that snapped with an answer in response to every letter that arrived, every

article that appeared in the newspaper, and every person who asked for a favor. He had to calculate how her candidacy would affect Franklin's path to the White House. The answer had to be that it couldn't help. It would confuse the electorate, most of whom were probably still trying to figure out his relationship to the late Theodore Roosevelt, and more recently, TR's politically active son, Theodore Jr. A run by Eleanor would also lend the impression that Franklin was out of politics for good.

The idea that Eleanor was discussed as a viable candidate reflected how far she had come in her seven months in the political sphere. She had a valuable name, of course, and expert tutelage by Howe, but on the eve of the convention, she was on her own in the thick of delegate negotiations and caucus meetings. Two days before the convention's opening session, the female delegates held a general meeting and spontaneously voted on a resolution demanding that two of the seven statewide offices should go to women. Specifically they named Caroline O'Day or Marion Dickerman for secretary of state and Eleanor Roosevelt or Harriet May Mills for comptroller.[26] If they had wanted, they could have ensured that women receive those slots by offering their votes to whichever gubernatorial candidate would, in turn, throw his support to them. They didn't lose sight of the top-tier fight, though, voting in approval of another resolution that pledged their votes to Alfred Smith.[27]

———————

The next day Alfred Smith arrived in Syracuse unable to walk. An attack of neuritis was confining him to his hotel suite—or so he said. In view of the struggle at hand, the neuritis may have been a convenient excuse to force people to come and see him, so that he could exert that much more control: seeing only those people he wanted to see. As the convention began, Smith was the front-runner, but leaders wanted to avoid a floor fight and unify the party. They calmly suggested that Smith run for governor and Hearst for Senate. He stopped the party leaders cold by refusing unequivocally to run on a ticket with Hearst. Smith repeated his own reason, stemming from the Hearst press's ridiculous accusation that he had purposely starved babies of their milk. Belle Moskowitz was just as adamant, arguing that Republicans would defeat them both simply by repeating excerpts from their three-year-old feud.

"Alfred E. Smith will never consent to join with Mr. Hearst," she said to reporters, "but he will be nominated just the same, and he will be elected."[28]

The Smith contingent of Democratic women staged a dinner on the night before the convention. Expecting two hundred and fifty people, they ultimately had to find ways to accommodate an overflow crowd of five hundred. Caroline O'Day, serving as the emcee, whipped the room into a cheering, stomping frenzy with her rollicking endorsement of Smith. At one point she introduced Alfred's wife, Mrs. Catherine Dunn Smith, who timidly stood up and waved. "Mrs. Smith couldn't be induced to say a word," wrote a reporter. Harriet May Mills was glad to be the next speaker. Mills, who could be very funny, "carried enthusiasm to a high pitch," according to the same report.[29] Then it was Eleanor's turn. O'Day and Mills had been at their best. The room was electric, they were a hard act to follow. Mrs. Smith had probably done the smart thing, to wave and muster a smile. Eleanor, however, stood up. She went to the front of the room. She didn't try to continue the rousing style or repeat the crowd-pleasing messages of the previous speakers. Trained by Howe's advice, she took her own route, to "have something to say, say it and then sit down."[30]

Eleanor was all for cheering, but it was organization that won elections. She had seen that with her own eyes in Franklin's unceasing efforts to encourage leadership and structure in every forsaken corner of the state. "Democratic men," she began, "have suffered from apathy and laziness. They have felt so long that no matter what they do they can't win their local tickets, that they are all out of enthusiasm. They lose sight of the fact that every Democratic vote cast, increases the minority. Go back to your counties and be enthusiastic. Give the men something to work for hopefully."[31]

The next day, Eleanor's speech was quoted in newspapers around the state and received banner coverage as well: "Democratic Male of Species Apathetic, Says Mrs. Roosevelt," ran one headline.[32]

———◆◆◆———

The following afternoon, just before the convention was to begin, the Democratic women held another meeting out of sheer frustration at being denied a role in the preconvention deliberations, which were tense and critical—and very exciting. Party leaders visited Smith in his suite and begged him to agree to allow Hearst on the slate. He wouldn't budge. Most of the leaders wanted him to capitulate, but not all of them did. One old crony opened the door, put his head in, said "stick," and then shut the door.[33] Smith did stick, as the pressure mounted.

The female delegates played no part in the deliberations, but then neither did the majority of the male delegates. The real action was behind closed doors. And so the women went behind closed doors, too. They were not hostile, however. Quite the opposite: in the interest of harmony, they withdrew their resolution concerning the two slots on the ticket. Anyway, the common wisdom predicted that it wouldn't have carried at the convention. The women did, however, want the men to notice that "they were a force to contend with and a force of which effective use could be made."[34]

Once again, speeches were made to express the excitement and the frustration of the women at the convention. A number of the speakers used Eleanor's message from the night before about building up local organizations. When Eleanor was called on to address the crowd, her new speech shifted in topic. "Stand up and praise whenever you can," Eleanor said. "How on earth are your elected representatives going to know what you want them to do unless you tell them. Praise them when you can and when you can't be sure to make it clear to them why you can't."[35]

In the hotel suites where the real business of the convention was under way, Alfred Smith was still refusing to run on the same ticket as William Hearst. Charles Murphy finally weighed in after keeping his counsel for days. He sent an emissary to try and persuade Smith to cooperate with Hearst. In previous years and with other candidates, Murphy's word was law. Smith, however, sent the emissary away. He knew that he had the delegates to win the nomination and that he had the hearts of New Yorkers to carry him through the general election. It was a watershed moment in New York politics. A Tammany man was ignoring a Tammany boss.

———◆———

During the day, Conners sent a telegram to Hearst, who was in New York awaiting developments; aloof by nature, Hearst preferred to rely on seconds to bring him the results he wanted. The telegram expressed Smith's position and his refusal to change it. Hearst calmly sent a return wire withdrawing his name from consideration for statewide office. The effect was momentarily stunning. The convention had been girding for a brawl of historic proportions. Instead, Hearst bowed out without rancor or hullabaloo. He simply sent a message stating that he wouldn't have wanted to be on a ticket with a conservative such as Smith anyway.

Smith had the satisfaction of permanently destroying Hearst's political aspirations. Whether Hearst was outwardly angry about that, as the convention started in Syracuse, no one recorded, but, as he would prove, he was always a patient man when it came to returning a favor.

A few hours later at the convention, amid wild cheering, Alfred Smith's name was placed in nomination for governor. "Your missus led the Dutchess County delegation with the banner three times around the hall," Howe wired to Franklin that night.[36] He then continued with a whole line of points and observations, reminders, and witticisms, intended to blow a bit of the confetti into the empty room of the man who loved the game more than anyone.

During the election, Roosevelt dispensed advice and made his first public appearance since his paralysis at a reception he and Eleanor hosted for Alfred and Katie Smith on the lawn of Springwood. After Smith won the governorship in November, Roosevelt wrote to a Democrat in New York City. "We can all congratulate ourselves upon the fine results of election day," he started. "I had quite a tussle to keep our friend Hearst off the ticket and to get Al Smith to run, but the thing went through in fine shape."[37]

From Louis Howe's standpoint, it had been a sublime campaign. Franklin Roosevelt was in the "tussle" and even masterminding it, according to the picture in his own mind's eye. That was all right, considering where Roosevelt had been the year before. Howe had been politicking hard, working the floor to support the perception of Franklin. With hundreds of delegates—local party workers of the type Howe considered invaluable—the convention offered more than enough for him to do.

At the Democratic women's general meeting the first day of the convention, Eleanor had had no speech prepared. She had simply said what she knew at that moment. "You can accomplish a lot if you go ahead with a stout heart and are human," she told them.[38] The audience was rapt, and reporters took to their pads to write down what she said. In the back of the room, sitting in a familiar place where Eleanor knew to look, would be a man content, as she held her own, just to listen with the rest.

CHAPTER THIRTEEN

THE SMITH ERA

After the autumn of 1922, the relationship between Louis Howe and the Roosevelts did not change materially. That is not to say that the two quite different friendships weren't tested as all three grew busier and crowded more people into their lives, but with Franklin, on one hand, and Eleanor, on the other, Howe's dealings remained stable, after the seminal transitions of the previous thirteen months. Eleanor came to him for advice; Franklin received a constant stream of it, whether he asked or not.

The relationship that did change was that of the Roosevelt family to Springwood. In part because of Howe's pressure to use it as a meeting place for Democrats of all types, the family didn't feel quite as much at home there as they once had.[1] Anna was still struggling with jealousy and resentment, regarding her mother. "I felt that when I wanted to see her, she and Louis would be in very deep conversation, talking about things," she later recalled, "Obviously I wasn't wanted, when these conversations were going on, and it was hard."[2] Though Anna's hurt feelings were lessened at Springwood, where the woods offered a retreat, Sara Roosevelt's ill will was, if anything, intensified there, with Howe living under the same roof. Both Anna and Sara would change their minds about Howe, but not until they learned to live with a different sort of household, for the sake of Franklin and Eleanor. That wasn't easy—not even for Franklin and Eleanor.

In response to the year of transition, both Roosevelts needed new scenery, or were ready to exert individual preferences. Franklin, whose love of Springwood was in his blood, was the first to break out in search of a place that was carefree, quiet, and private. Not so long before, Springwood had been all three. In 1923, he rented a motor yacht in which to ply the waters off of Florida. Howe was onboard for one cruise through the Florida Keys. That summer, he also convinced Franklin to stay with him at Horseneck Beach, which was as rustic as ever and just as inaccessible. Roosevelt enjoyed himself, but his idea of a vacation cottage was the eighteen-bedroom house at Campobello. He termed the Horseneck house "wee."[3] For Howe, though, the snug simplicity of the place was a large part of the attraction. For the duration of the stay, he hired two servants to help because at times Roosevelt had to be carried. Eleanor paid a visit, while touring New England with Marion Dickerman and Nancy Cook. Howe was pleased to play the host to all. "It was a very crude camp on the sand there," Dickerman recalled. "Franklin went and stayed with him quite a long time. They were practically alone and he could crawl down to the water and he could crawl on the sand, crawl back and nobody would be watching him."[4]

When the winter of 1924 arrived, Roosevelt was more enthusiastic about Florida than ever, buying a houseboat with a friend from Harvard. Howe was a regular guest on the boat, called the *Larooco*, which typically sailed with a few friends onboard. Eleanor gave it one try and thought it was much more trouble than it was worth. Franklin would eventually come to the same opinion, but for a time, it seemed to offer a sense of freedom he hadn't felt since his illness. Howe looked on the *Larooco* as a floating funhouse, to which he contributed more than his share of gags and homemade entertainment. On one trip, he put himself in charge of keeping the ship's log, which was highly decorated as a result, and also a bit bawdy.[5]

When Roosevelt was away from New York, Howe took his place, watching over the insurance business at Fidelity & Deposit and carrying on much of the general correspondence that went out under Roosevelt's name. As to the law firm, Roosevelt resigned from it in September of 1924. Not only was it a money-losing venture for him, but the work itself was unappealing, as he wrote to one of his partners. He reflected that his background equipped him for "practical management of business of one kind or another." In the meantime, he continued to rebuild his political credentials, he speculated in a small way in business propositions and he even tried a new profession, writing a scenario for a movie serial on the life of John Paul Jones.[6] Submitted to Paramount Pictures, it was never produced.

"Louis," wrote Eleanor in her second memoir, "worked unceasingly in New York."[7] To a friend, Howe described his life in the city with wry humor. "I am wasting my young life looking at 90 story buildings that need washing," he wrote, "trying to make believe that what I am breathing is real air, although I know better."[8]

Howe watched over the F & D in a general way and facilitated contact between the sales force and people in government. He devoted most of his time, though, to meetings with anyone who might eventually help Roosevelt. Howe's master plan called for Franklin to re-enter politics in the early 1930s and so he was layering support far in advance, with those in the party and in other fields, as well: lawyer John Davis; the influential clergyman Harry Emerson Fosdick, and Boston mayor James Curley, for example.[9] "Mr. [Van Lear] Black has asked me to go over to Baltimore tomorrow," Louis wrote to Franklin in 1924, "for a conference with Gov. Ritchie."[10] Albert Ritchie, the governor of Maryland, was a popular, well-established Democrat with presidential aspirations of his own.

Serving as Roosevelt's surrogate in private meetings with people of all personalities, most of them powerful, Louis Howe couldn't afford to fail. Apparently he didn't. The man that so many in the Navy Department disparaged as ill-kempt and bad-mannered presented a better picture with those he courted on behalf of his boss. In fact, he seemed to revert to his Saratoga days, when mixing with celebrities and charming strangers was his summer sport. In 1925, Howe called on *New York Times* publisher Adolph Ochs and wrote to Roosevelt about it afterward:

Ochs paid me the compliment of giving me a half hour and then sending out word to the people who were waiting that he had an important matter on and settling down for a two hour talk instead. I think he is thoroughly sold and has promised the support of the "Times," editorially and otherwise.[11]

Every few days, Howe would send Roosevelt a letter rounding up the latest incidents in the spheres of business, politics, and the newspapers. In effect, they constituted Howe's own newspaper, written for one person. "I took lunch with some of the Albany boys," he wrote in a juicy tidbit in his February 25, 1924, dispatch, "and they told me in one way at least Smith is much drier than he used to be." Smith's friends, including Roosevelt, were often forced to deny publicly that the anti-Prohibition governor liked to drink. "How long he has sworn off this time, God knows," Howe wrote. "Let us trust until after the national convention."[12] Roosevelt, onboard the *Larooco*, answered Howe's letter from "My-am-eye" (as he playfully spelled "Miami") in twelve points, the longest of which pertained to the boat and the cruise. Roosevelt's letters were invariably shorter and less concerned with politics than those he received from Howe, who still bore the burden of leaning his boss into a political frame of mind when other distractions presented themselves.

As Elliott Roosevelt pointed out in his memoir, his parents often used Howe as a conduit for messages. The temptation would be strong to do so: Franklin corresponded with Louis regularly and Eleanor saw him on a daily basis at East Sixty-Fifth Street. "Your family are all well and flourishing," Howe added to a letter of political news in 1924, in advance of the Democratic National Convention, "and your Mrs. is having a gorgeous scrap trying to get Nancy [Cook] made an alternate."[13]

"Try to persuade Eleanor to bring Anna," Franklin wrote to Louis in March, when he was hoping to arrange a visit from his wife to the *Larooco*.[14] He included contingencies regarding which of the children might come along with or instead of Anna. Eleanor, however, didn't manage any visit that year. By early 1924, Eleanor Roosevelt was deeply involved in her work with the Women's Division of the State Democratic Committee. She was also a committed supporter of Alfred Smith.

———◆———

Smith was widely regarded as the vanguard of a reshaped Democratic Party. He had compiled a dazzling record in his second term as governor, finding ways to improve housing, care for the elderly, labor practices, and human rights as his administration served as a testing ground for a strong, even insistent, social agenda. Smith's leadership was controversial, of course, but enough people across the country admired his priorities to shift the party for good, giving it a liberal strain that could not be ignored. Even more than most newly crowned heroes, though, Smith had his debts. Edward Flynn, a Tammany man known for clear thinking, gave Boss Murphy credit for Smith's success. "Mr. Murphy has been sadly neglected in so far as progressive legislation is concerned," Flynn said later, in relation to the histories being written of the era, "None of the progressive legislation in Albany could have been passed unless he urged it and permitted it to be passed."[15]

As a Tammany boss, Murphy needed support from the neighborhoods. To get it, he could either fool the people or serve them. He chose the latter. Perhaps it was easier in the long run. While others at the 1922 State Convention—notably Alfred Smith—were locked in combat over William Hearst's ambitions, Tammany district leader Jeremiah T. Mahoney was taking Murphy's direction in rewriting the party platform, stacking it with ideas for social reform, from unemployment insurance to old age pensions. "We created the foundation upon which others built," Mahoney said, "This all started with Charles F. Murphy."[16]

Smith had even stronger influence from inside his camp. With Mrs. Moskowitz as his primary adviser, Joseph Proskauer as a close second, and Frances Perkins as head of the Department of Labor, he could not have looked away from neglected parts of the population even if he had wanted to. Frances Perkins, in a conversation with Proskauer, later reminisced, "When Smith was Governor, he and I and you and Belle Moskowitz framed and fought for all the social legislation that made New York the pioneer."

"It was true," Proskauer replied in recalling the story.[17]

Flynn was more pointed, regarding Smith's legacy. "Belle Moskowitz was, without any question," he said, "the one person who did mold his opinions to the extent that she showed him the awful conditions that existed."[18]

Roosevelt often wrote to Smith early in his term as governor, giving him specific suggestions on handling personnel and legislation. Smith's replies were polite, but uninterested. Both of the Roosevelts were wary of Smith—but not of his leadership in state government. Eleanor believed that his liberalism derived from political expediency, and she doubted his sincerity as a humanitarian. Yet she was completely in accord with his record and the team of reformers with whom he surrounded himself.

In February 1924, Governor Smith made it known that he was seeking the nomination for president. Pressed by Mrs. Moskowitz, he calculated that his stellar record as a reformer in New York would overshadow the prejudice of some voters—many voters in 1924—against a Roman Catholic, and one who advocated the repeal of Prohibition at that. When Roosevelt returned to New York in late March, after putting the *Larooco* in storage, he was asked to serve as chairman of the Smith for President Committee. Smith considered it an honorary title, however, and ran his own campaign in tandem with Mrs. Moskowitz. That was probably to be expected. Roosevelt and Howe continued to work on the governor's behalf, though, using an extensive list of contacts to swing support to him.

Roosevelt had long placed a high value on realignment of the political parties. The optimum scenario in any political battle, of course, would be to find a way to lump the electorate into two neat categories: people who agree on every single issue and people who believe the opposite on every issue. In reality, the parties contain people of all stripes, which is frustrating to the professional politician who has less than a year to sort them all out. "If we can get the people to understand," Roosevelt wrote, "that the Republicans are hopelessly split between the ultra-radicals and the ultra-conservatives, and that the Democracy is the true party of liberal progress there will be every chance for a victory in 1924."[19] Aside from considerations of loyalty, Roosevelt's support for Smith reflected the fact that the New York governor was doing more to carve out an avenue of "liberal progress" than anyone else who was active in the party in the mid-1920s.

One loyal supporter wrote to Roosevelt and expressed the wish that he would enter the race for president. Roosevelt replied quite cheerfully that he wouldn't run for any office, "not even dog catcher," until he could walk without crutches.[20] Still Roosevelt, could hear the bell. Writing to a friend before Smith announced his candidacy, Roosevelt had predicted, "The Democratic candidate will be somebody in whom neither you nor I have given a passing thought." Then he added wistfully, "What an opportunity for someone to capture the public imagination in some sound and forceful way."[21] Howe was thinking the same thing, only he knew that the opportunity didn't necessarily have to be in the form of a candidacy.

———◆———

The Smith campaign needed someone to deliver the nominating speech for the governor at the Democratic National Convention to be held at Madison Square Garden in New York City in late June. It wasn't a matter of overwhelming importance, mostly because Tammany Hall was already planning a spontaneous outburst, just like the one that had greeted Smith's name at the 1920 convention—only that one had actually been spontaneous. In 1924, Smith's name would be greeted with riotous cheering, no matter what. Nonetheless, the person who made the nominating speech would have a moment in the spotlight before fourteen thousand of the most prominent Democrats in the country.

Howe decided that Roosevelt should give the speech and Eleanor agreed. The two of them worked together to convince Smith, each using their contacts to move the idea up to him. Eleanor, working closely with Mrs. Moskowitz at the Women's Division of the State Democratic Committee, was probably in the better position to make the point heard. When Smith was finally approached with the idea, he was skeptical at first. He was concerned about Roosevelt's health and his ability to deliver a major speech.

Having the nominating speaker trip or fall or faint or simply look ill on the platform would be detrimental to Smith and make any cheering at the sound of his name seem crass and insensitive. Howe rose to action at that point and arranged a meeting with Smith to assure him that Roosevelt could indeed move around very well. It wasn't exactly true, but Howe had faith that Roosevelt would somehow carry the day. Smith agreed.

Howe had yet to close the back end of the deal, which involved telling Franklin. He relied on Missy LeHand and on Eleanor to help with the job of selling the idea. Roosevelt was as afraid as Smith had been of the risk involved. If he should collapse while approaching the rostrum, his political career might never recover. Roosevelt was probably right about that, but he was also tempted. Finally, he said that if he were able to stand at the rostrum without assistance, he would make the speech. Howe promised him that he could. The two of them planned and practiced for weeks—not the speech, but the walk leading up to it. As with many people who appear confident and even nonchalant in public, Roosevelt was meticulous in his preparation behind the scenes—as the convention approached, he was certainly not confident and anything but nonchalant. "Nobody knows how that man worked," Marion Dickerman said in an interview at Columbia University. "They measured off in the library at the 65th Street house just what that distance was, and he struggled and struggled and struggled."[22]

The speech itself was ultimately written by Joseph Proskauer. To Roosevelt's annoyance, Smith and Moskowitz turned down his draft in favor of Proskauer's, which was more straightforward, except for one literary reference. Roosevelt capitulated, though not without resistence. After the convention began on June 24 at the old Madison Square Garden in New York, he arrived early each day so that he could be seated before any of the other delegates spotted him walking on crutches. On June 26, the convention was scheduled to hear Smith's nomination, and Roosevelt's speech. Seventeen thousand people were packed into the Garden—which had a maximum capacity of fourteen thousand, according to the fire department. People were in the aisles, sitting on barricades, and watching from the outer hallways, as best they could.

Roosevelt was expected to nominate Smith when the delegation from New York was called in a roll-call of the states. Just before noon, as the roll-call was proceeding, Connecticut yielded to New York and, suddenly, it was Roosevelt's moment. With help, he rose from his chair and started on his way to the platform a short distance away. It wasn't a speedy process. The delegates at the deeply divided convention began to cheer and didn't fade.

James, who was sixteen at the time, walked his father to the front of the hall. Roosevelt used one crutch and leaned on James. "I was afraid and I know he was, too," James wrote. "As we walked—struggled, really—down the aisle to the rear of the platform, he leaned heavily on my arm, gripping me so hard it hurt."[23]

Marion Dickerman was in the audience as a delegate. As she recalled, "Franklin walked, with the aid of Jimmy and a crutch, to the podium. Then the sun came out, and as it shone through the skylight, it struck his head, and you know what a handsome person he was. It was very dramatic."[24] Only after Roosevelt was securely standing at the podium did the delegates, escorting him with their voices, grow quiet, at least for a moment. Roosevelt's old family friend, Huybertie Pruyn Hamlin, was sitting on the side of the speaker's platform. "Franklin stood at the desk on the platform as if nothing was wrong with him—his fine height and superb head showing in silhouette from where we sat."[25]

"Leaning forward," James continued, "he rested one crutch against [the rostrum] and raised one arm to wave at the crowd. He was still smiling. The crowd gave him an ovation." Smith's daughter, Emily, was in the audience, caught up in the moment. "I shall never forget the thrill I felt as I sat on the edge of my chair and watched him grip the rostrum firmly with both hands and begin to speak," she wrote thirty years later.

"I never in my life was as proud of father as I was at that moment," James said. "And he never again was as popular, as he was in that instant. It has been dramatized, but no re-enactment could capture the intensity of the drama that was played out that day."[26]

Roosevelt started the speech in his usual friendly way, expressing his pleasure being with so many people he had not seen since the last nominating convention, four years earlier. There was no mention of his condition.

And then he began to make the case for Smith. The speech itself was well received, becoming famous in its own right as the origin of Alfred Smith's nickname, "the Happy Warrior" (an expression taken from a poem by William Wordsworth). But it was the delivery that overwhelmed the delegates. Noting that Roosevelt had been ill, the *New York Times* beamed that, "There was nothing wrong with his voice, or with his enthusiasm."[27] Alfred Smith was listening on the radio in another location in the city. In his opinion, Roosevelt "was probably the most impressive figure in that convention."[28]

The ovation afterward lasted for an hour and thirteen minutes—a new record. Part of the credit for the outburst belonged to Tammany Hall, but the impact of Roosevelt's speech made the news throughout the country. Nearly a month after the convention, the Bismarck, Montana, *Tribune* printed a syndicated column by Harry B. Hunt, which began:

> Washington's I-remember-when brigade, which seeks to compare each new political circumstance with some previous similar situation, preferably to take disadvantage of the newest development, finds itself stumped in seeking an occasion when more "fuss and fury" was made over the presentation of the name of a candidate for president than that which attended Franklin Roosevelt's speech at New York, nominating Gov. Al Smith.[29]

Someone had indeed captured the public imagination in some sound and forceful way.

After the speech, Eleanor and Caroline O'Day cohosted a reception at the house on Sixty-Fifth Street for delegates and others in the Democratic Party. When Marion Dickerman arrived, the butler told her that Franklin was in his room and wanted to see her. "I went up," she said, "and he was sitting up in bed. I remember him so vividly. He held out his arms and he said, 'Marion, I did it!'"[30]

———•·•———

The Happy Warrior speech is often regarded as a turning point for Roosevelt, signifying his return to political activity after his paralysis. It was more like a promise, to himself and the party, of an eventual re-turn. At the time, he reverted to the balance of pursuits that had sustained him for the previous year or two: rehabilitation, relaxation, politics, and business, in approximately that order. James' excellent account of the speech in his memoir, *My Parents,* contains a description that puts the speech in its proper perspective; he called it an "hour or so stolen from his sickness."

Louis Howe was at the convention, but left no impressions of the occa-sion he had helped to arrange: Roosevelt's appearance at a public event. The speech had accomplished Howe's goal, convincing Democrats everywhere that Franklin Roosevelt was physically able to return to public life and men-tally able to make a valuable contribution. But he didn't mention it after-ward. To remind people of the emotional greeting accorded to Roosevelt that June day was to remind them that he had been paralyzed, and that was something Howe didn't want to do.

At the convention at Madison Square Garden, Smith eventually lost the nomination, largely over the issue of Prohibition. John W. Davis, the corporate lawyer and diplomat, was chosen as the Democratic candidate. Davis, a former congressman from West Virginia, was a kindly, intelligent man, but he ran a lackluster campaign against the incumbent, Calvin Coolidge. Eleanor worked on Davis' behalf through the Women's Division, but Franklin and Louis were only peripherally involved in the campaign, by Davis' preference and theirs. Davis had his own campaign managers. Any-way, Howe and Roosevelt held out no hope for a Democratic victory, given the Republican climate and the sense of satisfaction with Coolidge. The two returned to Horseneck Beach for a second summer vacation there, though Roosevelt rented his own house, next door to Howe's "wee" cottage, so that he would have a bit more space than he'd had the year before. Roo-sevelt was still convinced that water was key to his recovery, but he was dis-illusioned by his attempts to establish a second home in Florida. Almost from the start, the *Larooco* had proven too expensive to maintain.

Within the span of about two months in the later half of 1924, Franklin and Eleanor would each find homes, two very different places that they each wanted—and wanted to own, as a statement of identity. They no longer vacationed together, except in the course of short, friendly visits, each to the retreat of the other. Even before their relationship became a disappointed one in 1918, Franklin often went on trips with relatives or friends. That tradition fit naturally into the lifestyle adopted by the Roosevelts and, for that matter, the Howes.

———•◦•———

In September 1924, Eleanor decided to build a house on a rustic spot near a creek, about two miles from Springwood. The idea was, in fact, Franklin's. He suggested that Eleanor could share a cottage there with Marion Dickerman and Nancy Cook: a retreat for all of them.[31] Franklin, who had strong opinions about architecture, helped with the planning and oversaw the construction. Louis, who was always available to advise Eleanor on matters of politics or anything else she cared to discuss, had little to contribute regarding homebuilding and steered clear of the cottage project. Eleanor stayed out of the planning stage herself, leaving the details to her husband, in consultation with Cook.

The following month, Roosevelt discovered Warm Springs, Georgia, courtesy of a tip from investment banker George Foster Peabody, who had grown up in nearby Columbus. A nineteenth-century resort along the lines of Saratoga Springs, the old spa was dilapidated by the 1920s, but as soon as Roosevelt slipped into its pool and felt the eighty-nine-degree waters invigorate his legs, he felt at home. The only thing that excited him more than using the pool was sharing it with others who were paralyzed. Roosevelt made plans to reopen the resort as a rehabilitation center.

Howe was not especially encouraging about the new venture. Franklin, having left New York in search of a second home, had come back with a medical treatment facility. After Roosevelt purchased the property in 1927, it was administered by a charity that he launched, the Warm Springs Foundation. Howe served on the board of directors, and visited occasionally. The adoption of Georgia as a second home could not have been motivated by politics, yet settling in Georgia proved to be a master stroke for Roosevelt. His association with the rural South let him understand a part of America entirely different from the Hudson River Valley. Howe probably felt remiss in not having thought of it first.

Howe continued to spend most of his time in New York, going to Fall River on weekends when he could. He and Grace had given Mary a formal wedding in 1924; his new son-in-law, Robert Baker, was an astronomy professor at the University of Illinois. Mary and her husband lived in Urbana. "I would love to come on for Thanksgiving," Louis wrote one year in the mid-1920s, "but don't honestly see how I can afford it."[32] The fact that he was strapped for money, even as Roosevelt was spending it liberally on his own travels, was underscored by the pleas he included in various letters to Roosevelt. Some were funny and some were blunt, but they seemed an echo of the days when he worked for Thomas Mott Osborne and continually badgered him for money.[33] He was in an uncomfortable position, but then, when it came to money, so was anyone who hired Louis Howe. He was typically impecunious and they were invariably the first to hear about it. Roosevelt found outside jobs for Howe as often as he could to lay off some of his responsibility for the entire salary.

According to Howe's timetable, Roosevelt would run for the New York governorship in 1932 and the presidency in 1936. In 1928, Alfred Smith was at last the presidential nominee for the Democratic Party, and Howe had reason to fear that Smith would want to use Roosevelt on the New York ticket as a vote-getter, one who might very well get unnecessarily battered in a Republican year. With his own timetable in mind, Howe thought that he had done his job well when he encouraged Roosevelt to leave for Warm Springs just before the 1928 New York State Democratic Convention in July. If Roosevelt could not be reached, he couldn't be nominated. Howe figured correctly: Smith did want Roosevelt on the ticket as the Democratic candidate for governor. He needed a strong name on the ballot to help him win New York in the presidential race. But Howe did not anticipate just how insistent Smith would be; the governor turned the state convention into a Roosevelt rally, ready to nominate him by acclamation.

Smith put Eleanor in an uncomfortable position. As a party leader, she was pressed hard to accede to Smith's request that Roosevelt be reached by telephone. As Mrs. Roosevelt, she knew that her husband had gone away for a reason. Under pressure, she agreed to call Franklin on the telephone, but not to try to influence him in any way.

By that point, Smith didn't need her skills of persuasion. He had a trump card in the argument that for Roosevelt to reject his party's ardent call to run as governor of New York would be worse for his career than losing the race in the fall. When Smith telephoned Roosevelt in Warm Springs, he and his seconds tried a number of arguments to elicit a commitment to run, but Roosevelt didn't volunteer anything. Finally, Smith asked him bluntly whether he would accept the nomination if the convention voted for it. Smith listened for a reply. He didn't hear anything. Roosevelt couldn't seem to say a word—and Smith interpreted that as a commitment.

In that moment, Roosevelt simultaneously returned to his political ambitions and silently abandoned those for a complete physical rehabilitation. Forsaking the resolve he expressed in 1923—not to run for office until he could do so without crutches—Roosevelt revealed that he knew he would not walk again unassisted.

The state convention in New York nominated Roosevelt for governor by acclamation. Smith may have ordered the nomination, but the excitement it inspired when it was announced at the convention belonged entirely to Roosevelt.

In Roosevelt's own circle, the response was not as joyous. Never, in fact, was the mood surrounding a successful candidacy so bleak. "Regret that you had to accept, but know that you felt it obligatory," Eleanor wrote in a telegram, reflecting what she thought was her husband's own attitude. Howe was devastated, believing it a terrible setback and that Roosevelt would lose in a Republican landslide.

CHAPTER FOURTEEN

THE WHITE HOUSE

Louis wrote a letter to Grace from New York City on the day that the State Democratic convention drafted Roosevelt as its candidate for governor. He had to cancel his weekend in Fall River with her and Hartley, because he was going to meet Franklin at Hyde Park to make plans for the campaign. He and Roosevelt had already been in close communication about the prospects for the election. "We are much upset," Louis wrote, and then he proved the point by continuing, "& are praying that we get licked, but it looks bad." He apparently forgot the word, "don't," as in "we are praying that we don't get licked, but it looks bad." Two sentences down, he spelled his son's name wrong, calling him "Harley."[1] He was, as he noted, upset.

Eleanor listened to Louis' misgivings and teased him for trying to dominate situations. She, on the other hand, embraced the demanding turn of events without even forming an opinion. Instead, and with her usual reflex, she accepted that "one adjusted one's personal life to the developments in other people's lives."[2] Each came to Franklin Roosevelt from different directions, when his decisions controlled their lives. Eleanor was passive, Louis exacting. Neither approach would stave off frustration, once they found themselves in the wake of a man on the move again.

When the one-month campaign was underway, Franklin proved to be a marvel, delivering speeches regionally on behalf of Smith and then embarking on a nineteen-city tour within the state. At least, it was planned for nineteen. In practice, he stopped nearly anywhere there were people to listen, and talked with them from the back of an open car.

As in the 1920 vice presidential campaign, Roosevelt gathered able assistants for the tour and, as before, he earned the friendship and loyalty of each. Unlike 1920, he wasn't trying to be popular with his staff, and didn't need to enjoy himself playing games. The campaign was the joy, or so he made it seem. As with an actor who derives energy from an audience, Roosevelt was invigorated by the process of meeting voters.

For seven years, he had been to some degree cloistered. In purely political terms, the timing was good; he had been conserving his energy through an era dominated by Republicans at the national level and by Alfred Smith in New York State. Roosevelt's seven-year hiatus from active campaigning may well have saved him from either early defeat and oblivion, or exhaustion. "I had heard stories of his being something of a playboy and idler, of his weakness and ineffectiveness," said Samuel Rosenman, a lawyer and speechwriter who accompanied the tour. "That was the kind of man I expected to meet. But the broad jaw and upturned chin, the piercing, flashing eyes, the firm hands—they did not fit the description."[3]

Eleanor Roosevelt didn't accompany her husband's campaign tour. She remained in New York City with important responsibilities as the head of the Women's Division of the National Democratic Committee. Frances Perkins remembered her as "a very capable executive. . . . She never forgot anything. If she promised to do so-and-so, it was done. She could keep three or four threads in mind at once, pick up the telephone, carry out that agreement, carry out another."[4]

Louis Howe didn't accompany Franklin Roosevelt in the campaign, either. He also stayed in New York City, with two jobs. Continuing work that he and Franklin had started for the Democratic Party, he worked for the Smith campaign as a liaison to business, soliciting support—or at least discouraging outright rejection. He was even more active as head of Roosevelt's independent campaign committee.[5] He soon had a staff of typists, stenographers, and facile letter writers, who could compose responses to incoming correspondence in the Roosevelt style. Howe was loath to use preprinted form letters, believing that politics was most effective when it had a personal touch.

Roosevelt's official campaign was subordinate to that of Alfred Smith, who supplied the campaign manager, Van Namee, and other high-ranking personnel.[6] Howe chafed at the idea of being the unofficial manager, serving under or beside Smith partisans. In reality, both he and Eleanor were also working under the direction of Belle Moskowitz, who was directing publicity for the Smith campaign, although her influence didn't stop in that capacity. She was expected to oversee the Roosevelt campaign and she undeniably knew something about the subject, after helping to put Smith in the governor's mansion four times.[7]

Belle Moskowitz had taken the strongest hand in steering Smith to the presidential nomination. In the general election, she had a lesser role, but was still Smith's most trusted advisor, just as Howe continued in that capacity for Roosevelt, whatever his other titles. One of Smith's liabilities in the 1928 campaign was his religion, and Moskowitz tried to beat anti-Catholic rumors, disseminating campaign biographies to present Smith in a statesmanlike way and not at all like a man who would *really* build a tunnel from New York City to the Vatican, so that he could talk to the Pope in secret. Or who would immediately void all Protestant marriages. Or build a castle for the Pontiff in New Jersey.

Several people tried to convince Howe to listen to Moskowitz' advice, but it was futile. The two didn't get along.[8] Their respective candidates may have been on the same ticket and very friendly in public, but Howe and Moskowitz knew they were in competition and that it could become cutthroat at any time.

In November, Smith lost the presidential election. He and Moskowitz were charged with underestimating the anti-Catholic prejudice in other parts of the country, but he also lost the state of New York, which was probably even more painful. Franklin Roosevelt was the surprise victor of the day, narrowly winning the governor's office. Rather suddenly, Eleanor prepared to leave her own career as a political activist behind and move to Albany in the more subdued role of the governor's wife.

Louis Howe, who wasn't offered a post in Albany, was to remain in New York City. All of the plans called for him to visit Franklin and Eleanor often. Above all, Franklin wanted a fresh start and a chance to prove himself in the governorship. If he hadn't wanted the office badly, he wouldn't have hobbled all over the state during the campaign—making sure, all the while, that he made it look effortless. The move to Albany reflected the assumption of power, but in a unique case—by a man who did indeed have something to prove, to himself and to all. While Roosevelt established himself in his new office, Howe stayed on the course he'd set for himself years before, as a political advance man. Under other circumstances, Howe might have moved to Albany, too, and taken a quiet job in the administration. The results in 1928, however, left a greater imperative.

Franklin Roosevelt may have won his election by only a whisker, but he emerged as a hero in the Democratic Party, having prevailed where Smith hadn't: in his own home state. Howe's new responsibility was to encourage that momentum and direct it toward the 1936 presidential election. It was a goal that sustained Louis' connection to Franklin and Eleanor, without actually tying him to the two any longer. He had been magnificent, but it was time for Louis Howe to take the trip that he had postponed seven years before, and go home for good.

The Howes' financial situation finally relaxed as the 1920s neared an end. In Fall River, Grace had received a windfall that put her name into a certain corner of history, far from the Roosevelts and Democratic politics. Grace's notorious cousin Lizzie Borden died in 1927, leaving her a diamond-and-amethyst ring and a half share in a large office building in Fall River.[9] Once the will was probated, the income from the building was enough to maintain her in comfort. Louis might still be scrimping, but Grace had the wherewithal to take Hartley, by then a teenager, on trips all over the world. They especially liked to visit England and see the Shakespeare plays at Stratford-Upon-Avon. Hartley, a good student, was looking forward to entering Harvard University in the fall of 1929. Grace rented a medium-sized apartment in Fall River and filled it with the antiques that she and Louis had collected through the years. An article in a Fall River newspaper featuring Grace and the apartment was titled, "Atmosphere of Comfort and Charm Characterizes the 'House of Howe.'"[10] At long last, the Howes had a place; that is to say, Grace did.

Louis Howe didn't opt to join her there, except on occasional weekends. More typically, he took a train up the Hudson and stayed with the Roosevelts on weekends. Grace could have moved to New York City, especially after Hartley entered college, but she didn't. After a lifetime of giving themselves and each other excuses for living apart, none was necessary. Louis stayed in New York and that was all.

———•✦•———

Roosevelt's election ended his friendship, such as it was, with Alfred Smith, who for a time after the election stayed on in Albany to offer advice to Roosevelt. One of his first suggestions was that the new governor retain Belle Moskowitz as his adviser. He called her "the smartest person he knew."[11] Mrs. Moskowitz was willing; she and Eleanor had long been friends. And Roosevelt's administration would get off to a quick start with the benefit of her advice. Yet Roosevelt declined the offer. Howe had influenced the decision, undoubtedly taking a dim view of the notion that he would be shuffling letters in New York City, while Moskowitz was at Roosevelt's elbow in Albany. But Roosevelt probably would have turned down anyone recommended by Smith. Despite the fact that Roosevelt himself had peppered Smith with advice six years before, when Smith was newly elected, Roosevelt didn't want to hear anything in return. That reflected the sense of competition that had risen to the surface between the two. In terms of policy, though, Roosevelt was deeply influenced by Smith's administration and indeed he continued most of the social and economic initiatives launched by Smith—or by Moskowitz.

The stock market crash in October 1929 and the subsequent deterioration of the economy gave impetus to Howe's timetable for a Roosevelt run at the White House. As the financial crisis rocked New York State in its earliest days, Roosevelt was called back to Albany from a trip to Warm Springs. He met Howe and the lieutenant governor, Herbert Lehman, in his office to discuss the fast-moving events. Lehman, the scion of a banking family (his father was a founding partner of Lehman Brothers), was agitated and nervous. Eleanor told the story afterward of how much Franklin was annoyed by Lehman's nervous pacing all over the room. Franklin was sitting quietly at his desk, and Louis was curled into one end of the sofa, barely moving as he thought about what was being said. Roosevelt was at the point of demanding that Lehman stop pacing, but he held himself in check. Then, when the phone rang, Louis stood up to answer it and Roosevelt exploded. "Louis, will you please sit still and stop moving around so much!"[12] It was a story Eleanor loved to repeat.

Howe laughed when someone noticed that he and Franklin were on a first-name basis, "Oh," he said, "we call each other lots of things—some of which aren't repeatable."[13] In fact, Howe was said to be the only person who could have an all-out row with Franklin. "He never feared to argue hotly with the Chief," recalled Lizzie McDuffie, a cook, of Howe and Roosevelt. "Sometimes the argument would go on for days," she continued, "with neither of them giving an inch. They had one such discussion at Warm Springs that lasted most of the night. The next morning Howe packed his bags and left! [My husband] said to me, 'Well, that was one argument that Louis Howe lost!'"[14]

Howe didn't pull any punches with Roosevelt, and Roosevelt paid him the same compliment. What worried Howe from time to time was whether his unhidden devotion to Roosevelt was also returned.

* * *

Starting in 1930, after Roosevelt's easy reelection as governor, Howe began to work more feverishly than ever, building a pathway for the 1932 presidential campaign. Howe and Roosevelt had originally anticipated that Herbert Hoover would remain in office for two terms, through 1936. That prediction had hinged on continuing prosperity. Roosevelt had, however, been expecting an economic reversal as a result of Republican policies (which he felt favored business to a degree that was unsustainable). He hadn't anticipated the Great Depression, the worst financial crisis of the century—but once it arrived, he and Howe knew that Hoover was doomed and that 1932 would be a Democratic year.

"Franklin did not tell me when he decided to run for the presidency," Eleanor recalled, "but I knew from Louis Howe that he, Louis, had decided and had long been working in his own way to prepare the ground."[15] With the advance in the timetable, Howe was more pressured than ever, arranging alliances and gathering an organization.[16] If Roosevelt was to be elected president in 1932, Howe couldn't make any errors in 1931.

In May, a family crisis struck the Executive Mansion. Sara Roosevelt, visiting Paris on her annual European trip, was stricken with pneumonia. The prognosis was grim, and Franklin immediately booked passage on a transatlantic liner, traveling with his son, Elliott, who was then twenty years old. Just before the liner left port, Roosevelt wrote Howe a letter unlike any other.

> Dear Old Louis,
>
> Just a line to send my love & tell you if it does any good to take care of yourself—try not to overdo or worry. All is really coming out so well & you are the main spring! Before you know it I'll be coming into the harbor again! Don't hesitate to telephone if anything comes up.
>
> As ever,
> FDR[17]

Roosevelt was normally jocular and casual in his letters to Howe, covering their current business, but with humor perched above nearly every line. He certainly never sent him his love. In the letter from the ship, that tone slipped and Roosevelt addressed Howe as he would his son, father, brother—as a blood relative. Heartened by the visit from Franklin and Elliott, Sara recovered from her bout with pneumonia. She remained in France after they returned to the United States.

As the 1932 presidential election drew closer, a new man was brought on board to help manage the growing campaign. James A. Farley, another upstate New Yorker and secretary of the New York State Democratic Committee, was an expert politician with an outgoing personality. He made a strong, positive impression and was, in short, much that Howe was not. In fact, the first test of Farley's smooth charm was Louis Howe. They had known each other for years, but never in such close proximity to Roosevelt. Farley had the instincts of a diplomat, though, and Howe accepted him.

Howe's jealousy reared up on occasions when he thought Farley was cutting him off from important discussions with Roosevelt. In response, Farley made it a point to inform Howe of his every contact with the candidate.

Starting with the campaign for the presidential nomination, Farley took over as Roosevelt's surrogate on the road and in meetings, while Howe remained in his office in New York City, organizing the states as though they were cards in a game. The 1932 Democratic Convention in Chicago was to be a showdown, perhaps an inevitable one, between Roosevelt, who had announced his candidacy early, and Alfred Smith, who entered late on the assumption that Roosevelt would defer to his seniority and withdraw. That was a miscalculation.

Smith campaigned tenaciously, discouraged by some party veterans, who reminded him that he had had his chance in 1928. As loyal as ever, Belle Moskowitz regarded his candidacy differently. Referring to the nomination in what was obviously going to be a Democratic year, she insisted, "he's entitled to it."[18] Moskowitz worked as hard as ever, and Smith gained ground quickly, painting himself as the more experienced candidate and the only one who could handle the crisis of the Great Depression.

As Marion Dickerman and Nancy Cook made their plans to go to Chicago, Howe insisted that they travel with him on the train. They chatted through the evening and then retired for the night. In the morning, Howe did not appear for breakfast. "No Louis, no Louis," recalled Dickerman. "Finally we got so concerned that we asked the conductor to go to his room. Louis was there, but he was a sick man."[19] Suffering from an attack of asthma, Howe was gasping for breath and would continue to do so throughout the convention. The condition may have been exacerbated by nerves; everyone in the Roosevelt camp was operating under high tension—even Roosevelt, who was back in Albany.

Howe had undertaken to install an open telephone line from the governor's mansion to Howe's suite. Roosevelt, chain-smoking, sat down each day in the Executive Mansion and listened to events unfold on the radio and via the open line. When Farley, working the floor, found a delegate who was wavering toward support of Roosevelt or, better yet, away from Smith, he brought that person to Howe's suite for a personal chat with Governor

Roosevelt—over the wire. Days passed. Howe's condition appeared to be bad, as he lay on the floor or even on the dresser, seeking good air and a comfortable position for his lungs. According to Dickerman, "The only part of him that seemed absolutely alive were his eyes. They seemed to blaze out of their sockets."[20]

After two ballots, Roosevelt was leading, followed closely by Smith. John Nance Garner of Texas was trailing. Roosevelt's position was weaker than it may have looked, though. Not only was Smith aggressively courting the Garner delegates, but Garner himself was angling to become a compromise candidate. Garner's support consisted of the delegations of Texas, California, and Illinois. The California delegation was headed by former treasury secretary William McAdoo and controlled by William Randolph Hearst. That alone ought to have given Alfred Smith pause.

Approached by Farley, Garner suddenly agreed to throw his support, and that of the Texas delegation, behind Roosevelt, in exchange for a place on the ticket as vice president. That would still leave Roosevelt just shy of the nomination. At that point, McAdoo abruptly took the floor. Everyone waited to hear what he would say—thousands of people at the convention, Louis Howe listening in his hotel suite, Franklin Roosevelt listening in his office in Albany. McAdoo pledged California to Roosevelt, who would, with that, then be nominated as soon as the formality of the ballot was complete.

Much speculation ran through the convention as to the cause of McAdoo's sudden jump. The word on the floor was that William Randolph Hearst was still angry about Smith's refusal to allow him on the ticket at the 1922 New York State Democratic Convention. Told that the convention could swing to Smith, he told McAdoo to hand his delegates to Roosevelt as a means of stopping Smith. Garner was presumed to have been apprised of the Hearst move, leading him to strike a deal with Farley. "Last night's sensational break in the balloting for President," the New York Times reported, "furnished revenge on Alfred E. Smith for William Randolph Hearst."[21] Of course, Hearst was happy to claim credit for acting the part of the hidden force behind the Roosevelt nomination—but then, so were many others. Even if Hearst played only a small part in influencing

McAdoo, for the purpose of stopping Smith, it indicated the fact that his grudge was finally laid to rest.

Once the nomination was secure, Franklin Roosevelt broke with precedent by flying to Chicago. No presidential candidate had ever appeared before a convention that had nominated him—and, moreover, few people of any calling had ever flown from Albany to Chicago, as of 1932. At the convention, jubilation had already enveloped the Roosevelt supporters, whose numbers suddenly exploded. Dickerman and Cook were part of the celebration, until they were suddenly stopped short. They opened a letter they had received from Eleanor. "She had said she did not want to be First Lady and could not live in the White House," Dickerman recalled.[22] With the nomination official, the odds were good that Eleanor would indeed be First Lady in a matter of months. Cook showed the letter to Louis Howe and asked his advice. "He ripped it into shreds," Dickerman said, "and told us not to breathe a word of it to anyone."[23]

Amid the Roosevelt celebrations, Alfred Smith left Chicago, never to return to politics. In fact, he bore out Eleanor's suspicions by soon adopting a conservative, business-oriented point of view. Belle Moskowitz called the Chicago convention "a most trying and difficult set of circumstances for all of us." Defeated and broken, she said, "I have learned much which I hope I may not have occasion to apply in a hurry again."[24] Moskowitz still had her family, but she didn't rebound easily, and in 1933, when she fell off the steps at her home in New York, breaking her arm, she died from her injuries.

———— ·◆· ————

Louis Howe often protested that he didn't care for attention. Even in his own home, he put the focus elsewhere, keeping very few papers related to his career. The walls featured oil portraits of his ancestors, but no framed photographs of him shaking hands with world leaders. One file that he did keep among his personal possessions, though, was a rather thick one, overstuffed with letters dated from 1932, when Franklin Roosevelt was elected president. While Roosevelt was the victor, letters of congratulation addressed to Louis poured in. And he kept them. Some were from party officials with whom he'd worked out strategies for Roosevelt. Some were from friends, such as Francis Perkins. "Yours was a great job," Perkins wrote from her office as New York's secretary of labor, "and I cannot tell you how appreciative are those of us who have knowledge of what you were doing. Particularly because I disagreed with you about some things, I want you to know how fine I think the total is."[25]

The letters Howe kept were from people he had courted when they were powerful—and when he was a hack drumming for his candidate. With the election over, they wrote on thick stationery to honor him, to pay court themselves. Financier Bernard M. Baruch wrote to Howe, "There are few people who know of your devotion and unswerving loyalty to [Roosevelt] during the past many years. You had the vision." It was a letter worth keeping, and rereading. "It is seldom one sees such unselfishness," Baruch concluded.[26] "You had a vision," the newspaper editor Herbert Bayard Swope wrote, reiterating the word Baruch had used.[27] "You certainly are entitled to a large amount of the credit," acknowledged former Boston mayor John F. "Honey Fitz" Fitzgerald. "I want to add my name to the large number who undoubtedly feel the same way as I do."[28]

According to Howe, securing the presidency for Roosevelt hadn't been so hard. He once said in an offhand way that he just set the timetable and then watched events meet it on schedule. It hadn't been quite that simple, although he was present at every step of the way. After Roosevelt won in November, Louis Howe moved into the White House—and so did Eleanor, of course, though not without trepidation. As Howe's stack of congratulatory letters deepened, it reflected the impression in some quarters that Howe had served his purpose: having put his man in the White House, he was no longer necessary, a holdover. That, however, was another role that Howe was used to: he had been a holdover and a hanger-on at every stage of Roosevelt's political career, but that didn't undermine his position. Even his enemies admitted that Roosevelt needed Howe: he could relax with Louis as with no one else outside his family, with the exception of Missy LeHand. But Howe could tell the president when he was wrong and sometimes hold him in check. Howe was responsible for several projects in Roosevelt's first term and was a major proponent of the Civilian Conservation Corps (CCC), but his greatest contribution to the New Deal lay in all of the programs that no one ever heard about. They never heard about them because Howe shot them down in the privacy of the Oval Office before Roosevelt could start them, or, more important, regret them. He called himself the president's "no-man."[29] He saved Roosevelt from himself, preventing two of his great strengths from destroying him: keeping his enthusiasm from becoming irrationality and his self-confidence, mere egotism.

Close friends, and also unadmiring acquaintances, had long suspected Howe of having a towering ego of his own, despite subsuming himself to Franklin Roosevelt. After the election, even strangers could see it, too, as he became more irascible than ever, a man in a position of power at long last and playing the part. As he became a celebrity in his own right, he even had his own radio show, in which he commented on national events.

Officially, Howe served as secretary to the president, a familiar role after twenty-one years. Unofficially, he was chief advisor to Eleanor. At first, Eleanor found herself reverting to her basic way of life thirty years before, when she was a society girl, engaged in a revolving circle of receptions, luncheons, and parties of which she was the host. For many women, that would be a delightful way of life. But Eleanor had forged a different sense of purpose for herself, as an activist and political worker.

Louis told her that he could make her president in ten years, just as he had Franklin. It was a bit of bragging, but it was pressure of the right kind for Eleanor. And it may have been true. For the time being, he was trying to tell her all of the things that she could do as First Lady, rather than let her dwell on those she couldn't. Howe assured her that she didn't have to be like the First Ladies who had preceded her; she could forge a different role for herself, just by sharing her sensitivities with the American people. First he told her, and then, finally, he showed her.

———◆◆◆———

In March 1933, the riverfront along the Potomac was crowded with veterans of World War I, mostly penniless and hoping for early payment of a one-time bonus that had been promised by Congress in 1924 (which, by law, was not redeemable until 1945). A similar gathering of "Bonus

Marchers" during the Hoover administration had been dispersed by the army in June 1932, using violent tactics as though they were attacking an enemy.

Howe, who had been strapped for money for most of his life, had splurged on a glamorous KB Lincoln convertible roadster.[30] Unfortunately, he often wasn't feeling strong enough to drive it, and asked Eleanor to take the wheel when they went on rides in the afternoon. On one occasion in 1933, Howe invited Eleanor to take a ride in his new car and directed her to the veterans' encampment along Potomac Drive. When they arrived, he prepared for a nap and told her to walk around. "Very hesitatingly," she recalled, "I got out and walked over to where I saw a line-up of men waiting for food. They looked at me curiously and one of them asked my name and what I wanted. When I said I just wanted to see how they were getting on, they asked me to join them."[31]

Eleanor toured the camp and returned to the White House. Before long, the men were given the opportunity to join the CCC, and they dispersed voluntarily. Howe had given her the liberty and confidence to see things for herself and still remain First Lady. In her work as First Lady, she went to see how Americans of all walks of life were getting on. Because of Howe's experience as a reporter, he also encouraged her to cultivate the media, especially as she expanded the role of First Lady. He encouraged her to write and taught her how to market what she wrote. In time, she earned a good living for herself through her books and her syndicated newspaper column, "My Day," in which she recounted her thoughts and activities.

When Louis' health deteriorated in 1934, the Roosevelt family feared for his survival. He was admitted to the hospital, suffering from heart disease and respiratory failure. All of the Roosevelts were concerned: the children, leading their own lives as young adults, nearly as much as Franklin and Eleanor. Telegrams kept each member of the family apprised of his condition, at times on an hourly basis. Grace came to the White House for an extended stay, also fearing the worst. Without Louis, the relationship between Franklin and Eleanor was more distant. According to

Marion Dickerman, he was "a vital link between Eleanor and the President—the sole means, in some instances, for their sympathetic working communication with one another."[32] Howe recovered, though, and while he was more debilitated than ever, he returned to the White House. Grace returned home and visited Louis only occasionally after that. The Roosevelts were responsible for him.

In September 1935, Howe went into the hospital for the last time, and even in his weakened state he almost tore the place apart when he found out that there was no telephone by his bed. Franklin had one installed. In an oxygen tent much of the time, Howe would pull the receiver under the plastic flaps and call members of the administration, hoarsely barking orders and advice. Because he sometimes grew confused—something he had never been before, in spite of all of his maladies—Roosevelt quietly told staff members to check with him before acting on Howe's orders. By the beginning of April 1936, Howe could no longer hold the telephone. He was barely conscious some of the time, as his strength seeped away.

With that, the Roosevelts waited, knowing that Louis Howe had at last done all that he could for them.

ACKNOWLEDGMENTS

I n 2006, the Franklin D. Roosevelt Library opened the Louis Howe Personal Papers to the public for the first time. Having been intrigued with the role and the persona of Howe for many years, I visited the library, in Hyde Park, New York, and found that Chief Archivist Bob Clark had done a masterful job in preserving the materials in that collection, while leaving them very much in an original state. I enjoyed a rare sense of discovery looking through the letters, drawings, poems, clippings, and pictures left by Howe, in relation to his family.

The Roosevelt Library also houses the Louis Howe Official Papers, which reflect his working life with Franklin Roosevelt before and during the White House years. This book is also based on many other collections at the library, and I am deeply grateful to the entire staff for helping me to find my way through them all. Virginia Lewick, Mark Renovitch, and Mr. Clark made every trip very productive, as well as enjoyable.

The papers of Belle Moskowitz are housed at the Lear Center for Special Collections and Archives, at Connecticut College, where Benjamin Panciera was instrumental in helping me to gain the most from them. The Osborne Family Papers are at the Bird Library of Syracuse University, where I consulted them. Other institutions that were important in the research are the New York State Library in Albany, the Fall River Public Library, the Columbia University Oral History Research Office, the Firestone Library at Princeton University, the New York Public Library, and the Library of Congress. The Onondaga County Public Library, near my home in Central New York, came through, as always, in obtaining obscure newspaper microfilms for me.

Faye Musselman, who is an authority on Lizzie Borden and Fall River, was generous and very helpful in talking about the relationship between Borden and Grace Howe. Faye operates a website dedicated to the Borden case (http://phayemuss.wordpress.com), which I recommend.

I want to thank Alessandra Bastagli, the editor of the book, for her excellent guidance. I can barely express my debt to Alan Bradshaw and Nancy Hirsch, whose assistance in the final stage of the editing process was invaluable to me. My agent, Joelle Delbourgo, believed in this project from the start and was instrumental in bringing it to fruition.

My father, Warren Fenster, and my dear friend, Lillian Schwartz, Princeton '11, served as my research assistants. They exhibited great patience with both me and the copying machine at the FDR Library, for which I am grateful. It would be impossible to complete this list without thanking Richard Harfmann, who listened to incessant chatter about Louis Howe, Franklin Roosevelt, and Eleanor Roosevelt for the better part of two years. And always, Neddy.

ENDNOTES

PROLOGUE

1. "President Visits His Ship Model Exhibit," *New York Times*, Apr. 19, 1936, p. 3.
2. Frederic J. Haskin, "President Roosevelt as a Collector," *Kokomo (IN) Tribune*, Apr. 17, 1936, p. 4.
3. "President Visits His Ship," *New York Times*.
4. Margaret Durand, letter to Grace Howe, 1936 [undated], Louis Howe Personal Papers, Box 15, Durand, Margaret, Franklin D. Roosevelt Library, Hyde Park, New York (hereafter, FDRL).
5. Eleanor Roosevelt, "My Day," Apr. 19, 1936.
6. Margaret Durand, letter to Grace Howe, 1936 [undated], Louis Howe Personal Papers, Box 15, Durand, Margaret, FDRL.
7. Associated Press, "Mrs. Roosevelt Sees U.S. Crime Museum with School Group," *Syracuse Herald*, Apr. 19, 1936, p. 6.
8. Associated Press, "New Deal Is Burlesqued by Gridiron Club," *Syracuse Herald*, Apr. 19, 1936, p. 6. The C.C.C. was a New Deal program. The lines were sung to the Irving Berlin song "We Saw the Sea" (1936).
9. Roosevelt, "My Day."
10. "New Deal Is Burlesqued by Gridiron Club," *Syracuse Herald*.
11. "Death of Howe," *Time Magazine*, Apr. 27, 1936.
12. "Gridiron Diners Fill Band Wagons," *New York Times*, Apr. 19, 1936, p. 8.
13. "Gridiron Diners," *New York Times*.
14. Eleanor Roosevelt, letter to Grace Howe, Jan. 23, 1936, Louis Howe Personal Papers, Box 22, Roosevelt, Eleanor, FDRL.
15. Margaret Durand, letter to Grace Howe, 1936 [undated], Louis Howe Personal Papers, Box 15, Durand, Margaret, FDRL.
16. Roosevelt, "My Day."
17. Associated Press, "Political Strategist Succumbs at 64 in Naval Hospital . . ." *Syracuse Herald*, Apr. 19, 1936, p. 1.
18. "Death of Howe," *Time Magazine*.
19. Roosevelt, "My Day."
20. "Roosevelt Will Go to Burial of Howe," *New York Times*, Apr. 21, 1936, p. 23.
21. United Press. "Roosevelt Stands in Cutting Wind for Howe Burial," *Modesto (CA) Bee*, Apr. 23, 1936, p. 9.
22. Reminiscences of Herbert Lehman, 1961, Columbia University Oral History Research Office Collection (hereafter CUOHROC), pp. 249–50.

23. Gabrielle Forbush Reminiscence, 1967, Small Collections, Oral History Interviews, A-O, p. 19; FDRL.
24. Franklin D. Roosevelt, letter to Ralph Cropley, Apr. 21, 1936, PPF 620, Cropley, Ralph, FDRL.
25. Frank Polk, letter to Franklin Roosevelt, Apr. 24, 1936, PPF 1006, Polk, Frank, FDRL.
26. Franklin Roosevelt, letter to Frank Polk, May 14, 1936, PPF 1006, Polk, Frank, FDRL. Lily was Polk's wife.
27. Associated Press, "Returns to Capital," *Florence (SC) Morning News*, Apr. 23, 1936, p. 1.
28. Eleanor Roosevelt, "My Day," Apr. 23, 1936.
29. Charles W. Hurd, "Last Howe Tribute Paid by Roosevelt," *New York Times*, Apr. 23, 1936, p. 24.
30. United Press, "Roosevelt Stands in Cutting Wind," *Modesto (CA) Bee.*

CHAPTER 1

1. Anne Ward Gilbert, interview Sept. 20, 1978, Eleanor Roosevelt, Oral Histories, FDRL, pp. 33–34.
2. U.S. Federal Census, 1870, Indianapolis, Ward 2, Marion, Indiana; Roll M593_340; p. 48, image 96.
3. *Presbyterian Memorial Volume* (New York: DeWitt C. Lent, 1870), reprinted in Albert H. Davis, *History of the Davis Family* (New York: T. A. Wright, 1888), pp. 107–08.
4. U.S. Federal Census, 1860, Indianapolis, Ward 2, Marion, Indiana, Roll M653_279, p. 110, image 112. *Indianapolis City Directory and Business Mirror* (Indianapolis: H. N. McEvoy, 1858).
5. James K. McGuire and Martin Wilie Littleton, *The Democratic Party of the State of New York, Vol. III* (New York: United History Co., 1905), pp. 89–90.
6. McGuire and Littleton, *The Democratic Party, Vol. III*, p. 90.
7. Lela Stiles, *The Man Behind Roosevelt* (Cleveland: World Pub. Co., 1954), p. 5.
8. McGuire and Littleton, *The Democratic Party, Vol. III*, p. 91.
9. Joseph Brucker, *The Chief Political Parties in the United States: Their History and Teachings* (Milwaukee: Chas. Webster & Co., 1880), pp. 71–74.
10. U.S. Federal Census, 1870, Indianapolis, Ward 2, Marion, Indiana, Roll M593_340, p. 48, image 96.
11. J. G. Sharpe, letter to the editor, *Indianapolis Star*, 1936, Louis Howe Personal Papers, Clippings 1932–33, FDRL; U.S. Federal Census, 1870, Indianapolis, Ward 2, Marion, Indiana.
12. Sharpe, *Indianapolis Star.*
13. *Presbyterian Memorial Volume*, reprinted in Davis, *History of the Davis Family*, pp. 107–08.
14. Sharpe, *Indianapolis Star.*
15. Theodore Roosevelt, *An Autobiography* (New York: Macmillan, 1913), pp. 32–33.
16. Sharpe, *Indianapolis Star.*
17. Theodore Roosevelt, *The Strenuous Life: Essays and Addresses* (New York: Century, 1905), p. 3.
18. "Dr. Strong Dead," *New York Times*, Feb. 3, 1891, p. 1.
19. Charles Newhall Taintor, *Saratoga: An Illustrated Visitor's Guide* (New York: Taintor Brothers, 1892), pp. 26–27.
20. Louis McHenry Howe, "Saratoga Springs," *New England*, June 1905, p. 474.
21. "Saratoga Springs," *Harper's New Monthly*, 53–315, Aug. 1876, p. 387.
22. Howe, "Saratoga Springs," pp. 476–79.
23. Howe, "Saratoga Springs," p. 480.
24. Lela Stiles, "Silhouette," *Jeffersonian*, Feb. 1933, p. 16.
25. McGuire and Littleton, *The Democratic Party, Vol. III*, p. 90.
26. Stiles, *Man Behind Roosevelt*, p. 15.

27. Howe, "Saratoga Springs," p. 485.
28. Howe, "Saratoga Springs," p. 482.
29. "A Friendly Chat with Mrs. Louis Howe," *New Bedford (MA) Sunday Standard,* undated clipping; Folder: Rollins, Alfred; Small Collections, FDRL.
30. Deborah Allard-Bernardi, "Grace Howe: Postmaster," *Fall River Herald News,* Mar. 21, 2004, p. 11.
31. D. Hamilton Hurd, *History of Bristol County, Massachusetts* (Philadelphia: J. W. Lewis, 1883), p. 380.
32. Stiles, *The Man Behind Roosevelt,* p. 15.
33. Alfred B. Rollins Jr., *Roosevelt and Howe* (New York: Knopf, 1962), p. 74.
34. Louis Howe, letter to Grace Howe, July 9, 1915, Louis Howe Personal Papers, Louis Howe to Grace Howe 1915–1922 FDRL.
35. "Mrs. Louis McHenry Howe Is a Lively 80," *Boston Sunday Globe,* June 27, 1954, p. 67.
36. James I. Clarke, letter to Louis Howe, Nov. 10, 1932, Louis Howe Personal Papers, Congratulations 1932–33, FDRL.
37. Reminiscences of Frances Perkins, CUOHROC, Part IV, p. 456.
38. "Atmosphere of Comfort and Charm Characterizes the House of Howe," newspaper clipping, 1933, Alfred Rollins Collection, Small Collections, Clippings.

CHAPTER 2

1. Louis Howe, letter to Grace Howe, 1899, Louis McHenry Howe to Grace Howe, 1898–1899, Louis Howe Personal Papers, FDRL.
2. Grace Howe, letter to Louis Howe, Jan. 23, 1900, Grace Howe to Louis Howe 1898–1900, Louis Howe Personal Papers, FDRL.
3. Louis Howe, letter to Grace Howe, May 1900, Louis Howe Personal Papers, Louis Howe to Grace Howe, May 1900, FDRL.
4. Louis Howe to Grace Howe, June 27, 1900, Louis Howe Personal Papers, Louis Howe to Grace Howe, June 1900, FDRL.
5. Thomas K. Brindley, "Political Grab Bag," *Fall River Herald News,* Apr. 23, 1936.
6. Eleanor Roosevelt, *This Is My Story* (New York: Harper & Brothers, 1937), p. 27.
7. Roosevelt, *This Is My Story,* p. 7.
8. Franklin D. Roosevelt, letter Dec. 4, 1903, in Elliott Roosevelt, ed., *F.D.R.: His Personal Letters, Early Years* (New York: Duell, Sloan, Pearce, 1948), p. 518.
9. "William Randolph Hearst States His Platform," *Syracuse Post-Standard,* Oct. 7, 1902, p. 1.
10. Harry Thirston Peck, "Twenty Years of the Republic," *The Bookman,* vol. 23, May 1906, p. 320.
11. "William F. Sheehan Dies, Ex-Lieut. Governor," *New York Times,* Mar. 15, 1917, p. 11.
12. "Like a Bomb," *Washington Post,* July 10, 1904, p. 1.
13. *The Riverside History of the United States* (Boston: Houghton Mifflin, 1915), p. 306.
14. Gustavus Myers, *The History of Tammany Hall* (New York: Boni & Liveright, 1917), pp. 215–16.
15. Edward J. Flynn, *You're the Boss* (New York: Viking, 1947), pp. 10–11.
16. Myers, *History of Tammany Hall,* pp. 290–293.
17. Sara Roosevelt, *My Boy Franklin* (New York: Ray Long and Richard R. Smith, Inc., 1933), p. 65.
18. Eleanor Roosevelt, *This I Remember* (New York: Harper Brothers, 1949), p. 14.
19. James Roosevelt, *My Parents: A Differing View* (Chicago: Playboy Press, 1976), pp. 19, 39.
20. "Mrs. Louis McHenry Howe is a Lively Eighty," *Boston Sunday Globe,* June 27, 1954.
21. Reminiscences of Frances Perkins, CUOHROC, Part I, p. 427.
22. Rudolph Wilson Chamberlain, *There Is No Truce* (New York: Macmillan, 1935), p. 155.
23. Francis A. Willard, letter to T. M. Osborne, Nov. 7, 1906, Syracuse University Special Collections, Osborne Family Papers, Box 62, correspondence, Nov. 1–10, 1906.

24. Louis Howe, letter to Grace Howe, Oct. 26, 1906, Louis Howe Personal Papers, Louis Howe to Grace Howe 1905–1911, FDRL.
25. "Mr. Conners Presides over a Palace of Quiet," *New York Times,* Oct. 11, 1906, p. 3.
26. Louis Howe, letter to Thomas M. Osborne, May, 27, 1907, Syracuse University Special Collections, Folder: May 16–31, 1907, Box 65, Osborne Family papers.
27. Charles Evans Hughes, David J. Danelski, Joseph S. Tulchin, eds., *The Autobiographical Notes of Charles Evans Hughes* (Cambridge, MA: Harvard University, 1973), p. 85.
28. Lela Stiles, *The Man Behind Roosevelt* (Cleveland: World Pub. Co., 1954), p. 21.
29. Francis A. Willard, letter to T. M. Osborne, Nov. 7, 1906, Syracuse University Special Collections, Osborne Family Papers, Box 62, correspondence, Nov. 1–10, 1906.

CHAPTER 3

1. Louis Howe, letter to T. M. Osborne, Nov. 29, 1906, Syracuse University Special Collections, Osborne Family Papers, Box 62, correspondence, Nov. 21–30, 1906.
2. Louis Howe, file to T. M. Osborne, "Report No. 5," May 27, 1907, Syracuse University Special Collections, Osborne Family Papers, Box 65, correspondence, May 27, 1907.
3. Louis Howe, letter to Grace Howe, Nov. 1906, Louis Howe Personal Papers, Louis Howe to Grace Howe 1905–11, FDRL.
4. "Mrs. Louis McHenry Howe Is a Lively Eighty," *Boston Sunday Globe,* June 27, 1954, p. 67.
5. Reminiscences of Herbert Lehman, CUOHROC, p. 249.
6. Franklin Roosevelt, letter to Sara Roosevelt, Sept. 7, 1907, Elliott Roosevelt, ed. *F.D.R.: His Personal Papers* (New York: Duell, Sloan and Pearce, 1948), p. 136.
7. Roland Redmond, interview Oct. 27, 1978, Eleanor Roosevelt Oral Histories, FDRL, p. 19.
8. Eleanor Roosevelt, *This Is My Story* (New York: Harper and Bros., 1937), p. 148.
9. Eleanor Roosevelt, letter to Lorena Hickok, quoted in Blanche Weisen Cook, *Eleanor* (New York: Viking, 1992), p. 180.
10. Franklin and Eleanor Roosevelt, letter to Sara Roosevelt, July 19, 1907, Roosevelt, ed. *F.D.R.* p. 136.
11. Rudolph Wilson Chamberlain, *There Is No Truce* (New York: Macmillan, 1935), p. 157.
12. U.S. Federal Census, 1900, Cambridge Ward 2; Middlesex, Massachusetts; Roll T623–656, p. 1A.
13. Chamberlain, *There Is No Truce,* p. 157.
14. Chamberlain, *There Is No Truce,* p. 159.
15. "The Two Peace Parties," *Syracuse Post-Standard,* Apr. 17, 1907, p. 4.
16. "The Two Peace Parties," *Syracuse Post-Standard.*
17. Jackson P. Searle, letter to the editor, *New York Times,* Oct. 12, 1906, p. 8.
18. "The Satanic Majesty of William R. Hearst," *Current Literature,* vol. 47, no. 6, Dec. 1909, p. 618.
19. "Democracy's New 'Leader,'" *Syracuse Herald,* Oct. 4, 1906, p. 12.
20. Will Irwin, "The Rise of 'Fingy' Conners," *Collier's,* July 11, 1908, p. 10.
21. T. M. Osborne, letter to Louis Howe May 14, 1907, Syracuse University Special Collections, Osborne Family Papers, Box 65, correspondence, May 1–15, 1907.
22. "Authors at Home," *New York Times Saturday Review of Books and Art,* Nov. 12, 1898, p. 750.
23. "Syracuse Democrats Swinging to Sulzer," *Syracuse Post-Standard,* June 27, 1910, p. 7.
24. "Syracuse Democrats Swinging to Sulzer," *Syracuse Post-Standard.*
25. "Mrs. Louis McHenry Howe Is a Lively Eighty," *Boston Sunday Globe.*
26. Louis Howe, letter to Franklin Roosevelt, 1912, reprinted in Lela Stiles, *The Man Behind Roosevelt* (Cleveland: World Pub. Co., 1954), p. 24.
27. Louis Howe, letter to Franklin Roosevelt, 1922?, Louis Howe Official Papers, Correspondence with Franklin D. Roosevelt 1921–28, FDRL.

28.   Frances Perkins, *The Roosevelt I Knew* (New York: Viking, 1946), p. 3.

CHAPTER 4

1.   Franklin Roosevelt, letter to "Clarkson," Aug. 20, 1923?, private collection; also, Franklin D. Roosevelt, letter to Lewis B. Emmerman, Jan. 8, 1925, Roosevelt, Franklin D., General Correspondence, 1920–28, "E" FDRL.
2.   W. A. Warn, "Senator F.D. Roosevelt Chief Insurgent at Albany," *New York Times Magazine*, Jan. 22, 1911, p. 11.
3.   "Perkins Had Varied Career in Banking, Railroads, Politics," typescript of newspaper article, July 23, 1952, Papers of Philip Mylod, Small Collections, FDRL.
4.   S. H. Troy, letter to Mrs. Perkins, Nov. 12, 1953, Papers of Edward Perkins, Small Collections, FDRL.
5.   Nancy Joan Weiss, *Charles Francis Murphy, 1858–1924* (Gluckstadt, Germany: J. J. Augustin, 1968), p. 22.
6.   Stephen J. DeCosse, "Edward J. Flynn: The Political Boss and Social Reform," Edward J. Flynn Collection, Biography by Stephen J. DeCosse, FDRL.
7.   Reminiscences of Edward J. Flynn, CUOHROC, pp. 5–6.
8.   Reminiscences of Frances Perkins, CUOHROC, Part I, p. 425.
9.   "Caucus Again Ballots in Vain," *New York Times,* Mar 29, 1911, p. 2.
10.   Louis Howe, Baby Book 1910, quoted in Alfred B. Rollins Jr., *Roosevelt and Howe* (New York: Knopf, 1962), p. 84.
11.   Eleanor Roosevelt, *This Is My Story* (New York: Harper Brothers, 1937), p. 148.
12.   Warn, "Senator F. D. Roosevelt."
13.   Warn, "Senator F. D. Roosevelt."
14.   Franklin D. Roosevelt, *The Happy Warrior* (Boston: Houghton Mifflin, 1928), p. 4.
15.   "Mr. Sheehan Now Faces Big Revolt in Senate Fight," *New York Herald,* Jan. 25, 1911, p. 3.
16.   Lela Stiles, *The Man Behind Roosevelt* (Cleveland: World Pub. Co., 1954), p. 27.
17.   Warn, "Senator F.D. Roosevelt."
18.   Warn, "Senator F.D. Roosevelt."
19.   Alfred Smith, *Up to Now* (New York: Viking, 1929), p. 71–72.
20.   Reminiscences of Jonah Goldstein, CUOHROC, p. 18.
21.   Perkins, CUOHROC, Part II, p. 84.
22.   Roosevelt, *Happy Warrior,* p. 6.
23.   "Patronage Cry Raised by Insurgents," *New York Herald,* Jan. 27, 1911, p. 3.
24.   Warn, "Senator F. D. Roosevelt."
25.   Roosevelt, *This Is My Story,* p. 30.
26.   Frances Perkins, *The Roosevelt I Knew* (New York: Viking, 1946), p. 11.
27.   Meredith Stebbins, "Mrs. Howe Says President Dies as Martyr to Both World Freedom and Peace," *Fall River Herald News,* Apr. 13, 1945.
28.   Louis M. Howe, "Behind the Scenes of the National Campaign," *The Jeffersonian,* vol. 2, no.8, Nov. 1932, p. 18.
29.   Stiles, *Man Behind Roosevelt,* p. 31.
30.   Howe, "Behind the Scenes of the National Campaign."

CHAPTER 5

1.   "Caucus Again Ballots in Vain," *New York Times,* Mar. 29, 1911, p. 2.
2.   "O'Gorman Elected Senator," *Middletown Daily Times-Press,* Apr. 1, 1911, p. 3.
3.   "O'Gorman Elected Senator," *Middletown Daily Times-Press.*
4.   "Senator Roosevelt Satisfied," *New York Times,* Apr. 2, 1911, p. 6.
5.   "James A. O'Gorman," *Middletown Daily Times-Press,* Apr. 1, 1911, p. 1.
6.   "A Friendly Chat with Mrs. Louis Howe," *New Bedford (MA) Sunday Standard,* undated clipping, Alfred Rollins, Small Collections, FDRL.

7. Meredith Stebbins, "Mrs. Howe Says President Dies as Martyr to Both World Freedom and Peace," *Fall River Herald News,* Apr. 13, 1945, p. 4.
8. Louis Howe, letter to Grace Howe, Oct. 1911?, Louis Howe Personal Papers, Louis Howe to Grace Howe 1905–11, FDRL.
9. *Tribune Almanac and Political Register* (New York: Tribune Association, 1911) pp. 719–724.
10. "New York Assembly Solidly Republican," *New York Times,* Nov. 8, 1911, p. 2.
11. Eleanor Roosevelt, *This Is My Story* (New York: Harper Brothers, 1937), p. 175.
12. Frederic Harris, interview Apr. 7, 1948, Small Collections, Oral Histories, Frank Friedel Collection, FDRL; Reminiscences of Joseph M. Proskauer, 1962, CUOHROC, p. 17.
13. Louis Howe, letter to Grace Howe, Louis Howe Personal Papers, Louis Howe to Grace Howe 1915–1922, FDRL.
14. Roosevelt, *This Is My Story,* p. 174.
15. George Haven Putnam, *Memories of a Publisher, 1865–1915* (New York: G.P. Putnam & Sons, 1915), pp. 360–62.
16. "Wilson Men Attack Murphy and Gaynor," *New York Times,* Jun. 25, 1912, p. 5.
17. Louis Howe, letter to Franklin D. Roosevelt, July 1912, reprinted in Lela Stiles, *The Man Behind Roosevelt* (Cleveland: World Pub. Co., 1954), p. 25.
18. Howe letter to Franklin Roosevelt, July, 1912, reprinted in Stiles, *The Man Behind Roosevelt,* p. 25.
19. Putnam, *Memories of a Publisher,* pp. 362–64.
20. "The Triangular Fight in New York," *American Review of Reviews,* 46–3, Sept. 1912, pp. 276–77.
21. S.J. Woolf, "As His Closest Friend Sees Roosevelt," *New York Times Magazine,* Nov. 27, 1932, p. 3
22. "Empire Democrats Name State Ticket," *New York Times,* Sept. 20, 1912, p. 4.
23. Louis Howe, letter to Franklin D. Roosevelt, Sept., 1912, reprinted in Stiles, *Man Behind Roosevelt,* p. 34.
24. Roosevelt, *This Is My Story,* p. 147.
25. Kenneth Davis, *FDR: The Beckoning of Destiny* (New York: Random House, 1971), p. 293.
26. Louis McHenry Howe, "Behind the Scenes of the National Campaign," *Jeffersonian,* vol. 2, no. 8, Nov. 1932, p. 18.
27. Jefferson Newbold Jr., letter to Franklin D. Roosevelt, Apr. 23, 1926; Folder: Newbold, Jefferson Jr., Roosevelt, Franklin D., Family, Business and Personal Papers, FDRL.
28. Howe, "Behind the Scenes."
29. Howe, "Behind the Scenes."

CHAPTER 6

1. Louis Howe, "Behind the Scenes of the National Campaign," *The Jeffersonian,* vol. 2, no.8, Nov. 1932, p. 18.
2. Robert Dallek, *Franklin D. Roosevelt and American Foreign Policy 1932–1945* (New York: Oxford University Press, 1995), p. 7.
3. Franklin D. Roosevelt, letter to Louis Howe, Apr. 9, 1913, Louis Howe Personal Papers, Roosevelt, Franklin D. 1913–1922, FDRL.
4. Roosevelt to Howe, Apr 9, 1913.
5. Lela Stiles, *The Man Behind Roosevelt* (Cleveland: World Pub. Co., 1954), p. 42.
6. S. J. Woolf, "As His Closest Friend Sees Roosevelt," *New York Times Magazine,* Nov. 27, 1932, p. 3.
7. Josephus Daniels interview, Small Collections, Oral Histories, Papers of Frank Friedel, p. 4, FDRL.
8. Louis Howe, letter to Franklin Roosevelt, June 28, June 30, 1913, Louis Howe Personal Papers, Correspondence Apr.-Dec. 1913, FDRL.
9. Eleanor Roosevelt, *This Is My Story* (New York: Harper & Brothers, 1937), p. 66.

10. Roosevelt, *This Is My Story*, p. 17.
11. Stiles, *Man Behind Roosevelt*, p. 53.
12. Mary Howe Baker, note, Louis Howe Personal Papers, Pre-1928, FDRL.
13. Samuel S. Adams, note, Louis Howe Personal Papers, Pre-1928, FDRL.
14. Mary Howe Baker, note, Louis Howe Personal Papers, Pre-1928, FDRL.
15. Louis Howe, letter to Grace Howe, undated, Louis Howe Official Papers, Letters and Materials 1912–32, FDRL.
16. Louis Howe, letter to Grace Howe, undated, Louis Howe Official Papers, Letters and Materials 1912–32, FDRL.
17. Louis Howe, letter to Grace Howe, undated, Louis Howe Personal Papers, Louis Howe to Grace Howe, 1915–22, FDRL.
18. James Richardson interview, Small Collections, Oral Histories, Papers of Frank Friedel, p. 2, FDRL. Richardson's opinion may have been colored by an intervening crisis in his career, when as an admiral he was recalled by then President Roosevelt in 1940 for claiming that Pearl Harbor, Hawaii was an indefensible place to move the U.S. Pacific fleet.
19. Stiles, *Man Behind Roosevelt*, p. 40.
20. "Ask Bids as Bill is Signed," *New York Times*, Aug. 30, 1916, p. 6.
21. Josephus Daniels, *Our Navy at War* (New York: George Doran, 1922), p. 12.
22. Louis Howe, letter to Thos. Durning, Jan. 23, 1924, Louis Howe Official Papers, Correspondence with Franklin D. Roosevelt 1921–28, FDRL.
23. R. H. Camalier, letter to Franklin Roosevelt, Nov. 9, 1922; Franklin D. Roosevelt, Family, Business and Personal Correspondence, "C," FDRL.
24. R. H. Camalier, interview May 28, 1948, Small Collections, oral histories, Frank Friedel Collection, FDRL, pp. 6–7.
25. Camalier, interview May 28, 1948, p. 6.
26. Reminiscences of Frances Perkins, CUOHROC, Part I, p. 428.
27. Elliott Roosevelt, interview June 20, 1979, Oral histories, Eleanor Roosevelt Papers, FDRL, p. 16.
28. Joseph P. Lash, *Eleanor and Franklin* (New York: W.W. Norton, 1971), p. 222.
29. "Lay Navy Scandal to F. D. Roosevelt," *New York Times*, July 20, 1921.
30. "Will Investigate Navy Prison Charge," *New York Times*, Jan. 6, 1920, p. 20.
31. Louis Howe, letter to Grace Howe, Oct. 9 1919, Louis Howe Personal Papers, Louis Howe to Grace Howe 1915–1922, FDRL.

CHAPTER 7

1. Alfred E. Smith, *Up To Now* (New York: Viking, 1929), p. 182.
2. Smith, *Up to Now*, p. 170.
3. Smith, *Up To Now*, p. 187.
4. Smith, *Up to Now*, p. 190.
5. Belle Moskowitz, typescript memoir, Lear Center for Special Collections and Archives, Connecticut College, p. 4.
6. Geoffrey Ward, *A First-Class Temperament* (New York: Harper & Row, 1989), p. 513.
7. Eleanor Roosevelt, *Autobiography* (New York: DaCapo, 1992), p. 150.
8. Elliott Roosevelt, ed., *F.D.R.: His Personal Papers, 1905–1928* (New York: Duell, Sloan and Pearce, 1948), p. 493.
9. Franklin Roosevelt, letter to Eleanor Roosevelt, July 17, 1920, in Roosevelt, ed., *F.D.R.: His Personal Papers, 1905–1928*, p. 493.
10. "Roosevelt's Aid May Succeed Him," *Brooklyn Eagle*, July 29, 1920; "Howe Urged as Daniels Aid," *New York Tribune*, Aug. 14, 1920.
11. "Expect Big Crowd to Hear Roosevelt," *New York Times*, Aug. 9, 1920, p. 3.
12. Edith Moriarty, "With the Women of Today," *Janesville (WI) Daily Gazette*, Aug. 27, 1920, p. 7.

13.   "Woodbury Takes Roosevelt's Post," *New York Times,* Aug. 27, 1920, p. 7; Thomas Madigan Jr., "Gordon Woodbury," *Proceedings of the Bar Association of the State of New Hampshire,* 1920, p. 220.

14.   "Roosevelt in Plane for Campaign Speech," *New York Times,* Oct. 10, 1920, p. 3.

15.   "Roosevelt Replies to Coolidge Speech," *New York Times,* Oct. 28, 1920, p. 5, "Roosevelt Talks in Rain," *New York Times,* Aug. 25, 1920, p. 5.

16.   Eleanor Roosevelt, letter to Sara Roosevelt, Oct. 19, 1920, in Eleanor Roosevelt, with Leonard C. Schlup and Donald Whisenhunt, ed., *It Seems To Me, Selected Letters of Eleanor Roosevelt* (Lexington: University Press of Kentucky, 2001), pp. 18–19.

17.   Eleanor Roosevelt, letter to Sara Roosevelt Oct. 19, 1920, in Roosevelt, *It Seems to Me,* pp. 18–19.

18.   R. H. Camalier, interview, Frank Friedel Collection, Small Collections, R. H. Camalier, FDRL, p. 7.

19.   Zoe Beckley, "Mrs. Franklin Roosevelt is Democratic Convert," *Waterloo (IA) Times-Tribune,* Oct. 8, 1920, p. 13.

20.   Conrad Black, *Franklin Delano Roosevelt* (Washington: Public Affairs, 2005), p. 127.

21.   Stephen T. Early, typescript, Stephen T. Early Collection, Cuff Links 1920–1933, FDRL, p. 3.

22.   Roosevelt, *Autobiography,* pp. 108–11.

23.   Roosevelt, *Autobiography,* p. 111.

24.   Franklin Roosevelt, letter to Adelbert M. Scribner, Jan. 10, 1921, Franklin Roosevelt, Family, General and Personal Correspondence, General Correspondence 1920–28, "Sa-SC," FDRL.

25.   Franklin Roosevelt, letter to James J. Hoey, Jan. 7, 1921, Franklin Roosevelt Family, General and Personal Correspondence, General Correspondence 1920–28, " Ho-Hy," FDRL.

26.   Llewellyn Howeland, letter to Louis Howe, Sept. 29, 1920, Louis Howe Personal Papers, Louis Howe and Grace Howe 1905–1946, FDRL.

27.   Hartley Edward Howe, "Autobiography," Louis Howe Personal Papers, Manuscript, undated, Microfilm #2, FDRL.

28.   Louis Howe, letter to Grace Howe, July 10, 1922, Louis Howe Personal Papers, Louis Howe to Grace Howe 1915–1922, FDRL.

29.   "Lay Navy Scandal to F.D. Roosevelt," *New York Times,* July 20, 1921, p. 4.

30.   "Newport Scandal Subject of Report," *Galveston Daily News,* July 20, 1921, 9.

31.   "Daniels Scored for Probe Plans," *Atlanta Constitution,* July 20, 1921, p. 2.

32.   Marguerite LeHand, letter to Eleanor Roosevelt, Aug. 23, 1921, Franklin Roosevelt Family, Business, and Personal, LeHand, Marguerite, FDRL.

CHAPTER 8

1.   S.J. Woolf, "As His Closest Friend Sees Roosevelt," *New York Times Magazine,* Nov. 27, 1932, p. 3.

2.   Eleanor Roosevelt, letter to James R. Roosevelt, Aug. 14, 1921, Eleanor Roosevelt Papers, Family and Personal Correspondence, Condolence letters to Eleanor Roosevelt, FDRL.

3.   James R. Roosevelt, letter to Eleanor Roosevelt, Aug. 20, 1921, Eleanor Roosevelt Papers, Family and Personal Correspondence, Condolence letters to Eleanor Roosevelt, FDRL.

4.   Frederic Delano to Eleanor Roosevelt, Aug. 28, 1921, Franklin D. Roosevelt, Family, Business and Personal Papers, Infantile Paralysis, FDR's attack and treatment, FDRL.

5.   Frederic Delano to Eleanor Roosevelt, Aug. 20, 1921, Franklin D. Roosevelt, Family, Business and Personal Papers, Infantile Paralysis, FDR's attack and treatment, FDRL.A 2003 research paper by a team of physicians in Texas concluded that Roosevelt's symptoms were less consistent with polio than with an auto-immune disorder called Guillain-Barré Syndrome, which was unknown in 1921. If that supposition is correct, then it is well that Roosevelt was not a man to harbor bitterness or regret regarding the circumstances

surrounding his attack, because all the massaging in the world wouldn't have affected GBS one way or the other.

6. Dr. Levine would have a storied career in cardiology after World War II.

7. Meredith Stebbins, "Mrs. Howe Says President Dies as Martyr to Both World Freedom and Peace," *Fall River Herald News,* Apr. 13, 1945.

8. Lela Stiles, *The Man Behind Roosevelt* (Cleveland: World Pub. Co., 1954), p. 77.

9. Eleanor Roosevelt, letter to Missy LeHand, Aug. 20, 1921, Franklin D. Roosevelt, Family, Business and Personal Papers, Lehand, Marguerite, FDRL.

10. Eleanor Roosevelt, letter to Missy LeHand, Aug. 20, 1921.

11. Marguerite LeHand, letter to Eleanor Roosevelt, Aug. 23, 1921, Franklin D. Roosevelt, Family, Business and Personal Papers, Lehand, Marguerite, FDRL.

12. Mrs. Charles Hamlin, "Some Memories of Franklin Delano Roosevelt," typescript, Eleanor Anna and Franklin Roosevelt, Small Collections, Reminiscences by Contemporaries, Hamlin, Huybertie, FDRL.

13. Eleanor Roosevelt to Marguerite LeHand, Aug. 30, 1921, Franklin D. Roosevelt, Family, Business and Personal Papers, Lehand, Marguerite, FDRL.

14. Sara Roosevelt, letter to Frederic Delano, Sept. 1, 1921, Franklin D. Roosevelt, Family, Business and Personal Papers, Infantile Paralysis, FDR's attack and treatment, FDRL.

15. Louis Howe, letter to Franklin Roosevelt, Sept. 30 1921, Louis Howe Official Papers, Correspondence with FDR 1921–24, FDRL.

16. S. J. Woolf, "As His Closest Friend Sees Roosevelt," *New York Times Magazine,* Nov. 27, 1932, p. 3.

17. Eleanor Roosevelt to Marguerite LeHand, Aug. 30, 1921; Franklin D. Roosevelt, Family, Business and Personal Papers, Lehand, Marguerite, FDRL.

18. Reminiscences of Frances Perkins, CUOHROC, Part IV, p. 455.

19. Reminiscences of Frances Perkins, p. 456.

20. Woolf, "As His Closest Friend Sees Roosevelt."

21. Marvin McIntyre, letter to Franklin Roosevelt, Sept. 20, 1921, Franklin D. Roosevelt, Family, Business and Personal Papers, McIntyre, Marvin, FDRL.

22. Armond S. Goldman et al., "What was the cause of Franklin Delano Roosevelt's paralytic illness?" *Journal of Medical Biography,* vol. 11 (2003), p. 232.

23. Franklin D. Roosevelt, letter to Frank Waters, Oct. 14, 1921, Franklin D. Roosevelt, Family, Business and Personal Papers, Waters, Frank, FDRL.

24. Franklin D. Roosevelt, letter to *New York Daily News,* Oct. 24, 1921; Folder: D, Roosevelt, Franklin D., Family, Business and Personal Correspondence, FDRL.

25. Claude G. Bowers, letter, excerpted in Elliott Roosevelt, ed., *F.D.R.: His Personal Papers, 1905–1928* (New York: Duell, Sloan and Pearce, 1948), pp. 496–97.

26. Stephen T. Early, typescript, Stephen T. Early Collection, Cuff Links 1920–1933, FDRL, p. 5.

CHAPTER 9

1. Anna R. Halstead, interview, May 11, 1973, Oral histories, Eleanor Roosevelt Papers, FDRL, p. 3.

2. Anna Roosevelt to Eleanor Roosevelt, Sept. 22, 1921, Eleanor Roosevelt Papers, Family and Personal Correspondence, Roosevelt, A.,FDRL.

3. Eleanor Roosevelt, *This I Remember* (New York: Harper & Brothers, 1949), p. 25.

4. Sara Roosevelt, *My Boy Franklin* (New York: Ray Long and Richard R. Smith, 1933), p. 103.

5. James Roosevelt, *My Parents: A Differing View* (Chicago: Playboy Press, 1976), p. 76.

6. Roosevelt, *My Parents,* p. 77.

7. Roosevelt, *My Parents,* p. 85.

8. Roosevelt, *My Parents,* p. 67.

9. Anna R. Halstead, interview, p. 3.
10. Anna R. Halstead, interview, p. 3.
11. Eleanor Roosevelt, *This Is My Story* (New York: Harper & Brothers, 1937), p. 336
12. Joan Morgenthau Hirschorn, Oral History, Eleanor Roosevelt Oral Histories, FDRL.
13. Franklin Roosevelt, New York State Income Tax Return, 1921 and Individual Income Federal Tax Return, 1921; Folder: Income Tax Returns, 1921, Franklin D. Roosevelt, Family Business, and Personal Correspondence, Financial Matters, FDRL.
14. Louis Howe, letter to Homer Ferguson, Dec. 1921, Fidelity and Deposit Company of Maryland, Correspondence of Franklin Roosevelt as Vice-President, 1921–1928.
15. William T. Briggs to Franklin Roosevelt, Oct. 3, 1921, Franklin D. Roosevelt, Family Business, and Personal Correspondence, "B," FDRL.
16. John B. Shearer to Franklin Roosevelt, Apr. 7, 1944, Folder: Jack Shearer, Franklin Roosevelt Personal Papers, FDRL.
17. Ellen McCormick to Franklin Roosevelt, Dec. 7, 1922, Franklin D. Roosevelt, General Correspondence, "Mac-Mo," FDRL.
18. Reminiscences of Dickerman, 1973, CUOHROC, p. 133.
19. Caroline O'Day, letter to Franklin Roosevelt, Jan. 20, 1922; Franklin Roosevelt to Caroline O'Day, Jan. 28, 1922, Franklin D. Roosevelt, General Correspondence 1920–1928, "O," FDRL.
20. Franklin D. Roosevelt, letter to George Ketchum, Sept. 29, 1921, Franklin D. Roosevelt, Family and Personal Correspondence, "K," FDRL.
21. "Hyde Park News," *Rhinebeck (NY) Gazette,* Jan. 20, 1922, p. 4.
22. Roosevelt, *This Is My Story,* p. 120.
23. Roosevelt, *This I Remember,* p. 30.
24. Roosevelt, *This Is My Story,* p. 336.
25. Anne Ward Gilbert; Folder: Eleanor Roosevelt Oral Histories, FDRL.
26. Dickerman, CUOHROC, p. 315.
27. Reminiscences of Frances Perkins, CUOHROC, Part II, Session 1, p. 299.
28. Perkins, CUOHROC, p. 329.

CHAPTER 10

1. Louis Depew, Oral History file, Small Collections, FDRL.
2. Franklin Roosevelt, Notes on Springwood History, reprinted in Eleanor Roosevelt, *Franklin D. Roosevelt and Hyde Park* (Washington: National Park Service, [n.d.]), p. 5.
3. Olin Dows, Eleanor Roosevelt Oral Histories, FDRL, p. 34.
4. "Mrs. Vincent Astor Closes Highway to All Except Friends," *Poughkeepsie Evening Star and Enterprise,* Aug. 13, 1921, p. 1.
5. Clara and Hardy Streeholm, *The House at Hyde Park* (New York: Viking, 1950), pp. 115–16.
6. Olin Dows, *Franklin Roosevelt at Hyde Park* (New York: American Artists Group, 1949), pp. 89–90.
7. Depew, Oral History.
8. Moses Smith, Small Collections, "P-Z" Oral History Interviews, FDRL.
9. Thomas Leonard; Small Collections, "A-O" Oral History Interviews, FDRL.
10. Lily Norton, letter to Miss Whidden, Nov. 14, 1921, Anna and Franklin Roosevelt, Reminiscences by Contemporaries, FDRL.
11. Henry Noble MacCracken, *Blithe Dutchess* (New York: Hastings House, 1958), p. 89.
12. MacCracken, *Blithe Dutchess,* p. 90.
13. S. J. Woolf, "As His Closest Friend Sees Roosevelt," *New York Times Magazine,* Nov. 27, 1932, p. 3.
14. Lili Rethi and Frederick L. Rath Jr., *Franklin D. Roosevelt's Hyde Park* (New York: Henry Holt, 1947), not paginated.

15. Elliott Roosevelt, Eleanor Roosevelt, Oral Histories, FDRL.
16. Grace Howe, letter to Mary Hartley, July 1922, Louis Howe Personal Papers, Grace Howe and Mary Hartley, FDRL.
17. Reminiscences of Marion Dickerman, 1973, CUOHROC, p. 315.
18. Depew, Oral History.
19. "Toy Yachts to Race Hudson," *New York Evening Post,* June 8, 1921.
20. Depew, Oral History.
21. Huybertie Pruyn Hamlin, "Franklin Roosevelt," *The New Republic,* Apr. 15, 1946.
22. Anna R. Halstead interview, May 11, 1973, Oral Histories, Eleanor Roosevelt Papers, FDRL, p. 7.
23. Lela Stiles, *The Man Behind Roosevelt* (Cleveland: World Pub. Co., 1954), p. 86.

CHAPTER 11

1. "All for Hearst, Will Win for Sure Says Conners," *New York Tribune,* June 4, 1922, p. 5.
2. "When You Hear Me, You Hear Hearst! He'll Run Says 'Fingy,'" *New York Tribune,* June 12, 1922, p. 3.
3. Marion Davies, *The Times We Had* (New York: Ballantine, 1975), pp. 34–36.
4. "'Vote for Hearst' Soap Is Put Out to Skid Him In," *New York Tribune,* June 22, 1922, p. 5.
5. "Westchester Women Will Bolt Hearst," *New York Tribune,* June 21, 1922, p. 1.
6. "Westchester Women," *New York Tribune.*
7. "Hearst's Ambitions Get Fresh Jolt at Women's Luncheon," *New York Tribune,* June 23, 1922, p. 3.
8. Grace Howe, letter to Mary Hartley, July 8, 1922, Louis Howe Personal Papers, Grace Howe and Mary Hartley, FDRL.
9. Reminiscences of Marion Dickerman, 1973, CUOHROC, p. 11.
10. Gabrielle Forbush interview, Small Collections, Oral History, Interviews A-O, FDRL, p. 8.
11. Dickerman, CUOHROC, p. 11.
12. Eleanor Wotkyns, interview Jun. 12, 1978, Eleanor Roosevelt, Oral Histories, FDRL. Mrs. Wotkyns was one of Eleanor's nieces. She attended many of Mrs. Roosevelt's speeches starting in the 1940s and left a description of her style: "It was always very simple, and yet it said such profound things in a way that everybody could understand . . . everybody in the room felt as though they were getting a letter from her."
13. Eleanor Roosevelt, *This I Remember* (New York: Harper Brothers, 1949), p. 32.
14. "Murphy Locks Wigwam Door Against Conners," *New York Tribune,* June 30, 1922, p. 1.
15. "Hearst Buys Albany Paper to Wage Campaign," *New York Tribune,* June 28, 1922, p. 1.
16. Franklin D. Roosevelt to Neal Brewster, June 30, 1922, Franklin D. Roosevelt Papers, General Correspondence 1920–1928, "Br-By," FDRL.
17. "Hyde Park," *Poughkeepsie Sunday Courier,* June 25, 1922, p. 4.
18. Adolph Caspar Miller was well known as an economist and a member of the first empanelment of the Federal Reserve Board. Grace Howe to Mary Hartley, July 8, 1922, Louis Howe Personal Papers, Grace Howe and Mary Hartley, FDRL.
19. Roosevelt to Brewster, June 30, 1922.
20. "Anti-Hearst Men Agree on Smith as First Choice," *New York Times,* July 8, 1922, p. 2.
21. Alfred E. Smith, *Up To Now* (New York: Viking, 1929), p. 85.
22. Samuel Rosenman, Oral History Interviews, Small Collections, FDRL, p. 43.
23. Rosenman, Oral History Interviews, p. 43.
24. Louis Howe, letter to Grace Howe, July 10, 1922, Louis Howe Personal Papers, Louis Howe and Grace Howe 1915–1922, FDRL.
25. Louis Howe, letter to Grace Howe, July 10, 1922.

CHAPTER 12

1. "Mrs. Hearst Home as Two Bands Play," *New York Times,* July 13, 1922, p. 13.
2. Alfred E. Smith, *Up to Now* (New York: Viking, 1929), p. 229.
3. Denis Tilden Lynch, "Conners Starts Hearst's Boom for President," *New York Tribune,* July 22, 1922, p. 1.
4. Franklin D. Roosevelt, letter to H. F. Morningstar, June 19, 1922, Franklin D. Roosevelt, Family, Business, and Personal Correspondence, "Mo-My," FDRL.
5. Josephus Daniels, interview, Small Collections, Friedel, Frank, FDRL.
6. Reminiscences of Joseph Proskauer, 1962, CUOHROC, p. 2.
7. Proskauer, CUOHROC, p. 3.
8. Franklin Roosevelt, letter to Susannah Thompson, July 31, 1922, Franklin D. Roosevelt, General Correspondence 1920–1928, Thompson, Susannah, FDRL.
9. Harriet May Mills, letter to Franklin D. Roosevelt July 28, 1922; Franklin Roosevelt to Harriet May Mills, Aug. 4, 1922; Franklin D. Roosevelt, General Correspondence 1920–1928, "M," FDRL.
10. Franklin Roosevelt, letter to Alfred Smith, Aug. 13, 1922, Franklin D. Roosevelt, Family, Business, and Personal Correspondence, Smith, Alfred, FDRL; also "Smith Urged to Act by F. D. Roosevelt," *New York Times,* Aug. 15, 1922, p. 13.
11. Alfred Smith, letter to Franklin Roosevelt, Aug. 15, 1922, Franklin D. Roosevelt, Family, Business, and Personal Correspondence, Smith, Alfred, FDRL.
12. "Al Smith's Letter Enlivens Contest for Governorship," *Buffalo Courier,* Aug. 17, 1922, p. 2.
13. George Foster Peabody, letter to Franklin Roosevelt, Aug. 17, 1922, Franklin D. Roosevelt, Family, Business, and Personal Correspondence 1920–1928, Peabody, George F., FDRL.
14. Armond S. Goldman et al., "What was the cause of Franklin Delano Roosevelt's paralytic illness?" *Journal of Medical Biography,* vol. 11 (2003),p. 234.
15. S. A. Woolf, "As His Closest Friend Sees Roosevelt," *New York Times Magazine,* Nov. 27, 1932, p. 3.
16. Eleanor Roosevelt, *This I Remember* (New York: Harper Brothers, 1949), p. 25.
17. Roosevelt, *This I Remember,* p. 25.
18. Lela Stiles, *The Man Behind Roosevelt* (Cleveland: World Pub. Co., 1954), p. 83.
19. "Dutchess County," *Syracuse Herald,* Sept. 27, 1922, p. 18.
20. Reminiscences of Marion Dickerman, 1973, CUOHROC, p. 105.
21. Dickerman, CUOHROC, p. 11.
22. Louis Howe, letter to Grace Howe, July 10, 1922, Louis Howe Personal Papers, Louis Howe and Grace Howe 1915–1922, FDRL.
23. Kenneth S. Davis, *Invincible Summer: An Intimate Portrait of the Roosevelts Based on the Recollections of Marion Dickerman* (New York: Atheneum, 1974), p. 19.
24. "Strength of Hearst on Steady Increase," *Buffalo Courier,* Sept. 8, 1922, p. 1.
25. "Along the Trails of Convention," *Syracuse Post-Standard,* Sept. 27, 1922, p. 6.
26. "Two Places on Ticket Wanted by New Voters," *Syracuse Post-Standard,* Sept. 29, 1922, p. 6; J. B. Watson, "Expect Democrats to Begin Casting Ballots at State Convention Today," *Buffalo Courier,* Sept. 29, 1922, p. 1.
27. "Two Places on Ticket Wanted by New Voters," *Syracuse Post-Standard,* p. 1
28. Matthew and Hannah Josephson, *Al Smith: Hero of the Cities* (Boston: Houghton Mifflin, 1969), p. 271.
29. "Smith's Name Cheered When Women Gather," *Syracuse Post-Standard,* Sept. 29, 1922, p. 1.
30. Stiles, *Man Behind Roosevelt,* p. 89.
31. "Smith's Name Cheered," *Syracuse Post-Standard.*
32. "Smith's Name Cheered," *Syracuse Post-Standard.*
33. Smith, *Up to Now,* p. 233.

34. "Women Fail in Effort to Get Post on Ticket," *Syracuse Post-Standard,* Sept. 30, 1922, p. 10.

35. "Women Fail in Effort," *Syracuse Post-Standard,* p. 10.

36. Louis Howe, letter to Franklin Roosevelt, telegram Sept. 29, 1922, Louis Howe Official Papers, Correspondence with FDR 1921–24, FDRL.

37. Franklin Roosevelt, letter to Louis Wehle, Nov. 18, 1922; Franklin D. Roosevelt, General Correspondence 1920–28, Wehle, Louis, FDRL.

38. "Women Fail in Effort," *Syracuse Post-Standard.*

CHAPTER 13

1. James Roosevelt, *My Parents: A Differing View* (Chicago: Playboy Press, 1976), p. 57–58.

2. Anna Roosevelt Halstead, interview, Oral histories, Eleanor Roosevelt Papers, May 11, 1973, FDRL.

3. Franklin Roosevelt to Livingston Davis, Sept. 3, 1924, Franklin D. Roosevelt, Family, General, and Personal Correspondence, Davis, Livingston, FDRL.

4. Reminiscences of Marion Dickerman, 1973, CUOHROC, p. 302.

5. Elliott Roosevelt and James Brough, *An Untold Story* (New York: Dell, 1973), p. 179.

6. Franklin D. Roosevelt, "John Paul Jones" [1923], Franklin D. Roosevelt, Family, Business, and Personal Papers, Writing and Statements, FDRL.

7. Eleanor Roosevelt, *This I Remember,* (New York: Harper Brothers, 1949), pp. 29–30.

8. Louis Howe, letter to A. P. Homer, Nov. 4, 1921, Franklin D. Roosevelt, Family, General & Personal Correspondence; Homer, Arthur P., FDRL.

9. Louis Howe, letter to Franklin Roosevelt [1927?], Louis Howe Official Papers, Correspondence with Franklin Roosevelt 1921–28, FDRL; Louis Howe, letter to Franklin Roosevelt, Feb. 27, 1925, Louis Howe Official Papers, Correspondence with Franklin D. Roosevelt, 1921–28, folder 1925–26, FDRL; Louis Howe to Franklin Roosevelt, Frb. 6, 1924, Louis Howe Official Papers, Correspondence with Franklin D. Roosevelt, 1921–28, folder 1925–26.

10. Louis Howe, letter to Franklin Roosevelt, Mar. 5, 1924, Louis Howe Official Papers, Correspondence with Franklin Roosevelt 1921–28, FDRL.

11. Louis Howe, letter to Franklin Roosevelt, Feb. 27, 1925, Louis Howe Official Papers, Correspondence with Franklin Roosevelt 1921–28, FDRL.

12. Louis Howe, letter to Franklin Roosevelt, Feb. 25, 1924, Louis Howe Official Papers, Correspondence with Franklin Roosevelt 1921–1924, FDRL

13. Louis Howe, letter to Franklin Roosevelt, Feb. 14, 1924, Louis Howe Official Papers, Correspondence with Franklin Roosevelt 1921–1924, FDRL.

14. Franklin Roosevelt to Louis Howe, Mar. 3, 1924, Louis Howe Official Papers, Correspondence with Franklin Roosevelt 1921–28, FDRL.

15. Reminiscences of Edward J. Flynn, CUOHROC, p. 5.

16. Reminiscences of Jeremiah T. Mahoney, CUOHROC, pp. 49–51.

17. Reminiscences of Joseph M.Proskauer, 1962, CUOHROC, p. 17.

18. Reminiscences of Edward J. Flynn, CUOHROC, p. 8.

19. Franklin D. Roosevelt, letter to Charles J. Edwards, Dec. 11, 1922, Franklin D. Roosevelt, General Correspondence 1920–28, "E," FDRL.

20. Franklin Roosevelt, letter to Sidney Gunn, Sept. 4, 1924, Franklin D. Roosevelt, Family, Business, and Personal Correspondence, Gunn, Sidney, FDRL.

21. Franklin Roosevelt to Bryon E. Newton, Dec. 20, 1922, Franklin D. Roosevelt, General Correspondence 1920–28, "N," FDRL.

22. Reminiscences of Marion Dickerman, CUOHROC, p. 22.

23. Roosevelt, *My Parents,* p. 93.

24. Dickerman, CUOHROC, p. 22.

25. Huibertje Hamlin, Reminiscences by contemporaries, Roosevelt, Anna and Franklin, Small Collections, FDRL.

26. Roosevelt, *My Parents,* p. 93.
27. Elmer Davis, "Outburst Beats M'Adoo's," *New York Times,* June 27, 1924, p. 1.
28. Alfred Smith, *Up to Now* (New York: Viking, 1929), p. 288.
29. Harry B. Hunt, "Dem Outbreaks Hold the 'Fuss and Fury' Record," *Bismarck (MT) Tribune,* July 23, 1924, p. 6.
30. Dickerman, CUOHROC, p. 22.
31. Marion Dickerman, "The Val-Kill Industries," Small Collections, Oral Histories, Marion Dickerman, FDRL.
32. Louis Howe to Mary Howe, undated; Folder: Howe, Louis, Letters to wife and children, Louis Howe Personal Papers, FDRL.
33. Louis Howe to Franklin Roosevelt, May 8, 1929, Folder: Louis Howe, FDR Governorship Papers, FDRL.

CHAPTER 14

1.   Louis Howe, letter to Grace Howe, Oct. 3, 1928, Louis Howe Personal Papers, Folder: Louis Howe and Grace Howe 1927–28, FDRL.
2.   Eleanor Roosevelt, *This I Remember* (New York: Harper Brothers, 1949), p. 46.
3.   Samuel I. Rosenman, *Working With Roosevelt* (New York: Harper, 1952), p. 16.
4.   Reminiscences of Frances Perkins, CUOHROC, Part I, p. 330.
5.   Alfred B. Rollins, *Roosevelt and Howe* (New York: Knopf, 1962), p. 240.
6.   "A. C. James to Head Roosevelt Drive," *New York Times,* Oct. 12, 1928, p. 6.
7.   "Mrs. Moskowitz Not in New Regime," *New York Times,* Dec. 29, 1929, p. 2.
8.   Elisabeth Israels Perry, *Belle Moskowitz* (New York: Oxford University Press, 1987), pp. 206–7.
9.   Lizzie Andrew Borden, Last Will & Testament, Jan. 30, 1926, Tattered Fabric website, Faye Musselman, ed. (http://phayemuss.wordpress.com/source-documents).
10. Lucie Adam O'Brien, "Atmosphere of Comfort and Charm Characterizes the House of Howe," Alfred Rollins Collection, Clippings, FDRL.
11. "Mrs. Moskowitz Eulogized as Woman of Rare Intellect," *New Castle (PA) Times,* Jan. 11, 1933, p. 4.
12. Reminiscences of Eleanor Roosevelt, May 17, 1957, CUOHROC, p. 3.
13. S.J. Woolf, "As His Closest Friend Sees Roosevelt," *New York Times Magazine,* Nov. 27, 1932, p. SM 3.
14. Lizzie McDuffie, "He called Me Lizzie," Folder: Lizzie McDuffie, Small Collections, Anna, Eleanor and Franklin Roosevelt, Reminiscences by Contemporaries, FDRL
15. Roosevelt, *This I Remember,* p. 65.
16. Louis Howe, "The 1932 Democratic National Campaign," Louis Howe Personal Papers, Transcripts of Articles 1932 FDRL.
17. Franklin Roosevelt, letter to Louis Howe, May 8, 1931, Louis Howe Personal Papers, Correspondences with Franklin Roosevelt, FDRL.
18. Elisabeth Israels Perry, *Belle Moskowitz: Feminine Politics and the Exercise of Power in the Age of Alfred E. Smith* (New York: Oxford University Press 1987), p. 211.
19. Reminiscences of Marion Dickerman, 1973, CUOHROC, p. 50.
20. Kenneth S. Davis, *Invincible Summer: An Intimate Portrait of The Roosevelts Based on the Recollections of Marion Dickerman* (New York: Atheneum, 1974), p. 104.
21. James A. Hagerty, "Smith-Hearst Feud Aided Roosevelt," *New York Times,* July 3, 1932.
22. Dickerman, CUOHROC, p. 52.
23. Dickerman, CUOHROC, p. 52.
24. Perry, *Belle Moskowitz,* p. 213.
25. Frances Perkins to Louis Howe, Nov. 11, 1932, Louis Howe Personal Papers, Congratulations 1932–33, FDRL.
26. Bernard M. Baruch, letter to Louis Howe, July 8, 1932, Louis Howe Personal Papers, Congratulations 1932–33, FDRL.

27.   Herbert Bayard Swope, Letter to Louis Howe, Nov. 9, 1932, Louis Howe Personal Papers, Congratulations 1932–33, FDRL.

28.   John F. Fitzgerald, letter to Louis Howe, Nov. 11, 1932, Louis Howe Personal Papers, Congratulations 1932–33, FDRL. John F. Kennedy was named after his maternal grandfather, John F. Fitzgerald.

29.   Woolf, "As His Closest Friend Sees Roosevelt," p. 3.

30.   District of Columbia, motor vehicle title, Mar. 3, 1933, Louis Howe Personal papers, Box 7, FDRL.

31.   Roosevelt, *This I Remember*, pp. 111–112.

32.   Davis, *Invincible Summer*, p. 143.

INDEX